Lost Where We Belong

C.L.Bell

To Vanessa
All the best
C.L.Bell

First published in Belgium in 2016 by Mr. Clinton

Copyright © C.L.Bell, 2016

ISBN 978-1-98187-455-2

Cover design by Zia Peter
Printed in South Africa by PixoPrint

Contents

Foreword

THIS BOOK WAS WRITTEN over five years from 2010-2015, in a time that I now think of as the years of silence. This was the time when South Africa was still pretending to itself that it had not been scarred by the shadows of apartheid, that Mandela's magic wand had made it all go away. We were the Rainbow Nation. Our youth were the Born Frees. We boasted and lamented that the young were not even interested in politics. They had escaped our haunted past. And then came March 2015 when the Born Frees woke up.

With the #RhodesMustFall and #FeesMustFall student protests, the silence was broken. As young people bandied together to demand the removal of colonial icons, to pressure the post-apartheid government to deliver on its promise of free tertiary education, and to hold a mirror up to the entrenched rules and systems that unconsciously still favour white lives over black, a new era was ushered in which shone a spotlight on the unexamined racism that continues to divide South Africa, making second-class citizens of many black South Africans.

At the same time, another voice woke up, that of white fear, white confusion, white disbelief. Until then this voice had been hushed and unexamined, whispered only among friends. But in early 2016, through the medium of social media, racist slurs and unchallenged racist tropes came out of the shadows and went viral. We were not who we had been pretending to be. But, deep down, we knew that anyway.

When I first pitched this book to publishing houses, they told me there was not a big enough market for a book that confronts racism from a white perspective. White people will not spend money to make themselves uncomfortable.

Some liberals, who supported the book, thought it would have more chance of success if it was less honest and did not document my earlier ignorance and naïvety.

"It will get people's backs up," they warned.

I disagreed, not because I wanted to vex people, but because I believe that forensic honesty can engender something else in people – compassion.

Apartheid was not a compassionate system. It was harsh and uncompromising. It prioritised order and economics over the human heart. Perhaps in many ways it is not dissimilar to the current capitalist system that values us for what we do, not who we are.

But if we genuinely want to heal as a country, white South Africans need to introspect, in their own individual minds, on the things we stand accused of: white supremacy, abuse of privilege, perpetuating a white centrist view of the world. We need to get comfortable with being uncomfortable. For a little while.

Lost Where We Belong is a tale about feeling like an outsider in your home country, about fear and ignorance, about prejudice, about that very human urge to belong and to matter – the things of every human life. Recently, black South Africans have argued that only white people can end racism. This may be true. No black person can understand the depth of fear, prejudice and white-is-best, that was instilled in us by the old political system, and by a system which continues to be replicated in action, if not in law, by systems that operate around the globe.

That said, *Lost Where We Belong* is not a political treatise, it is a memoir, a personal reckoning. I did not write it with the ambition of changing anyone's heart or mind. Rather I wrote it to shift my own. As Socrates once said, the unexamined life is not worth living. I wanted a life that I could value.

CL Bell
Johannesburg, July 2016

PART 1

Prologue

T HERE IS A WORMHOLE across the Mtamvuna River. It is disguised as a steel suspension bridge, but everyone that crosses it knows they have been catapulted back in time. To the north, the road is smoothly tarred and speeds on to the shiny shopping malls and beach resorts of South Africa's Kwazulu Natal province. To the south it narrows to a patchwork of potholes, delivering weary travellers to the *lali* of the old Transkei, the pastel painted African villages where Nelson Mandela grew up, and where people still live in round huts, with clay-brick walls and thatched roofs, under the rule of chiefs, many without running water and electricity.

It was 1995 when I first saw the Transkei. I say saw, because all I did was spy it through a car window. At speed. Doors locked. Windows wound up. Do not stop until you get to the other side. It was the year after South Africa's first democratic elections. I was a journalism student at Rhodes University, travelling with my boyfriend back to his parents' Kwazulu Natal home. Before 1994, most white students who lived in Kwazulu Natal made the long journey home via Bloemfontein, adding five hundred kilometres to their journey. Now the border posts that separated the Republic of South Africa from the Ciskei and the Transkei, the two so-called independent Homelands of the Xhosa people, were unmanned, and the unrest and bloodshed that had rocked both of these in the latter days of apartheid – internal coup d'etats of which I had understood nothing – was over. We were free to travel through this unknown land as long as, on strict parental instructions, we did not get out of the car.

As we drove I felt like a child who had broken into an old-fashioned sweet shop, where all the pretty colours are stacked on top of each other, behind glass, way out of reach. The Transkei is not a flat land. Hills grow out of more hills. Smartie-coloured thatched huts scatter across brilliant green hillsides. The road winds and curves, and chances are when it forgets to bend you are on a mountain plateau and at any moment the world either side will drop away to reveal a deep valley. It was a world away from the brown brick, block-like architecture favoured by the apartheid government. To my 19 year old eyes, it was as if someone had stolen my blindfold. But I would be lying if I said I wanted to get out and explore. If anything, I was relieved when we were spat out the other side on to the straight, smooth roads of Kwazulu Natal. It took another 15 years and 40 countries before I felt the urge to return.

It happened one wet evening in Glasgow, Scotland. It was raining. Again. A grumbling, misery-packed cloud had blacked out the sun and we had lit a fire in a rusty oil drum to keep warm. It would not have been so bad, except we were having a mid-summer's eve party. Fortunately the Scots are never ones to let a downpour dampen their spirits, but for me it was the watershed.

Like so many other young, restless souls, I had been using the Queen's sodden island and its Great British Pounds as a springboard from which to discover the world. I had notched up adventures that one day might impress my grandchildren, but as the rain made a mockery of my summer party, I became restless in another way. Restless for roots. Warm roots. There was just one problem: the country that raised me was not there anymore. Its neat, dull, whites-only streets had been replaced with vibrant, noisy,

African roads and going home for longer than a holiday meant facing up to an uncomfortable truth.

In Europe I can walk anywhere, go anywhere. In South Africa, my footsteps are controlled by invisible boundaries. The world remembers apartheid as the system that forbade black people from participating in white society, but there was a converse: whites were schooled to stay apart, keep away, don't get too close, and despite the dream of the rainbow nation, those self-imposed prisons still exist.

Sixteen years into our democracy I could count on one hand how many times I had been to a township – the suburbs of urban South Africa that apartheid designated for 'non-whites'. I tell myself I am educated, open-minded, liberal and yet I have no sense of how black South Africans think, feel, live, are. How can I crave for roots in South Africa, if I do not even know the country? At best, it would be nostalgia. At worst, it would be craving for a racist past.

I think about this while lying in a polished wooden bed in a 200-year-old farmhouse on the edge of a cold, wet city, in the north of the world. My feet are facing south. I am alone, but I do not just feel alone, I feel I am in the wrong place, like I have managed, by my own wilfulness, to hijack someone else's life. I begin slowly, methodically, to list the choices I made to move from South African suburbia to Glasgow. I am like a quality controller looming over a conveyor belt of memories, scanning for aberrations, seeking out imperfections. I am looking for moments in this Choose Your Own Adventure tale when I could have, should have, taken a different road. When I could have, should have, turned south. I reassure myself that every decision was a product of hopes and a dream. A young buck heading out into the world to discover, learn, grow. I tell myself that I acted with an open heart, that my decision to remain here was not reactionary. That I am not in hiding in the northlands.

It is a lie. I am hiding.

In the late nineties South Africa began haemorrhaging white people. This mass exodus to Australia, Canada, Britain, America was mostly the result of escalating crime levels – people did not want to live in fear – and a mistrust of a black majority government. At the time, I did not fall into either camp. I left because I was 22 and I was bored. I had grown up under sanctions. South Africa in the eighties had been an inward-looking, insular place, and even though it was already 1999 and we had elected our second democratic president, life felt stuck. Apartheid was like an old-fashioned folk dance, everybody had a part, everybody knew their steps, and although new music was playing, few knew how to dance any other way. I wanted out. A different life was out there, and I wanted it in here, filling the void in my head, so armed with a one-way plane ticket, a British passport and R700 (£70), I left for London.

My decision to leave was probably not that dissimilar to young people the world over who have grown up under conservative regimes. The reason I chose not to return was particularly South African. I was afraid.

From 1994 to 2002, the South African Police Service reported a 33% increase in violent crime in the country. Between April 2001 and March 2002, the statistics showed that 59 people were killed, 142 people were raped and 864 homes were broken into every day.

Statistics often bear little resemblance to reality but this is what they meant to me:
My father's workmate was tied up as his wife was raped and murdered in their home.
My husband's best friend was stabbed to death in his home.
My school friend's fiancé was killed, shot through the head in a car hijacking.
My brother's dogs were poisoned and his car stolen from his driveway.
My friend and her boyfriend had their car hijacked at gunpoint.

My friend's mother was hijacked and kidnapped in the car.
My friend's sister's was hijacked at gunpoint in her driveway.

All this happened while I was away, on the other side of the world. Safe.

Some black South Africans do not have time for lists like this. They accuse white South Africans of being paranoid. They point out that we were cosseted by a police state and it's only now that we are experiencing what it is really like to live in South Africa. And they point out – quite correctly – that most of the violent crime, the murders and rapes do not affect the white community, fortressed as we have become behind six-foot walls, electric fences, rapid-response security guards and distant shores. In 1999 the National Mortality Surveillance system data reported that black and coloured people accounted for 93% of all 6,800 homicide victims.

But while it may be true that the majority of crimes have less of a bearing on white people's lives, they perhaps have even more of a bearing on white people's minds, because we were the ones who were weaned on a diet of *swart gevaar* (black danger). And now it is as if all those old racist fears have come true, and our much lauded democracy that promised freedom for all, has robbed me of mine. In the north of the world I cower. Fearful, lost, feeling homeless.

This kind of confession is not permitted. Hush white girl. Hush with your nonsense. How can you talk of homelessness when some people are still without houses? We must celebrate the Rainbow Nation, not mourn it. Your woes are out of step with the world. *Maak toe* (shut up) or *voetsek* (fuck off). I am silenced by the canon. Made voiceless by a dream. Until, that is, providence intervenes.

It was raining again. I was sitting in my office reading the online *Mail & Guardian*, South Africa's weekly liberal newspaper, when I noticed an invitation for applications for a three-month journalism fellowship to investigate democracy in the new South Africa. During my years in Britain I had worked as a freelance journalist for the national newspapers and magazines, including the US news magazine *Time*. With the backing of an editor at *Time*, I pitch the idea of investigating how democracy had affected the lives of those who live in the old Transkei, the remote, rural villages where Nelson Mandela, Walter Sisulu and many other anti-apartheid leaders had spent their childhoods.

During apartheid, the white government in Pretoria did not want black people settling permanently on "white soil" and so they portioned off land that during pre-colonial times had been inhabited by the tribes, and designated this land as so-called independent "Bantustans" or "homelands"[1]. The homeland of the Transkei was created out of land that had "traditionally" been inhabited by the Xhosa, Thembu and Pondo tribes. According to law, only on this land, could black people own homes, develop their culture and a system of governance. Transkei citizens were permitted to work "abroad" as migrant labourers in the white-owned farms, mines and factories, but were not permitted citizenship of South Africa. To enforce this policy, the government deployed a policy of divide and rule whereby tribal chiefs were paid to be the "true leaders of Bantu people", transforming chiefs who had once been the representatives of the people, into instruments of the South African state.

Not all the chiefs saw it this way, though. In 1976, with the backing of Pretoria, the Transkei became an independent country – recognised neither by the African National Congress (ANC), nor the United Nations. In his book, *Independence My Way*, the independent Trankei's first head of state, Kaiser Daliwonga Matanzima, a relative of Nelson Mandela, and the Paramount chief of the Emigrant Thembus, a breakaway Thembu clan, argued that liberation would not come through the ANC, but through a coalition of independent black states. Whether Matanzima truly believed

1 Bantu Authorities Act of 1951

this or whether he positioned himself to enjoy the spoils from the table of Afrikaner social engineering – three quarters of the operating budget of this new country was paid by Pretoria – went to his grave with him. But what is certain is that the fight against apartheid was as divided and divisive as apartheid itself.

To the editors of *Time*, I frame this as a mission of objective reportage. It sounds credible, even to me. But it is not the whole truth. The fact is I am discontent with the second-hand diet of fear that I am being fed from afar. I am uneasy with how it shaping my heart and mind. As a child, I had grown up in ignorance. The truth about South Africa had been purposefully hidden in the eighties and it still feels that everything I know about South Africa comes through the prism of someone else's lens. There is an ever-widening schism between myself and my homeland and I have begun to realise that I am in danger of becoming permanently adrift and never finding my way back home.

So why the old Transkei? When I was feeling brave, I told myself that the Transkei was the epitome of the black African and thus symbolised the essence of what my apartheid childhood had conditioned me to fear and what I had to confront. I did not harbour the same unease towards the country's equally dark-skinned Indian or coloured communities. When I was feeling less brave, I told myself that the pastoral scenes that I had once spied through a car window belonged to a world unsullied by the opportunism and extreme poverty that were making no-go zones of our urban areas. My cowering self assured me that the Transkei would be a gentler place to probe at my scars.

Was this naïve? I was to find out it was. But at the beginning of this journey, my naivety was just another symptom of my ignorance.

Chapter 1

Another White Girl in Africa

I<small>T IS DAWN IN</small> Pondoland. The wild night orchestra, best known for its scratch and screech section, has finally put its instruments to bed just in time for my alarm. It has been one of those nights when your dreams are wracked by fears and you wake feeling like you have already lived the day that lies ahead. I fumble for my glasses, extract myself from the sheets and stumble onto the balcony to breathe in the cool morning air.

On the opposite side of the Umzimvubu River tiny curls of smoke are drifting above a pink hut. Between us, hanging heavy in the sub-tropical valley, is a thick early morning mist, as if Mother Nature has sent me an ethereal bridge to connect my world to the one across the river. If only. Today is the first day of my journey and I am already gnarled with self-doubt.

"Another white girl in Africa. Just what it needs," chides a voice inside my head. I shake my head and sigh. It is a voice I hope will be quashed by the stories of people I meet, but right now, as the world is caught between sleep and a new day, the monologue takes centre stage and commands its audience of one.

I get dressed and head down to the early morning chatter of the open-air kitchen.

I am staying with Thea Lombard, a single, blonde Afrikaans woman of a certain age who, with the help of waifs and strays, has turned a derelict old farm behind the sub-tropical coastal town of Port St Johns into a traveller's hideaway. Thea is a bit like a fairy godmother, only she would probably chargrill the pumpkin, transform her three dogs, Pablo, Mamba and Bombelina into footmen, and drive you to the ball in her 4x4.

The first time I ever drove with her she confessed she had nearly had four head-on collisions that day.

"I keep thinking this is my driveway, but it's not, it's actually a road," she giggled, as she steered down the one kilometre dirt track from the main road to her house.

"My poor neighbours," she cackled again, hooting and waving as a neighbour swerved and waved back. The local drivers are not renowned for their motoring skills, and as I cradle my morning coffee, I rest my chin on my chest, waking up somewhat belatedly to the fact that I am single-handedly going to have to navigate its gravel roads and mud ruts. If only for a chauffeur. Ironically, most people who live here do have drivers. Most people are crammed into the back of minibuses and bakkies, enduring hairpin bends and potholed roads with no say as to how fast or slow they go. Road accidents are one of the major killers in South Africa. In 2008, nearly 15,000 people died on the roads, with minibuses and bakkies responsible for a third of these casualties.

I had first stayed with Thea a few weeks before when I had joined a hike between Port St Johns and the marijuana-rich hippy hangout of Coffee Bay, following a 61km trail of forested goat paths, wind-dashed hills and isolated beaches. Each night hikers stay in a different Pondo village, sleeping with families in their homesteads and eating local food. Our guide was Jimmy Selani, a 38-year-old strapping Pondo man with dreadlocks and ceremonial tribal scarring on his face.

We started the hike at Umngazi River Bungalows, where Nelson Mandela and Graca Machel spent their honeymoon. We took a ferry across the Umngazi river and walked past free-range beach cows staring mindfully at the crashing waves, before heading up into the green hills beyond. Jimmy's English is excellent, fine-tuned by years of reading books and fielding questions from inquisitive tourists, and he has a way with words that makes him compelling to listen to. As we rested on the crest of the first hill, looking back over a crashing Indian Ocean, Jimmy mused about what it had been like to grow up in the old Transkei.

"When I was a child, I didn't even know we were oppressed. You saw that the white man came by in a fancy car and that the black man always drove an old broken car, but you thought that's just the way it was meant to be. You called the white man Nkosi which means boss and his son Nkososana which means little boss, and you lifted your hat when they went past. That was just the way it was. We enjoyed our lives. We didn't see the oppression. It was those people who went and worked in the cities who then came back and said that the situation you are in is not right. Most of the people then were not educated, they didn't differentiate that this is right and this is wrong. They just took it as this is what was supposed to be.

Jimmy's words threw me. Within South African it has become commonplace for white people to plead ignorance of the real apparatus of apartheid.

"We didn't realise what was really going on," we protest.

But a black South African? I had expected Jimmy to shake his head in a bid to block out memories of police brutality and dawn raids, similar to the kind that Mark Mathabane recounts in his soul-stilling 1986 autobiography *Kaffir Boy*, about life in the Johannesburg township of Alexandra. But of course Jimmy did not grow up as an unwanted interloper in a white-dominated world, he grew up exactly where the white government wanted him: on land demarcated for Pondos. And in ignorance.

I recognised the latter well because I had grown up in a similar place.

Benoni is a suburban town built among the gold mine dumps of Johannesburg's East Rand. Its two claims to fame are the Bunny Park – where feral ankle-nipping fluff balls chase carrots for the delight of small children – and the Hollywood actress Charlize Theron. It was still being built in 1982 when I arrived, the youngest child of economic immigrants fleeing the imploding hard industry of Yorkshire under Margaret Thatcher's government. My parents were not highly educated. They left school at 16, married at 19 and bore three children. On their first day in the country my parents befriended similar factory workers from the north of England and so it was that I grew up in a blue-collar Yorkshire-Lancashire bubble under the African sun. Of South African politics, there was no talk, no perspectives, no reflection. The TV news, unknown to us, was censored and the only newspaper that came though our door was the Benoni City Times, the weekly advertiser that carried stories of car crashes and children's badminton victories. When I read now of the "cauldrons of conflict" that exploded in Daveyton, the black township which was just five kilometres from our little house, it may as well have happened on another planet. I accepted the world as it was presented, and like Jimmy, I was still a child when South Africa changed forever.

"I remember the day Mandela was released," Jimmy recalls. *"We were already in class and the principal called an assembly and then he made a speech. He said: today Mr Mandela is free, that means freedom is just around the corner. We are going to get freedom and then that means there will be no more black people begging on the corners of the streets. That means there will be no more black people sweeping the streets. Life is going to change. There will be prosperity. And then they said we must go home because Mr Mandela today is free. We didn't even know who Mr Mandela was. At this stage in standard 10, it was the first time for us, when we saw the pictures in the newspapers, to see his face, I'd never seen Mr Mandela's face before."*

It was 1990 when I first heard about Mandela. I was 13 and in my second year of secondary school. My friend's big sister had dropped us at the Saturday morning Jo'burg Flea Market, outside the Market Theatre, and we had spent a tantalising few hours trawling through the African-style clothes and jewellery. It was so exotic, so far away from Benoni and I loved it. Afterwards the big sister took us for a Smartie Cup at a drive-thru ice-cream parlour in Hillbrow and on the way home she told us Nelson Mandela was going to be released from prison.

"Who's Mandela?" I asked.

The big sister was a student at Wits, the University of the Witwatersrand, a liberal campus at the epicentre of anti-apartheid protests. She said he had been sent to prison for plotting to kill people, but that he had had a reason. He was fighting for freedom for his people. It was the first time anyone had ever talked to me about South African politics and I remember replying: "Well, if people try to kill other people, then they should be sent to prison, and they should have to stay there." Case closed.

How my life was so sheltered, how everything was so contained and controlled and censored, it is hard to understand. I have South African friends who say to me "I can't believe you didn't know what was going on", but they were the children of professors and the politically astute. My parents came from a different world. And hence, so did I. I wish now that I had been old enough to protest in the 1980s and wear defiant T-shirts. But I was busy learning to swim.

Chapter 2

A journey with Jimmy

JIMMY SELANI IS WAITING for me on the shoulder of the main road to Mthatha, the capital of the Transkei. To the casual observer it is your stereotypical South African scene, past and present: a black man standing on the side of a hot road waiting for a white person in a bakkie to give them a job. The difference here is I need Jimmy more than he needs me. I have hired him to be my guide into the local villages and my interpreter, since I do not speak Xhosa. When I was at school it was compulsory to take Afrikaans as a second language, but black African languages were only taught once a week for half an hour and where I grew up in Benoni, Zulu was the only language on offer. *Sawubona. Unjani? Sikhona Wena Unjani. Ngubani igama lakho? Ngu Claire. Eish.* Hello. How are you? I am fine, how are you. What's your name? My name is Claire. Oh dear. That is the extent of it.

Jimmy jumps into the bakkie and at the next *shebeen* (unlicensed liquor store) he instructs me to turn left, and we are soon bumping and bouncing down a dirt road, potholed and scarred by years of rains and neglect. Cows stand lazily and stubbornly in our path, small children on their way to school skip and dance too close to the bakkie's wheels, yelling: "Sweets! Sweets!" and something in Xhosa.

"What are they yelling?" I ask.

"Umlungu," says Jimmy, laughing.

"What does it mean?" I ask.

"It means white person. Have you never heard that before?" he asks.

I shake my head. Over the next week I learn that umlungu is also the word for the white scum that rides the waves of the sea, a nod to the fact that white people first arrived on these shores via those waves. It is probably more derogatory than descriptive but I reckon it is preferable to Madam. Baas and Madam, Boss and Boss lady. What black people were once ordered to call white people.

We are on our way to meet Chief Ndamse of Gomolo. During our new year hike, Jimmy and I had been ambling along, talking about life in Pondoland. Jimmy had explained that, despite our democracy, the local villages were still ruled by unelected chiefs. I had idly wondered aloud if there were any women chiefs. Jimmy nodded. "This land you are walking on now is headed up by a woman," he said.

Visions of a bronzed Amazonian warrior princess who suffered no fools sprang instantly into my mind. I had asked Jimmy if he could arrange a meeting for when I returned.

As the last vestiges of urban South Africa vanish into the rearview mirror our conversation turns to rural life and how it is changing.

"The problem is the money. Everybody is focusing on the money. Look around and see how beautiful this land is. The land here is very rich, if you plant anything here it will grow. But the grant system has changed things. It's easier for people to buy *mielie* meal than to grow it," he says, referring to the social welfare grants for children and the pensions which have been introduced by the post-apartheid governments.

"The Xhosas are drifting slowly away from the old life to a western style of living. Before when you got new clothes you would say it smells of white men, and everyone envied you. Now people buy things all the time."

Around the next corner I see the first sign of the malady which kills hundreds of thousands of South Africans every year: a gaunt, weak man, his body emaciated by HIV/Aids walking slowly, painfully.

"Pull over!" Jimmy orders.

After a brief exchange in Xhosa, the man clambers into the back of the bakkie.

"We're not going the whole way now, but we can help him get closer to the clinic," Jimmy says.

"I'd like to go to there later," I say. "I'd like to see it for myself."

"You don't go there to get better," Jimmy warns. "If God permits you, you live, if not, you die."

As we bump along, I hand Jimmy my questions for the chief. Chief Ndamase does not speak English so Jimmy is going to have to translate. He reads them and scowls.

"Are you sure you want to ask these?" he asks.

"What's wrong with them?" I ask.

My questions span three A5 pages and include questions like: How does tribal life fit into the South African democracy? I have heard it is difficult for chiefs and government to work together – why is this?

Jimmy shakes his head. "In our culture, there are some things that a younger person should not ask of an older person, especially a chief."

"Okay, well just ask the ones that you are comfortable with then," I say.

We leave our ailing hitchhiker at the fork in the road, and continue on to Gomolo. At the start of the village we ask a villager for directions and he waves us up a hill, along a track barely visible beneath long, wispy grass. We pull up outside a metal gate. On the other side of the gate, a modern pink bungalow squats alongside two thatched cream coloured huts. A chalky blue Mercedes with matching blue hubcaps, the kind once popular with apartheid government ministers, shelters from the sun under the shade of a poplar tree.

"Molo!" Jimmy calls, getting out of the car.

At first nobody stirs. The only sound is the breeze rustling through the long grass.

"Molweni?" Jimmy calls again. I join him at the gate.

From behind the bungalow, a young woman in blue overalls and black wellington boots appears. She pops her head inside one of the huts and then beckons for us to open the gate and enter the hut. Jimmy and I glance at each other. I am also nervous.

An inner voice wakes up, hissing: "*What right does a white girl from Benoni have to ask for an audience with a Pondo chief?*" I take a deep breath, try ignore it, and plaster a smile on my face.

Inside, to the right of the doorway is a row of plastic chairs, one occupied by a man wearing blue overalls, holding a panga. To the left are two plastic chairs, both occupied by elderly women, one resting her upper body weight on a beach umbrella pole, her makeshift walking stick, the other in traditional Xhosa dress, her face covered in white clay, her head wrapped in a scarf, her wrists and ankles beaded. Further back from the door is a single bed covered with a pink throw. On it, an elderly woman, dressed in a silky leopard print blouse, a houndstooth skirt, a spotty green hat and pink fluffy slippers, is sitting holding a fat, contented baby girl. The young woman motions us to sit down next to the man.

I scan the room. The walls are painted the same colour as the Mercedes and the floor is covered with linoleum in a parquet pattern. There is a cabinet, displaying two clay pots, one cracked, against the far wall, a table draped in a blue and red floral tablecloth is laid out with coffee and tea, and hanging above it is a poster celebrating 10 years of the House of Traditional Leaders and a framed photograph of a serious man in a khaki police uniform and a younger version of the woman in the pink fluffy slippers. I look at her and smile. Chief Ndamse of Gomolo regards me coolly and addresses Jimmy.

"She wants you to introduce yourself," he translates.

My audience listens attentively, ears cocked and nodding, better able to understand English than speak it. I tell them my age, my profession, that I grew up in Benoni and that I would like to understand and write about how life in the old Transkei has changed under democracy. Seemingly satisfied, the chief instructs me to ask my first question. So I start with a simple one, I ask the chief her first name. She eyes me suspiciously, and asks Jimmy again, in Xhosa, to explain why I am here. A debate follows. The old women and the man with the panga chip in. I stare at the poster on the wall feeling like the elephant in the corner of the room that everyone *is* talking about.

Finally after much thought and discussion Chief Ndamase tells me her name is Nogcinile, but adds that she will not talk about government politics. I accept her terms and ask how long she has been the chief.

"I was the chief for 12 years, until last year. Now my son is the chief," she says.

This comes as a surprise. A couple of weeks before I had sat at the home of a 62-year-old matriarch, whose village falls under the rule of Chief Ndamase. According to the gossip, the reason Nogcinile was the chief was because her firstborn son was usually too drunk for the job.

"During my generation it was unheard of for a woman to be chief," the woman had told me, "but because the children of today drink a lot, now you have to look for the best possible person for the job."

The journalist in me had planned to ask if there was any truth to this, but as I sat in front of the proud grandmother in her pink fluffy slippers, I realized I could no more ask her if her son was a drunk than I could ask an old lady neighbour in Glasgow. Instead I ask her to tell me about what kind of person you need to be to be a chief.

Chief Ndamase thinks for a while.

"You cannot go to school to be a chief, you have to be born to a clan that is in line to be a chief, but the most important thing is that you must also get the western education. You need to be a good leader and a good listener. And you need to be a humble person, so that people can communicate with you, not fear you. As soon as I wake up there are many people who are waiting for my help. If someone is going to Jo'burg, I must write them a letter saying I know them, that I am their chief and they are from this village, so they can get a job or a bank account. I must make sure all is well, that the children are being educated, that they are not hungry and that the fields are being ploughed. Now we have a challenge because not everyone has oxen to plough the mielie fields and those oxen that are owned are not fit enough to plough the fields."

I ask if her job has become easier since the end of apartheid. She talks of the arrival of running water, electricity, and freedom of movement.

"Now no one is forced to go to the cities so they can have the privilege of electricity. Now the *lali* are like the urban areas. It means people are gradually starting to come back to their traditions. An example is that people are starting to wear their traditional attires when there is a traditional ceremony, doing the traditional dances, things they were starting bit by bit to forget."

"Is Zuma influencing this? I ask, sneaking in a political question.In April 2009 President Jacob Zuma, a Zulu, a proud African traditionalist emerged from a welter of corruption and rape charges to be elected as president of the African National Congress (ANC), the ruling political party, and president of the country. Zuma is a polygamist who has been married six times, is estimated to have 20 children, and often wears animal skins for important occasions.

She nods.

"The people are getting courage when they are seeing their leaders going back to their roots by wearing traditional attires and doing dances."

I find my eyes roll inwardly, my inner monologue clicks in. "*We have only just shaken off the gauntlet of pariah state, embarrassment of the world. Doesn't he realise that dancing around in skins will make us look like a banana republic?*"

I realise later, much later, that I would never judge a Scottish leader in a kilt like that. Though I knew enough then not to speak my mind.

Instead I change the subject.

"What is the most important thing to you?" I ask.

"The land of my people," she says. "I will never exchange it, no matter what price you come up with. I will never let people build roads or mines through it."

"What is your biggest worry?" I ask her.

She sucks her teeth and thinks.

"Hunger and starvation for my people. The people now are poor, they cannot afford to buy ploughs, and so they cannot afford to cultivate."

I feel myself bristle. From what I saw on the five days I spent walking the goat track between Port St Johns and Coffee Bay, there is no starvation here. Linah, a 29-year-old woman who we stayed with for a night told me: "Life here is good. Look around you, the people here are fat. If you have mielie meal you can get oysters or mussels or crayfish from the sea."

Is she saying this to make me feel guilty? Why do these words make me feel guilty? I bat away her reply.

"What else do you worry about?" I ask.

"The education of our children. The education of this country is not of a high standard. South Africans need to travel to other countries so that they can get broad-minded and learn how other people are doing things."

Finally her words soothe me. Suit me. The last thing I expected to hear from a Pondoland chief was an importance of overseas travel for expanding the mind. I feel like I have been handed a permission slip for my ten years of absence.

South Africans – especially those whites who have chosen to stay – often berate those who leave, branding them either as racists or traitors. You are either with us or against us. The fact is, apartheid was a rigid and uncompromising political regime that made us rigid and uncompromising in the way we view ourselves and each other. We are like the pieces on a chessboard, our identities are fixed, determining the way we move, act and interact. There is no space in that thinking for a young buck who wants to grow and explore and I am grateful for the Chief's alternative worldview.

Our visit is coming to an end. We head outside and take a few pictures of the chief sitting on a plastic deckchair, her granddaughter in her arms.

"Did you bring a gift?" Jimmy whispers as I focus the camera.

"A gift? Why? I didn't know I had to," I whisper back.

"It's custom to bring a bottle of brandy," Jimmy whispers.

I had already heard that during apartheid, white people would buy coastal plots of land for a case of brandy. On the hike we had passed white-owned cottages perched on the edge of cliffs, miles and miles from tarred roads, supposedly purchased in this way. The chief mutters something in Xhosa to Jimmy.

"Actually she wants some beers," Jimmy says. "Six bottles of Hansa. We can get them from the shebeen."

I nod and smile. Somewhat bemused, a little confused, happy enough to oblige. We wave goodbye and drive down to the local shebeen to put in our order. As Gomolo disappears into a cloud of dust, I cannot help but wonder if the beer is for the fluffy slippered chief, or for her son.

Chapter 3

....

The Sick Heart

I DID NOT REALLY HAVE a plan. I did not want to pre-arrange meetings with local experts or officials. I wanted to drift, follow my nose, letting serendipity lead. I wanted to wear my ignorance and see what this land would teach me.

"Where to next?" Jimmy asks.

"The clinic," I say.

Jimmy shakes his head.

"Are you sure?" he asks with a sigh.

"I'm sure."

We bump along another excuse for a road, arriving half an hour later at Isilimela Clinic. From the outside, it does not look too bad. Inside hope disappears. In the waiting room, there is a stagnant air, a heavy mood, as rows and rows of people sit quietly, blank eyes staring into blank space. We ask the receptionist if we can speak to one of the doctors, and after a wait Jimmy and I are ushered through to the office of the financial director who offers me a well-rehearsed smile and a chair.

"What can I do for you," he asks, holding onto his desk and rocking back in his chair. I explain my presence, he nods at the end of each of my sentences, and then like a man long accustomed to passing the buck, he picks up the phone and dials the Department of Health head office and hands over the receiver. I bend over the phone and endure ten minutes of being chastised by a health official for turning up unannounced. I politely accept the reprimand, carefully jot down the number of the person I should have called, and then leave by the front door and re-enter by the back to see if I can corner a doctor.

The wards are dispiriting. Frail, gaunt people lie weakly on grey, steel beds, their bodies loosely covered with white sheets. Jimmy is slightly optimistic though.

"It is cleaner than when I brought my father here," he whispers.

On the way over Jimmy had told me that they had taken his father home to die.

"In hospital you need encouragement, you need hope to get better, but the people who work here don't care. They are just here for the jobs and the salary."

Behind the wards is the Gateway clinic, a series of wooden sheds with paint peeling off the walls. This hosts the antenatal and well-baby clinic, as well as the TB and HIV/AIDS information clinics. Sitting outside are a few teenage girls who shy away when I say hello. Outside, in the afternoon sunshine, a few patients are lying on the grass, wearing striped hospital-issue pyjamas. Their eyes are empty, distant. They look more like inmates than patients.

We take a seat on the wide porch outside the wards and wait. After a few minutes a nurse and two orderlies walk by. Jimmy approaches the nurse, explaining why we are here. I expect her to dismiss us, to be too busy, but instead she takes a step forward, grabs my arm and pushes her face towards mine.

"What have you got for me?" she hisses. "You must give me something. Give me a sweet."

Her manner is unnerving. Her eyes are glassy and seem fixed on a place just beyond my ear and there is an energy to her which is as jagged and fraught as broken glass. The two orderlies at her side say nothing, but stare on with a similar crazed stare.

"I don't have any sweets," I reply.

"Then your pen," she says, "Give me your pen."

"But, but, you have a pen," I say, pointing at the pen in her shirt pocket. "I need my pen."

"But you *must* give me something," she insists. "What have you got for me?"

"Why *must* I give you something?" I ask.

Her words flick my inner switch. The inner monologue bites. "*Why does a black person always expect something from me? Why am I always seen as an opportunity first, a person second?*"She lets go of my arm, takes a step back, scowls, turns and walks away. The orderlies tail behind her.

"Do you think they were on drugs?" I ask Jimmy.

"I don't think so," he says. "Maybe it is the stress. They see so much suffering. Maybe it makes them a little mad."

We sit back down on the porch and it is not long before a tall man with an air of calm authority rounds the corner. He listens politely to our request but answers that he is a Nigerian doctor who has only been an Isilimela for a year – he cannot comment on how things have changed since 1994 but he knows someone who can. A few minutes later we are ushered into the office of Nurse Cynthia Qikani.

Cynthia has worked at Isilimela since 1987. She sits at her desk, the nurse's ledger open in front of her, and pulls no punches.

"Before 1994 everything was going good. We had doctors, nurses, equipment and services. In 1994 we thought the change was all for the good. But as time goes on there is a constant decline. We can't blame the government, but we are blaming them. We are in a dilemma."

I ask her to give an example.

"We have five wards but only two nurses. We need more staff, more doctors, and we need people who are actually well-trained and competent in charge of the tenders."

She is referring to the supply contracts between government and the private sector. "We used to order medical equipment from a central medical store. Now we have to use tenders and it takes from six months to a year to get new equipment. It is difficult for us to get basic equipment like blood pressure testing machines, urine sticks, blood sugar testing equipment. We are failing because the tenders are failing us."

Just over 120km from here is Qunu, the birthplace of Mandela and the ANC. Many men and women sacrificed their lives to fight for freedom, but what is freedom without decent healthcare? It seems a bitter pill.

"Do you think the government has forgotten about rural people?" I ask. Cynthia considers the question carefully.

"I think they do try and improve services, but I think the government needs to evaluate now the way it is going because we are going nowhere. If you were to draw a graph, it would go down, down, down. This part of the world is getting left behind the rest of South Africa. We have been more than ten years without nurses and we've been promised and promised a tarred road, but it is just talk. In November 2009 we got a visit from the Department of Health and they said they are going to fix the road. We believe them, but to say is not to do," she says.

Cynthia's account of failure is not isolated but rather symptomatic of a chronic condition poisoning the entire Eastern Cape healthcare system. A Special Investigations Unit (SIU) study into corruption in the provincial department showed that in the 18 months between January 2009 and June 2010, public officials and their associates stole more than R800-million.

Jay Naidoo, the founding General Secretary of Cosatu and former Minister in Mandela's government commented: "Its collapse has been presided over by a parasitic elite that has, for over a decade, abused the public trust and used our public coffers as their private slush fund."

As she escorts us outside I ask Cynthia if she still has hope. Her answer sends a chill through my heart.

"No, I don't have hope anymore."

She shakes her head and sighs.

"But thank you for coming, because that shows you care. Maybe you can tell people what it is like and maybe one day things will change."

I had wanted to find out about the beating heart of this country, and today I found it was on a life-support machine. Well, it would be if such high-tech equipment existed at Isilimela.

Jimmy and I climb into the bakkie in silence. As we drive away, Jimmy stares pensively out the window. I sense a storm brewing in him. After a few minutes Jimmy slams his fist against the dashboard.

"How can she say she has no hope? How can she say that?" he seethes. "If we don't have hope, we have nothing. If I didn't have hope, I would not be alive today."

As the bakkie bumps and lurches along the scarred road, he begins to tell me his story.

"It was not easy. It was not easy," he says, staring out of the window. "You know, if you are born out of wedlock, your mother is going to go away at an early age to work for a white family or an Indian family. Then you grow up in the village thinking that person is your mother, then you find out at a later stage that she is not your real mother. There are things that you want to share with people so they can assure you that everything is going to be fine, but you are invisible. Even if you have the courage to ask, they will scold you. When you are born out of wedlock in this part of the country, as a Pondo, you don't ask questions, you listen and you do as you are told."

"So who raised you?" I ask.

"My grandmother, but she was not my grandmother. And then when she got sick and died nobody cared how I felt, if I was healed properly inside, they just told me that I had to move, that I had to go and stay with the family of my grandmother. I missed her dearly, I was crying inside, I was not okay, and then you go to a new place and you have to adjust to a new way of doing things. Unfortunately the environment and culture I grew up in, if you make a mistake, you are going to be beaten up, that's how you learn. Even at school during that time, if you are not doing well at a certain subject you will just be beaten up or the adults will shout at you and tell you, you are an idiot. You grew up thinking you are an idiot."

"Are you saying there wasn't a lot of compassion towards children in Pondo culture?" I ask.

"I won't say it is that way because each home is different, but when I look around, it still happens in that old way. The child doesn't have an opinion. They don't care how you feel or if you see things differently," he says.

"So how did you hold onto your hope?" I ask.

"All that time – and this is why I believe everyone has a guardian angel – I had this thing inside me that is telling me: 'No Jimmy, everything is going to be okay one day. In the veld you see the birds, and they give you hope singing to you. You listen to the water, making its own music. I was more happy in the veld than I was at home. That keeps you going, that gives you hope. From nature you get the sense that these things are temporary'."

We fall silent, both retreating into our own thoughts. The peace and beauty of the land is one of the great ironies of South Africa. As we lit our fires and waged our wars, munificent Mother Nature went about her business, as generous and abundant as she ever was. We turn right onto the main road and drive along the banks of the Umzimvubu river, its banks dense with lush greenery, towards Port St Johns. This river starts as a trickle in the high mountains of the Drakensberg, where snow falls in the winter, coming to its grand finale in the eternal semitropical summers of Port St

Johns. My favourite story about the river is about a group of South African explorers who rafted from the source to the mouth. They set off in January 1990 and for a whole month they had no contact with the world. When they popped out on 9 February 1990, they discovered Nelson Mandela had been released from prison. "We had entered the Transkei from one era and came out into another," said the expedition leader.

I drop Jimmy next to the bustling market town.

"Go well. *Hamba kahle*," Jimmy says, as he gets out, banging his hand on the side of the bakkie and poking his head back through the open window. "And remember, you're a white woman alone, so no hitchhikers!"

Back at Thea's, I park the car behind her heavy wooden gates. Thea's dogs Pablo, Bombelina and Mambo are lying comatose in the late afternoon shade, not even bothering to lift up their heads as I walk past. Thea is in the kitchen, conjuring up tonight's dinner. As soon as I see her I start to cry.

"What's wrong my meisie? What's happened?" she asks, putting down her knife and gathering me in her arms.

"Nothing," I blubbed into her shoulder. "Everything's fine. It was a good day. It's just…" And the words tumbled out about the hospital and about what Jimmy said about God deciding if you live or die and how the nurse said she had no hope.

"Why is this happening? It's as if everyone has just given up," I sob.

Thea sighed and squeezed me a bit harder.

"I know my meisie, I know. But you have to understand, they have different expectations to us".

Those words hung in the air between us. They. Different. Us. That was the premise of apartheid. Black and white people were different. We wanted – *and expected* – different things. And so for us – the whites - to prosper, it was imperative that we kept apart.

That night John Costello comes to dinner. John is a local hotelier who speaks fluent Xhosa and spends his downtime travelling with his camera to remote Transkei villages, documenting the disappearing customs of the Xhosa people. "Think of it like this," he says, as we sit at the bar, drinking beer from the bottle. "The Transkei has never been part of South Africa. It's South Africa that is getting reabsorbed into the Transkei."

John tells me a story about a man called Thuthani who in 2009 was fighting to stop a road being built through his maize field.

First the local councilor accused Thuthani of caring more about the needs of trees than human beings. When Thuthani did not back down, he was then told that he was not the rightful owner of the maize field. When that did not douse Thuthani's ire, some heavy-handed police officers were sent to his home in the middle of the night, accusing Thuthani of hiding illegal weapons. While they searched, they covered his head in a plastic bag, and fractured his arm. Then his maize field was set on fire.

"It's as if a new tribe has formed," says John. "The tribe of the government elite who have access to the power and the money, and are dividing it up to make lives better for themselves at the expense of everyone else. The only people making money around here are the chain stores, the undertakers, and the municipal contractors."

I feel an anger rise inside me, but is not directed at government. It is directed at John.

Shut up, I want to shout. Stop talking like this. You are not allowed to criticize. We are not allowed to criticize. Only racists criticize. We must not be racists. But I don't shout. I say nothing. John keeps talking.

"What you have is a people lost and discovering themselves. The real Transkei, unaffected by Christianity or whites, is not here, it's down in the Willowvale area. There they still sacrifice to the ancestors. Here, it is about keeping up with the Dlaminis. The hut with breathable thatch roofs and wattle lattice and clay walls is not good enough. People want tin roofs and cement block walls. The old style makes you look like a peasant."

Chapter 4

....

The Healing Springs

THE NEXT DAY THE air is hot and heavy. Distant rumbles warn of a brewing storm. I pick up Jimmy and we head for the village of Chaguba where he has planned for us to spend the day, getting a feel for village life. Our first stop is the home of Mr and Mrs Mangala, an elderly couple in their seventies, the parents of Jimmy's business partner.

We arrive at their home, a peach bungalow at the end of a rutted track, as the grumbling sky grows louder. Mr Mangala points for me to park up the hill, but as I start to furrow his land with wheel spins, he elbows me out from behind the wheel and parks the bakkie himself.

Mrs Mangala is waiting for us in her garden, a hectare of peaches, guavas, maize, lemons, beans, pumpkin, bananas, mangoes and cabbage. As she shows us around she points wistfully to neighboring fields in the village, full of trees.

"All those fields were cultivated in the past," she says, shaking her head. "Now people are buying mielie meal from the shops. They are very lazy. In twenty years time nobody will be cultivating."

We are invited inside for coffee, served on a silver tray with thick slices of buttered bread. The Mangalas have six children and eight grandchildren, and the atmosphere is warm, relaxed, welcoming. We take a seat on a pink leather lounge suite. The television cabinet is lined with photographs of the children graduating from university and on the wall is a heart-shaped sign made of sea shells that reads: "Thank you for not smoking". I feel I am visiting my own grandparents.

Our conversation moves easily to all the positive changes the village has seen since 1994. Mr Mangala points to the running water – "we used to have to get water from the river, from the same places the livestock was drinking" – and to the toilets and electricity.

I reply that Chaguba is one of the lucky ones, that many villages are still waiting for these services and Mr Mangala nods, smiles and responds with a grandfatherly lecture on patience.

"There is no hurry. We have to wait. Rome was not built in a day," he says. "We persevered from 1948 when the apartheid system was introduced, and now we are still persevering. We got our independence in 1994 from persevering, so the older generation knows how to wait more than the younger generation."

I am not sure he is speaking his whole truth, yet, and as he relaxes, he opens up a little more.

"There's too many people at the top who are corrupt and they protect each other," he says, folding his arms and shaking his head. "Even if they do bad things, they cover it up. I'm not a member of the ANC, I'm a Christian. My organisation is the organisation of God. As a Christian I'm not supposed to lie, but the politicians lie a lot. I cannot vote for someone who is lying to the people. How can you vote for someone who is lying? Tell me that. When the ANC say they are going to do something, you know they are lying."

I ask him if he still has hope things will change.

"I live in hope that God is going to make sure things go as they are supposed to. Not the ANC. God is in charge and he will make sure things are getting better. We are waiting for God's kingdom," he says.

The sky erupts in a thunderous crack.

Mr Mangala walks onto the verandah and looks up at the sky.

"You should go," he warns. "The storm is getting closer. You cannot drive down this road after it rains. You could be stuck here for days."

As he speaks, the rain starts. Giant drops, faster and faster.

We dash for the bakkie, waving a hurried goodbye, and within moments it's as if the road has been smeared with Vaseline.

As we drive past the local school, Gungubele Junior Secondary School, a collection of mint green buildings on top of a hill, the children are also leaving, most of them dragging chairs with them. It is two hours before the end of the school day and Jimmy calls out, asking what is going on.

"It's pay day," shouts a little boy in Xhosa. 'The teachers leave early to get their money."

Jimmy clicks his tongue in disgust and anger.

"And the chairs?" I ask.

Jimmy asks again.

"They have to bring their own chairs to school," he translates.

This, in a country that exports gold, diamonds and platinum.

"What now?" I ask Jimmy. He thinks for a moment and then hatches a new idea.

At the bottom of Thea's road are the Isinuka healing springs. You smell them before you see them. A sickly, eggy odour leads you through the forest to a cluster of dilapidated shacks built alongside milky sulphuric ponds that bubble up from beneath the ground: the Transkei equivalent of Iceland's Blue Lagoon, except it is free, the only cost the price of a night's accommodation in the mud and wood huts. If you suffer from skin ailments, the advice is to bathe in the water and cake your skin in the white mud; if you have sinus problems you're pointed to the 'evicksini' (named after the Vicks nasal inhaler) to breathe in sulphur fumes; and if you have stomach complaints, you're instructed to drink the eggy waters.

We pull up in the clearing and at first there is no one to be seen. Then Nomvakaliso Solumani, the owner of the wood and clay-built spaza shop pokes her head out and waves us inside. We dash through the downpour and slip inside where at least 14 wellness seekers are huddled from the rain, sitting on a mixture of beds and benches made of old planks. Among them are an elderly tata and a mama, but most are in their 30s. A few look up and smile. Others just stare at the floor. I tell them why I am here and Ntombi Sobuza, a sharp 34-year-old woman, dressed in a funky outfit of a metallic blue peak cap, a blue T-shirt, a brown skirt and blue and white striped socks, speaks frankly.

"You want to know about the Tranksei? It's not working," she says, her voice thick with anger. "There are no jobs at all. I don't feel part of South Africa. I feel closer to a country like Somalia or Zimbabwe, countries suffering from starvation. We are getting poorer and poorer. You see people complaining on the TV about service delivery and instead of changing, things are getting worse. We've given up."

Listening to Ntombi, I realize I could be looking in a mirror. We are both in our 30s, both have strong opinions and a penchant for slightly ridiculous fashion, and we both get ourselves worked up when we are upset. It is sheer luck of birth that we are standing where we are.

"Would you still vote for the ANC?" I ask.

She folds her arms and shakes her head.

"I will never vote again," she says. "If a political party gives me work first, then I will vote for them. The political leaders want votes from us, then after they get the votes they forget about us and go and help other nations and other areas. If something is happening in Mozambique, they make sure they help out there, but they forget about the lives of the people in their area."

The rain is letting up and Ntombi is done talking. Her anger is too explosive for this small space and she storms outside to get some fresh air. Everyone sits in silent agreement, shoulders heavy, resigned. I feel guilty. Everyone has come here to get better and I have stoked up the fires of all the ills in the country. I too shuffle off outside.

A small queue has formed at the 'evicksini'. A couple of large bellied men have arrived in a big Mercedes and they are bending over the hole, snorting up the fumes. I turn and head into the forest to see the springs, trying not to gag at the smell. How anyone ever discovered the healing properties of this foul-smelling water amazes me. In Iceland, the story goes that the locals thought they had a national disaster on their hands when the sulphuric wastewater from one of their geothermal power plants spilled over. During their effort to stop the flood, one of the workers accidentally fell in. That night, he slept peacefully, for the first time in his life not bothered by the raw, itchy eczema that covered much of his skin. Today, the white sulphuric mud from those waters is bottled and sold at high prices to eczema sufferers around the world and the Blue Lagoon has become Iceland's top tourist attraction. I wonder if Isinuka will ever make it into South Africa's tourist brochures.

It is dark in the woods. There is a thick canopy of dense, green leaves, and as the light blocks out, I feel that anxiety that has been haunting me from the first time I decided to set out on this journey. I try to shrug it off and feel impatient with myself. What am I scared of? I am a stone's throw from Jimmy and a group of people who have sat peacefully alongside me and shared their thoughts and opinions. There is nothing to fear here, and yet this dread, this lingering dread rears up whenever I am alone. I urge myself forward to the edge of the milky waters, and then stop dead. Downstream, a lithe naked man crouches at the edge of the steaming spring, his head bowed. He is scooping water with a pink bucket and cascading it over his body. The dread inside me lurches again. Apartheid taught its white children to trust black women. They were the country's surrogate mothers, nurses and nannies, a symbol of nurture and care. But black men were not allowed in the house. They were not to be trusted. I take in a deep breath and release it slowly. Apartheid's divisions are in me, like an undetected cancer that lurks in the shadows, sickening you slowly. I turn on my heel and run back to the spaza shop.

Chapter 5

Fear and self-loathing

FEAR. WHAT CAN I tell you about my very South African fear? How can I explain this low-grade frequency that I tune in to whenever I am in the country? How can I make sense of this nervous anxiety that stops me walking alone through the buzzing streets of inner-city Jo'burg, even though there is no place on earth I feel more alive? Why is it that nearly twenty years after the end of apartheid I can count on my hands the number of times I have been in a township? How come it feels like the bars of Soweto and Khayelitsha and Gugulethu are off limits to me – that racial integration can only happen on my old turf? How come black South Africans can now walk without fear through formerly whites-only South Africa, but not vice versa? Is this fear, that has made exiles of thousands of white South Africans – sending them to Australia, Europe, Canada and America – all in the mind? How can I trace its past and its present?

I was not afraid as a child. I was often home alone. I often walked alone.

I do not remember fear. But I remember keeping clear.

I am 6. I am proud to be six. I get a Baby Angel for my birthday. You get white ones and black ones. My dad teased me and said if I was not good I would get a black one. I screamed in protest. I do not want a black dolly.

43

I take my dolly for a walk down the untarred road from my house to my friend's. A black man in a blue overall, carrying a plastic bag, walks along the road towards me. I can hear Max, our Rottweiler going crazy. He hates blacks. I cross to the other side of the road so that I will not walk too close to the black man. I do this because I think I must. That this is what I am supposed to do. Who told me to do this? I do not remember. Maybe it was my brothers. Maybe I heard it on the bus.

I am 8. We move to Neptune Street. Better than Uranus is the family joke. My favourite thing is a mint-flavoured Aero. You can get them on special in Clicks for 99 cents. There is a Clicks at the local shopping mall. I know a short cut, balancing on a grey pipe across a little river. There are only blacks and me that walk this way. I keep my eye on them, make sure they never come too close.

I am 10. Above the blackboard in my classroom are two big pieces of cardboard stuck with plastic landmines and hand grenades. We must keep our eyes peeled for these. There are also three alarms at school: the bomb alarm, the gun alarm and the fire alarm. We have to learn to tell them apart. For the bomb alarm, we must drop down under our desks and put our hands over our heads. For the gun alarm, we must drop to the floor and then roll to the edge of the classroom closest to the hallway. I hate this one because you get icky pencil shavings stuck to your legs. For the fire alarm, we must stand up quickly and arrange ourselves in pre-rehearsed alpha-betical order at the door. We file silently out of the building and into the playground. We giggle with joy at the fire alarm. Especially during maths.

I am 14. I am in high school. Two of the school nerds volunteer to be in the bomb squad. We laugh that it will be no loss if they get blown up. They scour the perimeter of the playground each morning looking for explosives. We live close to the school and I walk home alone every day. When I pass black men, walking home through tree-lined white suburban streets, they clasp one arm behind their back, they cross to the other side of the street, they look down, sometimes they nod. I too cast down my eyes, sometimes I nod. We walk past each other like shadows, as if neither of us is really there.

This was our world. We lived according to an invisible code built on mutual mistrust. The white man mistrusts the black man because he is the *swart gevaar*. At my whites-only school we learnt about the brave European settlers who fought their way into this land, from the Cape into the interior, matching guns to spears on new frontiers. On the way they came face to face with fearsome Xhosa and Zulu warriors, ferocious black men with spears. We are not taught to fear the brave British and Afrikaans men with guns. Only the black man must be feared and kept at bay. If he is not watched he will steal from you and kill you.

The black man mistrusts the white man equally. He mistrusts because the white men have the upper hand, because they have pushed them and squeezed them and they know that if they are not obeyed, they will imprison you, beat you, make you unemployed. In the white suburban streets he keeps his eyes down, because he is cowed, because it is safer that way.

The seeds of mistrust were nourished by apartheid and colonial politics. We are the products of a political system that had taught us to mistrust and fear each other. This is the fear's past.

So what is its present?

Seeds grow if they are watered. They grow tall and they bury their roots deep. Since the end of apartheid, escalating levels of crime, especially violent crime, have been like a tropical downpour on these old seeds.

Every year when I come home to visit, crime is the most popular topic of dinner party conversation. Just as during apartheid, when popular consensus had schooled us in race politics, popular consensus was now schooling us in fear and the only means I have to chart these fears is to rank them against the people who are telling me these stories. I put the crippling fears of those with weaker dispositions alongside the cavalier fears of those who keep the world at arms length, I weave in the resigned fears of the old and it-is-not-my-problem fears of the young, and the result is an ill-fitting patchwork blanket of little comfort. I have no barometer by which to really judge the real dangers of post-apartheid South Africa.

As the years go by my visits home are edged with a mixture of joy and anxiety. I begin to wish I was from somewhere else, another south. The south of France. The south of Spain. It begins to feel as if I am only ever one degree of separation from my worst nightmare. The question is not *if* you will be the victim of crime, but *when?* And you begin to hope that when your time comes, you will get off light. Rather a smash'n'grab than being tied up in your house in the middle of the night. Choose your favourite crime. Choose your own adventure.

Violent crime is the thunderstorm that nurtures these old seeds, keeping us fearful, keeping us apart. Our past is being grafted onto our present, growing tendrils that choke us. Violent crime validates our fears.

*

I am due to head north the following day to stay with Faith Hlakula. I first met Faith through a Zimbawean writer called Gerald Mtetwa, who works night shifts at the Cape Town apartment building where my husband had rented a flat. Gerald and Faith went to the same church and when I asked Gerald if he knew anyone who had grown up in the Transkei who might invite me to stay with them in their village, Gerald said he knew just the person. Faith and I are roughly the same age, both married to older men, and when I first met her in her Khayelitsha home – a small government-built

46

house in Kuyasa – I recognized in her an innate finger-up to authority and a playful kindness. Faith invited me to stay at her husband's kraal in Kanye, a small village two hours drive north of the old Transkei capital, Mthatha. Faith's husband is a distant relation of the legendary anti-apartheid struggle leader, Walter Sisulu, who had been imprisoned on Robben Island with Nelson Mandela. Faith explains that Sisulu was a Hlakula, but had changed his name to protect his family from the dangers of revolutionary politics. I was thrilled with the invitation - it was just what I had hoped for - but as the day for my departure grew closer, my excitement was dwarfed by my fear.

What did this fear look like? In my darkest, most paranoid moments I fear being raped and murdered in Faith's kraal by a shadowy stranger who wants to avenge the wrongs of apartheid. In my more sane moments I worry that someone might steal the bakkie. And in all the moments in between I am afraid of travelling into the unknown, of going to a place where I had been taught my whole childhood, by virtue of how my society was structured, that I did not belong. I fear that I will be scorned and hated. I fear that Faith has an ulterior motive for inviting me. I fear that this whole journey is the project of a fantasist who believes that by voyaging into her own heart of darkness, she will find a hidden light, but that in the end, the racists will be right and I will end up dead and foolish. And I fear what my fears say about me: I fear that despite my would-be liberal mind and heart, I am nothing but a common racist.

I decide to pay John Costello a visit to talk over these worries.

John lives in a beautiful old house with wooden floors alongside his hotel. It is a lair that once knew the touch of a woman but has now been resigned to male practicality. John offers me a cup of tea and then passes our order to his maid, instructing her that we will be out on the lawn. As we stroll outside, he jokes over his shoulder:
"Don't you just love being a colonialist?"

I smile and say nothing, uneasy with his humour.

Back when South Africa was a colony, a Brit with one foot in Africa and the other in the UK was called a Soutpiel – a Salty Dick – because as his legs stretched across the world, his dick would trail in the Atlantic. The other favourite was Rooi nek - Red Neck – after the colour the British soldiers would turn in the hot African sun. I have never minded these slurs. They were usually slung by Afrikaners and we would retaliate with our own treasure of slurs: Dutchman, Rocks, Boneheads, Crunchies. But I have never been called a colonialist before, and it did not sit easy with me. To my mind, colonialists are powerful people. Heads of industry and independent businessmen who exploit the labour and natural resources of South Africa to turn a personal profit. I am a writer funded by a grant, and my power extends only as far as my readers will bestow it.

We sit overlooking the mowed lawn. The grass is that spiky, tough local variety that FIFA rejected for the World Cup supposedly on the grounds that it is too green. It will also take the skin of your leg if you slide across it at speed, as every South African child will testify. As the maid pours our *rooibos,* John tells me he has just spoken to my husband.

I look at him, not comprehending.

"He called me. He's worried about you. He wants to know if he should fly up tomorrow and come with you to the village," John says.

My black-bellied fear surges into anger.

From the time I applied for the Open Society Foundation media fellowship, my husband has been uneasy. He did his best to sway me, telling me in graphic details of the violence he had witnessed in the South African townships in the late 1980s when he was a foreign correspondent for *The Times*, but I reminded him that I was not planning on going into the townships during the politically tumultuous last days of apartheid. Those days were gone. And besides, he had spent his thirties as a foreign correspondent, dodging bullets in war zones. What was good for the gander, had to be good for the goose.

My parents too had mixed feelings. Initially they were delighted to hear I was going to be back in South Africa for five months, using their home, close to the border of the Transkei, as a base. It meant they would see more of me since I left home at 17, but when it dawned on them that I would often be driving alone on roads they had never braved themselves, they became anxious. My dad though, came up with a plan. If he could not come with me, then he would send Tommy. My dad bought Tommy when he retired. For those first 18 months of freedom, Tommy towed my parents and their caravan around South Africa, seeking out a new place they could call home. For my father, Tommy was a symbol of strength and reliability, a sturdy workhorse that would protect you on rough terrain. If he could not look after me, his bakkie would.

But even after my family had warmed to the idea, my friends were still unsure. One of my close friends from my university days thought I was mad. "We grew soft in London," she warned. "When was the last time you saw a gun?"

My brother was equally sneering.

"Those Xhosas are hungry," he said. "Make sure you take a knife with you."

It irritated and unnerved me that everyone close to me assumed that I would be nothing more than a moving target. And that the only way I could mix with my fellow South Africans was if I was armed.

"What did you tell him?" I ask John.

"I told him you'd be fine. And that I'd come with you if you wanted me to," he says.

Did I want John to come with me?

"No," I said. "I don't want anyone to take care of me."

It was a lie. But I preferred it to the truth.

Chapter 6

You've got to have Faith

THEA SENDS ME OFF with *padkos*[2] and a hug.

"Go well my meisie. Don't worry, the stories are out there. You just have to listen," she says.

I am heading north, away from the dense sub-tropical humidity of the Pondoland coast, up to the grassy plains of the AmaXhosa. The road from Port St Johns up to Mthatha swings from left to right and back again, like a conductor's baton leading a gentle symphony. This morning the rhythm of the road is soothing, and as I drive, hooting at errant cows and goats and flashing my lights to warn fellow drivers of the beasts ahead, my fear momentarily ebbs and I breathe in the easy companionship of the open road.

I arrive in Mthatha in the morning rush hour. The cows and goats are replaced by laughing school children and busy women balancing maize and sugar on their heads and babies on their backs. A jolly policeman points me in the direction of the Ncgobo road.

"Are you traveling alone?" he enquires, a little surprised.

"My husband's coming tomorrow," I lie.

"*Eish*, he better keep an eye on you," he says with a laugh.

"Don't worry, he is," I say wryly.

---

2 A packed lunch

Ngcobo is eighty kilometres north of Mthatha along a narrow, roller-coaster type road that passes through grazing lands and forested hills. I drive with the window down, the soft air cooling my cheeks, smiling at the morning. An hour later, I arrive in the heart of the bustling market town. I park the car at the back of the petrol station and head out into the sea of humanity to find Faith. I have barely gone a few metres when a full-bodied turquoise figure sporting a wide smile, a stylish black bobbed wig and a matching blue headscarf appears out of the crowd.

"Your hair!" I exclaim, as we give each other a hug.

"You like it?" she asks.

"It looks fabulous," I reply, feeling a kinship with the fact that Faith had put on her glad rags to go home. When I first moved to London, I used to love sporting all the latest fashions on my trips back to Benoni. It was a sign to myself, and to everyone else, that I had got the hell out of that Hicksville. I got the sense that Faith had returned to Ngcobo with the same intent.

We climb into the bakkie, chatting idly about our journeys as Faith directs me out of town, past the new suburbia of identikit social housing built in neat rows, too close together, leaving little room for plants and people to grow, and onto a dirt track. The track splits and Faith is not sure which fork to take. Within a few minutes we are already lost.

"Sorry," says Faith. "I'm usually in the back of the bakkie. The driver always knows the way."

"Not this driver," I reply.

We reverse and try again, and are soon gathering speed down the best dirt road in the Transkei.

"Walter Sisulu built this road for us," Faith says with a hint of pride.

We drive on into a wide open landscape under big skies. After half an hour, we come across a bunch of teenagers thumbing a lift. We stop to ask where they are going. Faith shakes her head, winds up the window and indicates for me to keep driving.

"You didn't like them?" I ask.

Faith shakes her head. "Their village is at the far end of this valley. We can't take them there. This good road doesn't go all that way. It becomes bad later on."

The journalist in me says nothing. It is a big job to fix decades of neglect. But I also notice gritted teeth, and an inner eyeroll. Why is it that the ANC fought for equality of all South Africans, and yet equality of public services seem to stop at the driveways of the new political elite?

After three quarters of an hour, we arrive in Kanye. The village is built on a gentle slope overlooked by ancient volcanoes, their slopes carpeted with long grass and dense forest. Down in the village, puffs of smoke whirl up from thatched huts while sheep and mongrel dogs laze in fenced-in kraals. As we pull up, an old man rides by on a brown horse. There is a heavy silence in the air, perhaps the silence of a village that is used to keeping its voice down.

Faith opens the gate to her mother-in-law's homestead and directs me to park the bakkie outside her bedroom window. I edge forward, avoiding an old supermarket trolley lying on its side, three puppies, a dog, and a handful of chickens pecking at the ground.

"You have got an alarm on it, haven't you?" Faith asks as I climb out from behind the wheel.

This is the first time she has suggested there is anything to worry about. I nod.

"Oh, I'm sure it'll be fine," she says. "There's only one man in the village I don't trust. But it'll be fine. We'll ask him to look after the bakkie for us. If you want to stop a thief from stealing from you, ask him to help you."

Eight-year-old Anna, 9-year old Kamva (who everyone calls Junior), 12-year-old Thembi and 74-year-old Aunice Hlakula are standing on the steps of the hut waiting for us. Mrs Hlakula is tiny, wrinkled and is keenly aware of her place in the village hierarchy. We have barely put down our bags before she instructs us to get back in the bakkie and go visit Mrs Hlakula, the other one, the really important one, the one that is a daughter-in-law to the late Walter Sisulu. Faith and I both wrinkle our noses, tired from our journey, but Mrs Hlakula is insistent. "Go visit Mrs Hlakula. Then you can be sure no one will steal the bakkie," she says in Xhosa. So Mrs Hlakula and I take Mrs Hlakula's advice and go and visit Mrs Hlakula.

It is late afternoon and the clouds have drawn in, cloaking the rich green with a sleepy grey. Ellen Hlakula lives in a pink bungalow at the highest point of the village. As I wait for Faith to open the gate to the homestead, it strikes me how closely this scene resembles a Scottish Highland crofting village, except here the houses are brightly coloured, rather than white washed. As we approach the front door, a young girl is standing outside, staring up to the hills, unsmiling, her eyes empty.

"Come in, come in," Mrs Hlakula says, as she sees us approach. She is an elderly, rotund lady dressed in a blue and white wave-print dress and a red turban. She calls a young man to bring out a tray prepared with cups of coffee and slices of buttered bread.

We sit down and I thank her for inviting me into her home, commenting how beautiful the surrounding nature is. She nods, offers me coffee, and then gets straight to the point.

"What are you doing here?" she asks. Her face is now unsmiling. She stares me hard in the eyes.

I am unnerved. I am used to black women always being polite to me, always addressing me through a veneer of jolly kindness, but here in Mrs Hlakula's home, there will be no pretend deference. I have not been summoned here to be welcomed, I am here to be observed and have my motives assessed. The mood is of mistrust and suspicion.

I repeat my well-rehearsed monologue about wanting to understand how democracy has changed life for people in the rural areas, and she replies with her own well-rehearsed speech about the success of their new local primary school, built by Walter Sisulu, the advent of pensions for old people, the excellent road into town, and the fact that all the houses in Kanye now have access to running water.

As she talks, I scan the room, taking in the rich peach walls, the wall unit, the comfortable lounge suite, the sepia photo of a white-haired Walter Sisulu in his trademark 1960s-style spectacles with his wife Albertina, smiling, her hair coiffed into a stylish Afro. In most of the homes I have visited so far, there has been no art on the walls, just black and white portraits of family members and ANC posters, but here, propped up behind a crystal punch bowl is a stylised painting of an African woman, with a triangular Afro and a beaded necklace. It reminds me of the kind of painting a white tourist would buy as a souvenir of their safari holiday. The idealized version of the African woman. Proud. Noble. The exotic queen. I grew up in a home decorated with these images. Regal, carved African heads and beaded Zulu weapons – spears and knobkerries – mounted on the wall. Ironically heralding the same culture that we were oppressing.

My turn to speak again. I press Mrs Hlakula. Surely there must be something that worries her. Something that keeps her awake at night. She nods.

"Our problem is the bottle stores," she says. "There are so many bottle stores and they are disturbing our lives. Life is not all right because of alcohol. Our children are drinking and taking drugs, we are so worried about that. Even the girls are drinking. They start drinking age 12 and 14. They are drinking because they are bored. One day they beat the headman for no reason. They did it out of drunkenness."

Mrs Hlakula rises and I follow her out onto the porch where the little girl is still standing, looking out to the hills.

"She is not right," Mrs Hlakula explains, pointing at her head. "She is not my grandchild, but I am looking after her now. Both her parents are dead, and she has no one to look after her. It is a shame."

I realize what I am witnessing here is *Ubuntu*, the African philosophy that believes that our humanity is intertwined and that we gain our humanity through caring for each other. In a true African village, there are no orphans. I am because you are. It could not be further from the philosophy of apartheid: I am, because you aren't.

On the front steps a goat has curled up, soaking up the last of the warmth from the cement. We all laugh and I ask if I can take a picture.

"You can take a picture of the goat, but I do not want my house in the background," Mrs Hlakula says.

I nod. Dignity was hard fought for and won by this family and Mrs Hlakula will not have it undermined by a white woman with unclear motives. I respectfully zoom in on the goat, and then we say our goodbyes and climb into the bakkie.

"She didn't trust me, did she," I say to Faith as I start the engine.

Faith just laughs.

*

That night Faith and I get undressed by candlelight, and climb into her marital bed, giggling. Faith has placed a yellow bucket in the corner of the room so we can pee in the night without having to traipse through the mielie field to the long drop. As she changes into her pyjamas she gives me a brief lesson in how it is done, sound effects and all. I am relieved to be sleeping so close to her. My paranoid fear of being woken in the middle of the night by a dark prowler with a fancy for white flesh is ebbing away, and instead I feel like a teenager at a slumber party, Faith in her pink satin pyjamas checking her mobile phone for messages, me in my nightie, both too excited to go to sleep.

We have barely been in bed two minutes, when Faith leaps up, shrieking.

"What?" I whisper, sitting bolt up right, the terror ebbing back.

"Did you hear that?" she whispers.

"What?"

Outside the window a bird chirps.

"A snake!" she hisses.

"It's a bird," I say.

"Eish, I hate snakes," she says, grabbing the candle and scouring the corners of the room. "If one comes you must protect me."

"But… but… what do I know about snakes?" I ask.

"It doesn't matter. You're braver than me," Faith says.

At this point I start laughing. It feels good to laugh. In fact, it feels great. It is as if that deep fear that has been swirling around in my belly is pouring out of my mouth and vanishing into the ether.

Faith however, is not amused. Climbing back into bed, she blows out the candle and announces: "Then we'll just have to ask God to protect us both."

Faith is the wife of a preacher. At the end of our first meeting in her home in Khayelitsha, we stood in a circle and held hands and Faith asked God to bless me. Tonight, as she says her prayers out loud, I take the opportunity to have my own quiet word. I am not religious in any denominational sense, but I have experienced enough amazing co-incidences and helping hands when you least expect it and most need it, to believe that there is something which connects us all together, something far greater and more mysterious than our small, rational brains could ever hope to comprehend. Take the fact that when I was sitting in Cape Town, wondering how the hell I was going to get myself invited to a rural village, the universe sent me Faith. I love the poetry in that. So tonight, I close my eyes and say quietly: "Thank you for Faith."

*

The day starts early in Kanye. An enthusiastic cockerel wakes me up at 4am. And 5am. And 6am. I hope he tastes better than he sounds.

I stumble out of bed once the children are on their way to school. Faith is already in her mother-in-law's kitchen, a standalone yellow bungalow, the inside walls painted a bright pink. The floor is scrubbed with cow manure, as is the custom, and a mishmash collection of metal pans, tea pots and plates are spread between an old wooden sideboard and a Scotch dresser. Nothing is very clean. Old Mrs Hlakula is too frail to do housework anymore so Faith is getting stuck in. I help by taking our pee bucket down to the long drop inside a tiny corrugated iron shack, exchanging a cheery *"molo"* with our nextdoor neighbour. Over the next couple of days, we meet every time I have to pay a visit. Greater society might not think we have much in common, but our bowels would disagree.

Back at the house, Faith asks me if I want to bathe. I nod and she winks and hands me another bucket, just big enough to crouch in, and pops on the kettle. Faith is clearly enjoying all of this. The image of me balancing precariously over her bucket trying to scrub my bum will probably keep her amused for years to come. While the kettle boils, we sit down and do what most women do in the kitchen: *skinner* (gossip). Faith fills me in on the internal politics of her family, and of who will and will not inherit the Kanye homestead. The hot gossip is that although Thembi, Junior and Anna are the orphaned children of Faith's sister-in-law, meaning by tradition they should now be taken care of by the family's eldest brother, the brother has refused because the children were fathered by a man from the Venda tribe. The Hlakulas are Xhosa.

"He is a racist," Faith says disapprovingly, clicking her teeth.

"Really?" I say. "How can a black South African be a racist to another black South African?"

Faith shrugs. "He just is."

I am bewildered. Of course South African race relations are more complex than the international headline of whites oppressing blacks. The Indians, blacks, Cape coloureds, and all the white sub-tribes, the Lebanese, Greeks, Portuguese, Jews, Afrikaners and English have all to some extent harboured suspicion and dislike for each other, but I had no idea that the Xhosas looked down on the Vendas. Perhaps it should have been obvious that there would be prejudice between the nine black South African tribes. During the run-up to the 1994 elections, there had been bloody conflict between the Zulu IFP supporters and the mostly Xhosa ANC supporters.

But much of that bloodshed was later revealed to have been stoked by right-wing third-party meddling trying to derail the march to democracy, and I think I had naively, wishfully, filed that conflict in the past and adopted a belief that all black South Africans were now happily living side by side in our rainbow nation. Faith's confession smacked me around the head with my willful ignorance.

My inner monologue wakes up and goads. *"Why are you so bloody ignorant? Why has it taken you so long to ask questions? Why have you swallowed this ratified post-apartheid South African story of white men bad, black men good? Why do you avoid the grey?"* I push back, shutting down the voice in my head. Faith has moved on to another topic.

"The people in this house are educated, but nothing goes right for them because of the witches," she says. "The witches don't want anybody to succeed. They want to see you suffering day and night."

"What? Are there witches in this village?" I ask, now a bit bemused.

"There is one," says Faith, scrubbing furiously at a pot. "Once she told me that I must be quiet when I pray, that I pray too loud, but she lives on the other side of the village so she couldn't hear me. She could feel the power of the prayer."

"Is she a *sangoma* (traditional healer)?" I ask.

"She is used by the devil," Faith says firmly.

I laugh and openly roll my eyes.

"Would you ever go to a sangoma?" I ask.

Faith shakes her head. "My mother was a sangoma. When I was doing Grade 9, I lived away from home. My aunt passed away, and after that, at night, a bright light would come to my mother's house, like a ghost. There's no electricity in Tsolo, but when the ghost came it was like in the day, so bright. There was also a bad smell, like a dog had died. My mother tried to do some herbs. It didn't work. Then my family paid R1500 to slaughter two sheep and still the ghost didn't stop. I came home and I took all those things of the sangoma and burnt them in the name of Jesus Christ and it stopped. The sangomas just take money from people. I don't waste any money on sangomas. To cure a headache they can charge you R1000 or a sheep or a car. They charge according to how much money you have."

"What about the ancestors? Do you pray to the ancestors?" I ask.

"No. A dead person cannot pray for me. If he's dead, he's dead. Finished. Once when a family member dreamt that our ancestor was cold, we had to do a huge ceremony to make him warm. We had to buy a cow and have a big feast with brandy and African beer. Pah. If I dream an ancestor is cold I'll buy a new blanket for my bed."

We both laugh as the kettle for my bath boils.

I head off to wash my nether bits, rural style, while a modern African woman continues with her own scrubbing.

*

Old Mrs Hlakula is sitting on the steps of the hut she shares with Anna, Thembi and Junior, warming her face in the morning sun. At night, these steps are lit with a muted green light bulb since, much to Faith's irritation, old Mrs Hlakula does not like bright electric light. In fact, she does not like electricity at all. She still uses wood and paraffin for cooking, and thinks electricity is only really good for one thing: watching television. During my stay, we do not miss an episode of Oprah.

"It's nice to see the rest of the world in there," she says.

I join her on the step and she remembers the old days fondly. Old Mrs Hlakula's father was Walter Sisulu's brother. He died in 1957.

"It was nice before. Before things did not cost a lot of money. Now if you don't have money, you have nothing," she says. "People used to help each other. Now it's hard to help each other. If you've got nothing now, you are not sure someone is going to help you. When my mother died, it was too hard for me."

Faith finishes her chores and comes over.

"How is your head mama?" she asks.

Old Mrs Hlakula sighs a little.

"It's your fault," Faith says.

"Me? What did I do?" I ask.

"You brought that bottle of wine. You've given my mother-in-law a *babelas* (hangover)," she giggles.

Faith and I head off for a walk through the village. It is that quiet mid-morning hour, the sun is at half-mast, the children in class, and the adults, having just finished their morning chores are relaxing with a coffee in the sunshine. People smile and throw us a wave, and Faith giggles and says: "They think you are a millionaire."

"Why?" I ask.

"Every time a black person sees a white person coming, he thinks to himself: there goes a millionaire."

"I hope you don't think that," I say.

Faith shrugs.

We have not been walking long when an elderly man with a walking stick hobbles into our path. It is clear from his demeanour that this is not a chance meeting.

"Molo tata," greets Faith.

"Molo tata," I echo, trying out the customary Xhosa greeting for men older than you.

The old man gently chides Faith for not bringing me to visit him sooner, and then introduces himself to me.

Mr Khawulezile Hlakula is the elderly son of Walter Sisulu's brother. He lived in South Africa's major cities for 35 years, working in the goldmines of Johannesburg and as an asbestos foreman in Cape Town. Now back in the village he is one of the wise elders. We stand in the shade of a tree, next to the school fence, and talk. He starts with the usual musings on what has changed.

"Things are a little bit better, but we are crying about doctors," he says. "Here at All Saints Hospital there is only one doctor. People sleep there three days to see the doctor. The very important thing is for people to get clinics. We've got this HIV and we need a nearby clinic. All Saints is too far from us. Those with HIV have no power to walk."

"But what has improved?" I ask.

"We were the first to get electricity because Sisulu was born here and we say thank you for that, but we do not have toilets yet. We built these toilets ourselves. The municipality take a long time. This school, Sisulu built that with his own money.

We have water, but 15 houses share one tap. If each house can get a tap, then things will be better."

"So what has democracy meant to you?" I ask.

"It means that we are free. All of us. And that we should be together and we should share everything. But it's not going like that. He is rich, I am hungry, she has money, you don't want to share, that's the problem."

Something had been niggling at the back of my mind for a few days. I hadn't been able to put my finger on it, but as Mr Hlakula lamented the lack of sharing in South Africa, it hit me like a rock.

"Do you think we don't understand democracy in South Africa?" I ask.

"It's exactly like that. It confuses some people. The ruling government, they are ruling on their own, they don't use the democracy. They use their own constitution. They put their favourite people in place, they don't care of people who are hungry, they don't care of people who are suffering. You've come here from Scotland. Ask people here. They will say you are the first lady who comes here and asks us what we feel, what we need. The government didn't do that. There was not one single person here from government to ask, hey, what do you feel? What do you need?"

Mr Hlakula sighs. And then says something I never expected to hear from Walter Sisulu's relative.

"You must say the white government before was good because that government was keeping the pressure on, you grew up under pressure. That government was very good, really, because we were not suffering from work at that time. Now you can say I am free, but you get nothing.

There is no work, no money, no nothing. Now the young guys here have a Std 10 but they do nothing. They are drinking. It is our democracy that creates that. At that time when we were under pressure you would never see a young person go to the bottle store and buy a bottle of brandy. Now it is free for everyone to go get a brandy or beer to drink. Those things are going to spoil our children."

Faith agrees with him. She adds that, in the villages, pension money – hidden in the backs of cupboards in unlocked huts – has become easy pickings for drunk, frustrated youths, thirsty for another beer; some teenagers living under their grandparents' care have started stealing their child benefit grants to spend on alcohol. The children argue that the money belongs to them and because South Africa is now a democracy, they have "the right" to spend it as they choose. When the eldest of Faith's charges started pilfering her child benefit grant from the old Mrs Hlakula, Faith shipped her to Cape Town to live under her roof and give her a stern lesson that rights also come with responsibilities.

Close to where we stand chatting is the Pachu General Dealer, Kanye's local spaza shop and shebeen where groups of young men, aged between 18 and 25, mooch away the day. Mr Hlakula cautions me against approaching them, warning that they are not to be trusted and that if I want to speak to them, he will arrange a meeting for later that day. Though I appreciate his concern, I doubt they will speak their minds in front of one of the respected village elders, and so once Mr Hlakula is on his way, Faith and I head over in the pretence of buying a bottle of fizzy drink.

Heads turn as we walk inside. I order a bottle of orange fizz and Faith and I smile at each other as we hear giggles and comments start to be bandied about in Xhosa. It does not take long for one of the young men to approach us.

"Hello," says a young handsome face, sporting fake diamond ear-rings,

David Beckham-style. "We heard there was a white woman in the village. We heard you've come to find out what we need so you can help us."

I cast a look at Faith. This was the story she had made up and we had already had a disagreement over it. She said that people would not want to talk to me if they knew it was just for a book or an article. That they needed to believe they were getting something in exchange for talking to me. I was annoyed because as I saw it, I would only end up looking bad when I did not deliver, but she told me not to worry about that. No one ever delivers anyway, so it would not be much of a change. I resented getting tossed on the heap with everyone else who was systematically letting South Africa down, but Faith had her story and she was sticking to it. I started the conversation by telling them that I did not have the power or money to change anything, the best I could do was get their voices heard. This seemed agreeable. After all, there was not much else going on in Kanye at 11 o'clock in the morning.

The Beckham-styled young man introduces himself as Singalakha Mnquma, an 18-year-old from Bisho, who is in Kanye for the weekend to attend a funeral. From the smell of his breath, he has already had a beer. I asked Singalakha what he is doing with his life.

"Nothing," he says. "You go to school, you finish, then there's nothing to do. You have no cash so you go to town and you find a drunk man, then you steal some cash from him. The only way to get any cash is to steal."

Singalakha says this with a glint in his eye. I think he is playing up to me because I am white and because the stereotypical racist white point of view is, given a chance, all black people are thieves. But it is obvious from the depth in his eyes that Singalakha is a smart guy, that he is testing me, so I cock my head and raise my eyebrows.

"Oh really," I reply, taking out my notebook and starting to write. "So all young people nowadays just steal. The old people are right. You're all just

63

a bunch of thieves?"

The other guys start to disagree. Now everybody wants to talk.

"Look around you," says Singalakha, talking over everybody else. "There are more than 30 guys here who don't know what to do. There is no point going to school. After we finish there are no jobs, so we are just sitting here. Democracy brings a lot of things, but I don't know where they've ended up. It just brought grants for small kids, that's the only thing I know about democracy. That's a fact. There are no opportunities."

Now Singalakha is talking seriously. Sipheshle Hlakula, 21, chips in. After school he spent one year studying to be an electrician in East London, but failed and now his parents can't – or perhaps won't, it's not clear – pay for him to study further.

"Life was way easier for my father and grandfather. In those days there were job opportunities. The important thing is to have a job. All I want is to have a job. Democracy has made me unemployed."

I find his words shocking. If being herded onto a back of a truck to go and work underground for a pittance in the gold mines of Johannesburg, sleeping in men-only hostels far away from your wife and children is being romanticised as good times, then South Africa should start to shudder at the fury and frustration boiling in these young men's hearts.

"What about studying further?" I ask.

"We can't afford university. You have to pay to register, and then only you can apply for bursaries. Our parents don't even have the money to pay for the registration," he says. "What about student loans?" I ask.

"I don't believe in loans, I believe in bursaries," Singalakha says.

It was a bursary that helped me through university in South Africa. My dad worked in a factory, my mum in a shop, and their wages were not enough to pay for tertiary education. Rhodes University, however, awarded discounted tuition to students with top grades – for every A grade you got a R1000 deduction from the R4000 tuition bill – and so my father agreed that I could go, if I could get a 50% discount every year and if I got a job in the holidays to help pay towards the rest. I found out later that they also remortgaged the house. I was the first person in my family ever to go to university.

To hear Singalakha say that he believes in bursaries, not loans, unsettles me. It sounds like he believes someone else, not him, should be responsible for his education. And is he right? In Scotland university education *is* free. The government have assumed the responsibility for educating the youth and students only need take out loans to cover living expenses. In South Africa there is help for poor students through the National Student Financial Aid Scheme (NSFAS), but the bursaries do not meet the full cost of education and many students end up dropping out because they cannot make up the shortfall – even with the help of part-time jobs.

I think back to the secondary school I visited close to Port St Johns. A school with no furniture and teachers who knock off early to pick up their pay cheques. I think of village life where single mothers get by on R250 child benefit grants. The reality of being black and poor is at the root of Singalakha's thinking. He might sound like a socialist, a nihilist or a freeloader, depending on where you stand in the political spectrum, but perhaps his is just the voice of the pragmatist.

I look at these guys and feel their powerlessness.
"What gets you out of bed in the morning?" I ask. They shrug their shoulders.
"We do jobs for our families. We sit around. And we play football," Sipheshle says. "We have a league with the guys from the other villages. We train Monday to Friday afternoons, and we have matches on Saturday and Sunday."

"What do you guys think of the World Cup," I ask. "Are you looking forward to it?"

Singalakha shakes his head. "2010 means nothing to us here. It's the same as usual. I have a dream to meet David Beckham, but I won't meet him because we're stuck out here. They waste millions to build a stadium that will work for one or two days."

"Are you not going to support South Africa?" I ask.

"If I had R50, I'd bet it on South Africa not winning a single match," he says bitterly.

*

We head back to Faith's kraal for lunch.

"You know, those boys are right," she says. "Having a matric means nothing. During the apartheid times it was better because if you passed Std 7 you could be a nurse. Now to become a nurse you must pass matric and must go to the college for four years. Because of these people who were in prison, Mandela, Sisulu, everybody, they were highly educated so when they came back, they didn't want any more Std 7. Maybe they even want to send the Boers back to school. Because, you know, they weren't educated," she laughs.

I look up to the distant hills. Coming from the city, all that space makes your soul feel free. Strange that for those boys, these same hills feel a trap, a noose around their necks.

"I'd love to go for a hike into those hills," I say. "Shall we do it?"

Faith clicks her teeth and shakes her head.

"Eish, why do you white people always want to go hiking?" she says.

"I don't know," I laugh. "Maybe it's because we don't have to walk far to collect water so we have lots of spare energy."

"You know, I grew up among the Boers," she muses. "They used to call us baboons. I used to wonder why, I hadn't seen a picture of baboons and when I saw a picture I said: 'why do they call us that'? Do you know why they called us baboons?"

It was my turn to shrug my shoulders. I think I knew the answer but I was too ashamed to say it out loud, too afraid of being chucked back into the pot I was trying to scramble out of. Why were black people called baboons? Because baboons had black faces, because they were uneducated, and because they would attack you and steal from you if you did not keep up your guard. That, I think, is the racist stereotype in a nutshell.

Back in the kraal, I start playing with the puppies while Faith starts plotting to kill one of Mrs Hlakula's chickens for our dinner. I don't have much of an appetite for one of those scraggy old hens, and ask if we can have samp (dried corn kernels) and beans instead, my favourite African dish. Faith turns up her nose in disgust.

"What do you mean you don't like samp and beans?" I ask. "I thought all black people liked samp and beans."

"It gives me a bad stomach," Faith says.

"And you white people, why do you love dogs so much?"

"Don't you also like dogs? You've got four here" I say, tickling the puppy's stomach. "No, I hate dogs," she says. "I like chickens. You can eat chickens."

That night we gather around the television, watching soap operas. The next day is Saturday. During the week the kids are up at 5am to do their chores before school. Today everyone can sleep until 6am. As I stumble out of bed, Thembi is sitting washing clothes in a big bowl, Anna is sweeping the kitchen floor, Junior is off to fetch water, balancing a five litre drum in a wheel barrow, and old Mrs Hlakula is tidying the garden. Faith seems to have woken up on the wrong side of bed. We had planned today to attend the village funeral, but Faith wants to go to town instead. I notice my cue and give her R500 (£50) for her help so far. She scowls at me and tells me it is not enough. I am surprised and unsure what to do next, so I give her another R500. Perhaps I have underestimated the cost of living. She phones her husband and then tells me it is still not enough.

"How much were you expecting me to give you?" I ask.

"At least R1,500," she says.

Anger and disappointment flash in quick succession through my mind. When we first met in Cape Town, we agreed that I would use the fellowship money to pay for Faith's transport, mobile phone charges (both of which I had already paid) and to contribute towards food, but we did not put a number on it. Jimmy was charging me R250 per day for his translation services so it seemed unreasonable that Faith wanted R500 per day, the same price as an expensive guesthouse, to have me as a guest in her home.

I give Faith another R200. She takes the money begrudgingly.

"Do you want me to take you to town?" I ask.

"No," she says, and walks out the room.

I consider staying and going to the funeral without her, but I feel unwanted, unwelcome. With a disappointed, heavy heart I pack the bakkie. Faith does not try to persuade me to stay. An hour later I reverse out of the kraal and drive slowly and reluctantly back down Walter Sisulu's good road. As Kanye disappears into a cloud of billowing dust, I feel like I have pressed the ejecter button and been hurled from the warm, safe net of a family with all its routines and flung, unwanted, alone, back into the world. Back in Mthatha I check in to a bed and breakfast called the White House. The irony is not lost on me.

Chapter 7

How white is your heart?

I WAS ALONE AND I felt alone. I sat on a double bed in the White House, my hair and body wrapped in a white towel, staring at a white wall. What had just played out was the same thing that used to happen every day in the old South Africa. Black people were as useful to whites as the services they provided. White people were as useful to blacks as the cash they provided. Our relationships were transactional, defined by an invisible code. Perhaps it should have been obvious to me that I had set up my stay in Kanye to be that way. That by offering to reimburse Faith for her help I was creating a business relationship. And that in doing so, I had played out another famous old South African scene: where the white person underpays the black person for services due. Bravo.

But it was not obvious because it was not what I had wanted.

"What did you want? What are you doing?" I hissed under my breath.

I sighed, closed my eyes, feeling tears prick at their edges.

I grew up in a world where it was illegal for black and white people to make love to each other. The Immorality Act. To sit next to each other on park benches. The Reservation of Separate Amenities Act. Apartheid was so effective because it was insidious. It crept into every aspect of our lives, from the prosaic to the profound, and that is why it still hangs over us. It is like a gas cloud that we cannot see and cannot smell because we have been breathing it too long. The way white and black people interact in Britain and France and America is indistinguishable from the way most ordinary black and white South Africans interact. Foreigners will think I am talking neo-racist drivel. South Africans will understand. It is there in the way we greet each other with so much warmth, but know so little about each other's lives. In the way we want to get closer, but have no idea how. We do our best, some better than others, to manage our legacy, to wear our past with grace, but it is difficult to overcome something so intangible. It is like trying to stick a plaster on a ghost.

What did I want? I wanted Faith to like me. I wanted Faith to get to know me by the colour of my heart and not the colour of my skin. I wanted her to say that she did not blame me. That it was not my fault. I was just a child. My hands are clean. That she knows I am different *from them*. Better. That I am not one of *them*. Am I?

Chapter 8

....

Asimbonang' umandela thina
We have not seen Mandela

WHAT IS IT TO be ignorant of your country and yourself?

It is 1982. I am five, and I am on a plane, flying across the world. I am happy because I am wearing my burgundy velvet dress and long white socks with frills on top. My mum is happy because for the first time in two years, my dad is going to have a job and they won't threaten to put him in jail any more. On the plane they give me a toy giraffe that you can make dance. You get giraffes and lions and elephants in South Africa. I make my giraffe dance for hours.

The plane stops in Nairobi but we are not allowed to get off. My mum walks me to the open door to get some fresh air.

"Why are those men pointing guns at the plane?" I ask.

She does not know.

They are pointing guns because South Africa is an enemy state in Africa. Because it is hated for its political regime that oppresses the black majority under the rule of the white minority. We are going to live there and we do not know.

We buy a brand new house in Crystal Park where there are no crystals, no giraffes, no lions, no elephants and no tarred roads. The house is made of dark rough brick. My mum calls it clinker brick. Klinka. I like the way it sounds. And I like the way it smells. Of newness. Of nothing. Waiting to be filled by us. I go to a new school where they wear red uniforms. I take a blue PUTCO bus forty minutes each way, each day, and I am happy because I love the bus. I love looking out the window and mapping this new world in my head. Mielie (maize) fields, quarry pond, sweet shop, dam. Water tower, old-age home, chemist, vet, Spar. There are also brown PUTCO buses but I don't take them. They are for black people and they go to different bus stops.

On Sundays we go to Murray Park where there are trampolines, ponies, swimming pools and separate toilets for black people and white people. The toilets signs read *Geen Blankes* (Non-whites), *Slegs Blankes* (Whites only). Blanke is the Afrikaans word for a white person, but it looks a lot like the English word for black. Every time I need to go I get confused about which one I'm supposed to go to. I pee behind a tree.

The phone rings late one evening. It is my nanna and grandad calling my dad, all the way from England.
"What did they want," my mum asks, worried.
"They want to know if we're alright," my dad says. "They've seen some riots on the news."
"Riots here?" my mum says. "Are they sure it was here?"
There is nothing about it on the telly. There never is.

It is 1985. I am eight. My brother is dead. I woke up ten days ago to voices whispering on the phone. I crept through to the living room and listened from behind a wall. "There were two Richards travelling in the car. We know one of them is dead. Can you tell us which Richard is dead?" they are asking. It is our Richard. I creep back to bed and close my eyes and pretend

72

to sleep. When they tell me I pretend to cry. I feel numb.

Our house is in a shit storm. I'm not allowed to swear but it is true. My mum stops working because she cannot face driving every day on the motorway where her son was thrown out of a car to break his neck and die. Every day she takes a massive cream pill from a big brown glass bottle. These "big bombs" will help her get better, she says. She sleeps. My dad is torn apart with grief. He drinks. He drinks. He drinks. He drinks. He screams. He slams doors. He sits in silence.

The newsreader says there is a State of Emergency in the country. There is a state of emergency in my house.

My other brother goes to the army for two years. National service. We can't visit him for the first three months and then we go to watch his passing out parade.

"It has done him good," my mum says.

He gets sent away to South-West Africa to fight in a war on the Angolan border. When his letters come they have whole sentences scratched out. They don't scratch out the sentences where he asks about the dog.

The dog always goes crazy weird on the days my brother comes home from the border. The dog knows he is coming before we do. What else does the dog know?

One night a black man knocks on our door. Panicked. Breathing heavily.

"Please baas, please help me. Please can I use your phone?" he asks.

The phone is right by the front door. There is a debate. Should we let this man into our house? Should we let him use our phone? What could be so bad, what could have happened that he would need to use our phone? We ask him to explain. He said he can't explain. He pleads. My mum nods. Quickly. Phone calls are expensive. He stands by the door and uses the phone. He speaks in an African language. He disappears into the night.

It is 1990. I am 13. I am short, bespectacled and flat chested. I wear a bra anyway. I hope my boobs will grow by next year because my aunt is coming to visit from England.

Miss Bekker is our history teacher. In a prefab classroom on the edge of the school she teaches us about apartheid. Except she doesn't teach, she reads aloud from her notes and we have to copy, word for word, what she says into our history jotters. We take down the minutes of South African history. It goes something like this. "After World War 2, when nobody was looking, when all the English people were watching what was happening in Europe, the Afrikaners won the elections. They divided up the country so that all the different races in South Africa could all have a bit of it for themselves. They thought that everyone would be happier if they had their own land and their own rulers so that they could develop according to their own cultures and traditions."

It sounds fair enough. Why wouldn't you want to hang out all the time with people who are like you? I certainly don't want to hang out with those netball girls who are a total bunch of bitches.

16 June[3], 1991. I am 14. We have a bomb scare at school. Another one. We are marched down onto the big field and we sit there for hours in the hot sun. It is great because from where I am sitting I can stare at Jimmy whom I am madly, deeply in love with. We get sent home from school early. We must go home quickly. Once home, we must not go anywhere. No one tells us why. When I ask, our teacher tells me to just hurry up. I ask my mum why when she gets home from work later. She doesn't know why either.

---

3 Soweto day. In 1976, the year I was born, black high school students protested against the introduction of Afrikaans as the language of instruction. During the protest some students threw stones at the police. The police responded with bullets, killing an estimated 176 people.

It is 1992. There is going to be a referendum. A refer-what? All the lamp posts are plastered with big posters saying Yes! Ja! No! Nee! What is the question?

Officially it is "Do you support the continuation of the reform process which the State President began on February 1990 and which is aimed at a new Constitution through negotiation?"

But really it is "Do you want black kids to come to your school?" "Do you want black people living next door to you?" "Do you want change?"

"We have no choice," say the ones who know.

"We cannot go on like this," they nod and rub their beards.

Like what?

The referendum says YES.

We are taught to march. On Friday afternoons, the double period after second break, we are taken to the softball pitch, the no mans land that divides our school from the Afrikaans school next door and ordered to march. *"Left, left, left, right, Left my wife in New Orleans with sixty kids and a can of beans and I thought it was right, right, right for my country, whooopidee-dooo, left, left."*

This is nothing new for the boys – they have been learning to march since they were 13 – but this is new for us girls. At first we are outraged. It is dirty and sweaty and stupid. Then we hear that Anthony, gorgeous, dark-haired, olive-skinned Anthony, school heart-throb, is to be in charge of our squadron. We spend the better part of most school days following Anthony around with our eyes. Now we are being ordered to march after him around the playground. There is barely enough lip-gloss to go around.

A questionnaire gets sent home from school: "How long do you think it will be before Benoni High becomes mixed race?" 1 year? 5 years? 10 years? My dad and I hunch over it with a pen. It will never happen within a year. For a start, we don't speak the same language. It will take time. We circle 5 years. They come the next year.

It is 1993. My final school year. The matric history teacher is Mr Howarth. He has a big, thick brown moustache and wears tight-fitting brown trousers. He stands behind a podium and reads aloud a paragraph from our history textbook. It goes something like this: "Although apartheid has brought some economic challenges for South Africa, it is widely believed that it has been the best policy for the country."

"What do you think?" he asks me.

What do I think? *Think?* I do not think. I remember and repeat what I read in these textbooks. Just as you taught me to do. Nobody said anything about thinking.

"You should read more powerful books," my English teacher tells me. I tell her I've just read *Pandora's Box* by Jilly Cooper. It's a book about a powerful woman. She says that's not what she means. What does she mean? What are these books? Why are they not in our school library or on my parents' shelves?

It is 1995. I am 17. Nelson Mandela is the president of South Africa and I am at university. In wood-panelled lecture halls the light is starting to filter in. I learn that throughout the 1980s our press was censored and that when newspapers retaliated by printing empty white space where a banned story should have been, the government responded by making it illegal to print white spaces.

As part of a film studies course I'm required to watch *Cry the Beloved Country*, *Cry Freedom* and *A Dry White Season*, the latter of which had been banned. I do not leave the house for two days because I cannot stop crying, because for the first time I witness, if only on film, the truth about the fiction in which I have grown up. I realise that everything I thought and believed about the world was a product of a carefully fabricated bubble. I feel like I have been slapped in the face by a wet, spiked fish and had my heart broken. I feel like I am finding out something everyone else already knew. I do not talk about my feelings to anyone. I am ashamed of this country. I am ashamed of my ignorance. I sit alone with my grief.

The Truth and Reconciliation Commission begins. It is a forum for South Africans who were tortured and imprisoned during apartheid, and the families of those who were killed, to tell their stories, to ask questions, to demand answers, to come face-to-face with the perpetrators. Week after week, people come forward to share their darkest secrets and their ghosts, which are then broadcast on Special Report, an SABC hour-long programme dedicated to documenting this process. The stories make you sick to your stomach. People abducted in the middle of the night, taken to farm buildings in the middle of nowhere, beaten, electrocuted, suffocated, half-drowned, their faces smashed in with lead pipes, their bodies burnt on braais (barbecues) while the police drink beers and socialise. And while I slept soundly in my bed. My cocooned, silent, sun-drenched childhood is being exposed as a fairy tale built on the blood and corpses of others. Horror upon horror upon horror until you switch off the TV because you cannot face any more, because you do not know what to do with these new truths. My onion-like country is shedding its skins and my mind grapples to find understanding that engenders compassion.

Who is going to apologise for nurturing our minds in a country blanketed by censorship and propaganda?

Who is going to apologise for bringing us of age to believe that the way our society was arranged, whites to the right, blacks to the left, Indians and coloureds in the middle, was normal?

Who is going to say "Sorry, but the way our society was sold to you as a pragmatic idea that benefitted everyone, was actually poisonous and only possible because of torture, abductions, murder and rape"?

Nobody is.

Our ignorance is a minor injury in the face of lead pipe beatings and people being thrown out of windows.

There is no TRC for our ignorance.

We are carefully hand-reared racists that have been let loose and instructed to dance to a new tune.

We put on new hats made out of rainbow coloured paper and we smile and we do the same old dance.

We grow numb.

"What's on the telly?"

"The TRC."

"Not again."

"I'm sick of the bloody TRC."

We switch off.

Later that year, journalist Antjie Krog will pen these words: *When the Truth Commission started, I realised intuitively: if you cut yourself off from the process, you will wake up in a foreign country – a country that you don't know and that you will never understand.*

Krog is right. But I am too young and ignorant to realise or care.

Chapter 9

....

Mthatha Daze

February 2010

I HAVE NO PLAN. I leave the White House and take the bakkie for a slow drive around the streets of Mthatha. The city, effectively a big town, dates back to the late 19th century when British colonial forces set up camp along the Mthatha River and assigned British names to the roads they built: Sutherland, Durham, Leeds and York. During apartheid, it was the administrative and business capital of the Transkei, but after 1994, all of the city's black movers and shakers took their money and headed to Johannesburg, leaving Mthatha effectively to rot. Whereas the rest of South Africa has painted over its colonial and apartheid past with new, more politically relevant names, the residents of Mthatha still drive down Sutherland, Durham, Leeds and York streets, except today there is more pothole than street.

I stare through the window. I want to get out and explore, but a voice inside my head is chastising me:

White women do not walk these streets alone.

A lump of fear lodges itself in the back of my throat.

"Don't be pathetic, get out of the car," I goad myself.

I open the window. My acquiescence.

I drive up and down every street in Mthatha.

I do not get out of the car. I drive to a pizza parlour in a roadside mall. I park the car two metres from the doorway and scuttle inside. I order a pizza and pick up my phone.

I cannot do this alone. I need someone else's chutzpah.

I call Marc Shoul.

I had first met Marc at the bar at Thea's Wild Coast Kitchen. Marc is a hairy, chain-smoking Jewish boy from the South African coastal town of Port Elizabeth who was probably born with a mobile phone stuck to his ear. He is also a brilliant photographer. Marc was the first South African who understood what I was trying to do. He had spent over a year getting to know and documenting life on the streets of inner city Johannesburg, the Flatlands as he called them. He was mugged twice, losing two cameras, but the infectious energy of the city kept pulling him back.

"It's the excitement that overpowers the fear. Everyone is watching their back but going forward," he said.

I call him and ask if he will join me on the road for a few days. Marc is a freelancer like me, and as luck would have it, he is not busy. I offer to pay for his flight and he agrees to fly down the next day.

My heart relaxes. My confidence grows. I eat my pizza and head back into town. On my kerb crawl I had noticed a sign pointing the way to the Eastern Cape Arts and Crafts Hub. Craft, the realm of women. Creativity, a cocoon that I trust. I park outside and poke my head through the door. A woman is on the phone and waves me through to a showroom laid out with tables of Xhosa beadwork.

I spend a pleasant five minutes alone, admiring the necklaces until the woman is off the phone.

"Can I help you?" she says coming into the showroom and introducing herself as Bulelwa Bam, the manager.

Her accent flashes at me like an orange light on a dashboard. Inspection needed. She has the same accent as a white South African, which, when attributed to black South Africans of a certain age, is labelled a Model C accent. In the early post-apartheid years, Model C was the ranking given to the former whites-only government schools, and it was to these schools that middle-class black parents sent their children immediately after the end of apartheid. For a thirtysomething black person to have a Model C accent is a mark of black privilege. Bulelwa, however, is older than me. She would have matriculated before the end of apartheid. So how did she get that accent?

We chat about the aims of the hub, that it was set up to allow local crafts-women to sell their beadwork to the government to be used as conference gifts, and about how difficult it is because the women are uneducated and not used to deadlines, and though I am nodding and listening, I am more interested in hearing about Bulelwa's life.

"Where are you from?" I finally ask.

"Mount Ayliff," she says. A Transkei village on the edge of the N2.

"And did you go to school there?" I ask.

"I went to private school in Pietermaritzburg," she says.

The Bams, I discover, are one of the Transkei's wealthiest families. Bulelwa's grandfather ran the first black-owned bus company, Bam Brothers, and her father ran hotels and liquor stores. During apartheid, private schools were permitted to accept black pupils, and Bulelwa was one of only 15 black pupils in a school of 200.

"We looked down on the white kids from Pietermartizburg Girls High, because they went to a government school," Bulelwa laughs.

"And what was it like coming back to the Transkei in the holidays?" I ask.

"It was fine when I was little, but it got harder as I got older. You start internalising that white culture. These girls schools were prim and proper. I still have a problem with talking loud."

After school, in a bid to get back to her roots, Bulelwa enrolled at Fort Hare University, Nelson Mandela's alma mater.

"I wanted to go to a traditional black institution, but I didn't last. It was too much for me. When the lecturer asked questions, I would change my accent to an African accent to fit in. I ended up leaving and going to university in Durban instead," she explains.

"So what brought you to Mthatha?" I ask.

"I want to go live in a village. I've asked the chief for land," she says.

I look at her, bemused.

"A lot of my peers look at me like that," she says. "But I prefer being out there, you have your plot, you have your garden, you harvest your own water. Someone is going to advise me how to build a hut all eco-friendly."

"But aren't you worried that you won't fit in?" I ask.

She shakes her head.

"To get village people to accept you is simple, but we complicate it. You don't pitch up there in your jeans, no, you wear a skirt. If you go to a meeting and they say women on the grass, then you go sit with the women on the grass. You don't argue with a man. You can't say 'you are wrong', you have to find another way to say it. If they offer you samp and mealies, then you eat with them. Because we are educated, we tend to talk down to them, we don't even realise it. In the village there's a whole different culture of how to do things, how to speak to people."

I find myself smiling. I feel a curious kinship with Bulelwa. Another human who has been battered into an odd shape by our complicated, collective past, and who is doing her best to remould it into a shape that feels more true, more authentic, more bearable.

*

I pick Marc up from the airport. His is one of the first flights to land in a month. The runway landing lights had been broken. I tell him what happened with Faith and he is sympathetic.

"Happens all the time," he says. "People think I'm rich because I have a car and an expensive camera. But I'm not rich at all. It's hard to make a living as a photographer. It's hard to pay the bills. No one is going to give me a government house. No chief will give me land. I have to buy it. People don't realise that a western way of life isn't easy either."

82

We head into the heaving chaos that is Saturday afternoon in downtown Mththa. The streets are awash with shoppers, loud music and people hanging in the streets.

"So what do you want to do?" Marc asks.

"I want to walk these streets. Just be open and see what stories come our way," I say.

We park the bakkie, switch on the alarm, the steering lock, double check the doors, and head onto Eliot Street, where the pavements are lined with women street vendors, sat beneath rickety canopies, the floor covered with cardboard boxes, selling homegrown vegetables, colourful scarves and handmade African dresses. In this part of South Africa, where women make up 60% of the population and unemployment is off the scale, street trading is one of the few ways women can supplement the child benefit grants on which most households depend. The air is full of gossip, laughter and the whirring of sewing machines. Directly behind their stalls are the Chinese-owned shops selling imported clothes, bags, shoes and sunglasses at bargain prices.

I have mixed feelings about these stores. The girl in me delights that you can find a designer knock-off for less than the price of a sandwich while the nature lover reels at the heady stench of cheap synthetic fabrics and Chinese clothing dye. It is like the smell of the smog of Shenzen, shovelled into an airtight container and shipped halfway around the world.

I stop to admire an African skirt, patterned with blue and white fish.

"Hello my darling," says the stallholder, an elderly woman who speaks with an unusual accent – more English than African. She asks me where I am from and I tell her Benoni, but I have been living in Scotland.

"Oh goodness, my godmother was from Scotland, and I was educated at a Scottish missionary school," she says, gesturing for me to sit down next to her, and introducing herself as Moira Richards, a very Scottish name.

83

"You must have seen a lot of change over the years," I say.

Moira nods her head and smiles. "A lot, a lot, a lot. During apartheid, you know, it was very difficult for people to make a life. You were not allowed to make any progress with what you had or what you could do. Now, whatever skills you have, you can use them freely. Our problem is, we don't have enough money to buy in bulk.

"You see those shopping bags," she says, pointing to a nearby shop window, "We can't sell them anymore because the Chinese sell them at the price we bought them for. It's helping other people, but it's killing us vendors."

"Do you ever miss the old days?" I ask.

She smiles and nods.

"If we could get those days back – without the oppression – I'd take those days. In those years, there was not so much crime so we never used transport but now you cannot walk, because you are scared you will get hurt. Our children are living in a better world, but they don't really know what democracy is," Moira says.

"What do you mean?" I ask.

"Like with abortion," she says, pointing to one of the posters advertising 'Painless Womb Cleaning, Dr Mark, R200', roughly stuck onto a nearby lamppost.

"Our children don't understand why the government says abortion is legal. The abortion was put there so if I am raped, then I do not have fear. But now everybody, if they don't want the child, they just kill it. There's no balance."

"What do you think needs to change?" I ask.

"I think up there in the parliaments, they should not only sit with educated people, they should also take some people from the grassroots, so they can understand what is going on at our level," she says.

She tells me how the previous week, she buried a third member of her family. The young man had been planning to avenge the murder of his mother and his wife, and had been shot dead by their same killers before he could pull the trigger.

"The police say people must not take the law into their hands, but they are not arresting the people who are doing the killing, so then people do it themselves. It is just war," Moira says.

The voice in my head pipes up: "*It is just Africa. That is why they built the walls.*" I shake it away and buy a skirt from Moira. A shwe-shwe print with fish. It costs R60. Moira gives me a big kiss.

"Thank you my darling. I am so happy now," she says, giving me a hug. "Now I can buy milk for my grandson."

*

Marc has been sitting on the steps of a camera shop, showing his camera to some young would-be snappers. I give him a wave and we head on into one of the Chinese stores. I am curious to know what life is like for them here – are they welcome, or are they treated with hostility? At the back of the store, hunched over his computer, is a Chinese man in his thirties. "Hello," I say.

He looks at me unsmiling, blank. A voice cuts in. Disparaging.

"He doesn't understand English. None of them do."

The voice belongs to AJ Tahir, aka Raja, a 30-year-old Pakistani man who tells us he came to Mthatha from Lahore in 2003 to realise his dream of starting his own business. Raja owns SP Cellphone, a mobile phone sales booth in the doorway of the Chinese shop and a grocery and hardware store in the village of Mpekho, an hour's drive from Mthatha. We stand in the doorway and chat.

"Everybody is following the money," Raja says. "The Chinese sell mainly clothing. The Pakistanis sell electronics, hardware, phones and groceries."

"And is business good?" I ask.

"Yes. The people here spend the social grant money. On payday, the 3rd of every month, there is nice business. We send money home when we can."

Social grant money from Africa being sent to build villages in Pakistan.

That puts a new spin on globalisation.

"What do the locals think of you?" I ask.

"Some are happy, some of the educated ones are jealous," Raja says.

"And is it easy to integrate?"

"Not for everyone," he says. "But I married a black woman."

Marc and I look at each other and chuckle. During apartheid it was forbidden to marry across the colour bar. These laws were revoked in the 80s, even before Mandela was released from prison, but South Africans have been slow to intermarry. It is refreshing to hear how Raja was able to marry a local girl from his adopted hometown without having to filter any of the racist baggage of the past.

That night Raja invites Marc and I home to meet his wife. The couple live at the Grosvenor Hotel, which may still be an upmarket address in London, but has long lost its sheen in Mthatha. At the back of the hotel, an old storeroom has been partitioned to create makeshift rooms. Raja opens his door to reveal a small room, no bigger than 9m^2 crammed with a double bed, a wardrobe and a TV cabinet on which rests all their worldly possessions. His wife is sitting on the bed, a pretty young Xhosa woman, who smiles shyly and reaches for her burkha at the sight of Marc.

Raja apologises for the cramped conditions.

"I had my own house in the township for a while, but one night they robbed me, took R2000 and my bakkie. They said that if I had not been with the woman, they would have shot me. In Pakistan we have robbery, but if someone starts beating someone else, other people will come up and ask why are you beating him? Here, they start beating and they keep beating until he dies. We feel safer here all together," he says.

Raja invites us to sit on the bed and they tell us the story of how they met at a petrol station, and how Maya converted to Islam and changed her name – she was previously called Yandiswa – in order for them to marry.

"What did your parents think?" I ask.

"My parents said nothing. They cannot choose my husband for me," Maya says.

I ask if Raja had to pay *lobola*. In Xhosa tradition, the man pays the bride's family for her hand in marriage, proving that he has the means to support her financially and emotionally in the years to come. The *lobola* is often paid in cows, since cows are the most valuable assets in Xhosa society.

Raja nods.

But I paid in cash, not cows," he says. "And I did not pay it all."

Marc and I both laugh. In Pakistan and India it is de facto that you haggle over prices. I liked that that cultural rule stood up to the culture of *lobola*.

"And your friends? What do they think?" I ask.

"They did not like it at first, but now they see we're happy so they are happy for me. Love doesn't ask why," Maya says.

And they do seem happy. Raja speaks Xhosa and Maya is learning Arabic and has learnt to love hot curries. There is a lovely feeling when you sit together with them in the room. I ask if they plan to have children. They look at each other with lowered eyes and soft smiles. It turns out Maya is already three months pregnant.

"Will you stay living in Mthatha?" I ask.

Raja shrugs. "I can't say. It depends on the three Ws – work, weather, wife. They can all change overnight."

A face peers around the doorway. It is Raja's friend. He has overheard our conversation and offers his own reply instead.

"I will stay. It is so beautiful here. Where we come from in Pakistan, it looks nothing like this. We don't have these hills, the mountains like you see on the way to Port St Johns, the beaches. I've never known somewhere so beautiful. I am blessed because God brought me here."

His is the first truly positive voice I have heard in the Transkei. Strange how it takes an outsider to see what the rest of us cannot.

Chapter 10

....

The Black Widows

MARC AND I HAVE stumbled upon a story. My curiosity may have been fuelling this journey, but it was a fellowship backed by *Time* magazine that was bankrolling it; to satisfy the funders, I had to file a newsworthy story that gave some insight into the state of democracy in Mandela's homeland.

Our lucky break came after a morning spent at the Nelson Mandela Museum in Qunu, Mandela's home village. This impressive multi-million rand structure commemorates South Africa's first democratic president's long walk to freedom and includes in its grounds Mandela's actual child-hood playpark, a natural rock slide on the side of a hill worn smooth by generations of children's – and now tourists' – bottoms.

It was a typical Sunday morning in the Transkei. The air was hanging hot and heavy and the only thing moving was a dandelion, caught on a tiny thermal close to the tops of the long grass. Monde Mongodlana, the museum caretaker, had led us to the slide and there, on the open hillside, had pointed out the important homes of Qunu including Mandela's modest facebrick home and directly across the road, the small bungalow of Chief Nokwanele Balizulu, the village chief.

"You should stop in for a visit," Mondle said. "She won't mind."

"She?" I repeated, delighted. I thought I had already met the only woman chief in the Transkei.

Jimmy was with us. He had come from Port St Johns for the day to be our translator, and it was Jimmy that we sent first into the mint-green bungalow, peaked cap in hand, while we waited outside, watching goats graze. Behind us, the N2, the national highway connecting Cape Town to Durban, was quiet, disturbed only by the occasional rumbling of a taxi or a truck. A man lay sleeping on a bench in front of a wall of blue post office boxes – one of them surely Mandela's.

"*Molo*," Jimmy calls.

A small child pops her head out the door, followed by a woman dressed in a wide-brimmed floppy hat, stripey black T-shirt, long denim skirt and running shoes. She takes one look at Jimmy, then at Marc and I, and without missing a beat waves us all in. We file in, over her pink linoleum kitchen floor and are offered a seat in her lounge, on a green velour couch where a tiny white chicken, more pet than Sunday roast, pecks inquisitively at our feet.

Chief Balizulu sits down, surveys us, smiles and before I can ask a question, she disarms us with a welcome, spoken in Xhosa and translated by Jimmy.

"First I want to tell you that you are welcome to this area and I would like to apologise for things that have happened here, like the mugging of tourists in Port St Johns after 1994. At the moment it is quiet and I like it that you come and see the beauty and the warmth of the country, so that other white people can come as well," she says.

It is diplomacy but with a woman's touch and I am instantly charmed. I explain why we are here and ask her if there have always been women chiefs in this area. She shakes her head and smiles.

"It was unheard of before 1994 for a woman to become a chief. I was one of the first," she says, explaining that before 1994 the chief line would pass from father to firstborn son, and if the father died before the son was grown up, an uncle or cousin would hold the fort until he was ready. Mandela, however, changed all that.

"Mr Mandela insisted that the women as well become chiefs because everyone is equal in front of the people," she says.

"And do women make better chiefs than men?" I ask.

She contemplates and then nods.

"Women are more sympathetic, and that's what counts. In the past, if you had committed a crime, the chiefs would string you up by rope and start a fire under your feet so the smoke would envelop you. But that is not happening now. We give more fines than punishment. If you have impregnated a woman out of wedlock and the parents are complaining, you would pay five heads of cows and R200. In the past they used to beat them up."

"And does everyone accept them?"

Chief Balizulu nods tentatively: "Just a few people still have the mind of the past. Just a few think that only a man can be strong and capable enough to be a chief."

"And what of those people – how have they reacted?" I ask.

She shakes her head, clicks her teeth, and looks down at the floor. At first she says nothing. A short discussion ensues between her and Jimmy.

And then she says in English: "You should speak to Lindiwe Ngubenani." She scrolls through her mobile to find the number.

*

Lindiwe Ngubenani looks nothing like you would imagine a traditional African chief. Clad in a clinging, pink mini-dress, big loop earrings, black sandals dangling from painted toenails, the 27-year-old looks ready for a day at the beach. We meet at her relative's home in New Rest, one hundred kilometres from Mthonjana, the coastal village of which she is the head-woman. The house is a modern bungalow that would not look out of place in a Johannesburg suburb. The lounge windows are hung with orange frilly curtains, a stereo blaring pop music takes pride of place on the wall unit and the house is peppered with kitsch ornaments including ceramic swans, a pair of ceramic dogs and two handwoven raffia rondawels, the traditional Xhosa dwellings that still make up most Eastern Cape homesteads. On the wall is a simple prayer: "Dear Lord, Protect This House".

Lindiwe can speak English - she studied education at the Walter Sisulu University in Mthatha - but prefers to tell her story in Xhosa, with Jimmy translating. She shouts to her hosts to turn down the loud dance music that has been pulsating through the house since our arrival, and starts to nervously twirl her hair through her hands as she speaks.

"They assassinated my mother in September 2007. They shot her inside the hut and then burnt it with her body inside. She was the chief of our village, Mthonjana, near Hole in the Wall. She took over from my father after he died, but the villagers didn't accept her. They spread rumours that my brother was illegitimate, they insulted her, threatened her, and then the community selected four people to kill her. They said they could not be ruled by a woman."

The look on her face suggests her grief has long been replaced with anger.

"I am not at home now because people are not accepting me. Only 10 homes out of 74 support me. People are divided. They say they cannot be ruled by a woman, especially by a girl. They want a 60 year old man from a lesser house to become the chief, but it doesn't work like that. A chief is not chosen by the community. A chief must be born."

It is a strange situation where one of the key tenets of democracy – equality between the sexes – has been used to extend and entrench the influence of a political system that is at odds with the other key pillar of democracy – the right to choose and elect your leader. I try to imagine how I might feel if Lindiwe was my chief. It is not something a white South African would ever have to think about. In these tiny villages at the distant end of mud tracks, far from police stations and courts of justice, the tribal chief and their councillors have long been the bedrock of village life. The chiefs are the custodians of the culture, they are responsible for sorting out quarrels

91

and allocating land for homes and grazing. Since 1994, each village also has a municipally appointed ward councillor whose remit is to work side by side with the chiefs on issues of rural development, but many of these councillors live far from the villages and day-to-day life is still in the sphere of the chief. Over the next week I discover that Lindiwe and the villagers of Mthonjana are not the only ones caught in a fearful conflict between the past and the present.

*

"Thinking of your reason to meet me is very haunting. It is like digging what I want to forget. I think we need to arrange to meet face-to-face for your interview. We are about to go to lunch. Sorry to sound so complicated."

I had been trying to get hold of Senior Chief Nokhakha Jumba for two days. It was a case of broken wires and cross communication and when I eventually found her office in downtown Mthatha, she was not there. I felt like giving up. A few hours later she sent me this text, suggesting that we meet face-to-face at the conference centre at the Nelson Mandela Hospital where she was attending a rural development conference – the kind where people arrive in high heels and Mercedez Benz, not a tractor or trowel in sight.

Nokhakha Jumba is the chief of the Jumbas, a clan within Mandela's Thembu tribe. Like Chief Balizulu, Nokhakha became the chief after her husband died, a regent holding the position until her young son came of age. We meet during the conference lunch break, and she leads me to a quiet corner, beneath a plastic palm tree. Tall, regal, her hair covered by a colour-ful turban, her car keys dangling from an oxtail, Nokhakha looks every bit the modern African queen, but her story has more medieval undertones.

Nokhaha's husband was the chief of the Jumbas. When he died in 2003, the king of the Thembus asked that she quit her job in social development and take charge until her son came of age. At first she resisted.

"I was afraid. I knew a cousin of my father-in-law was desperate for the position, and I knew they would fight me and I was not ready to fight. I was still too fragile after my husband's death. I eventually took it because I thought I would have the King's backing, that I would have some people who would protect me. I decided not to disappoint them."

But King Dalindyebo is not known as a man of principles. In 2009 he was sentenced to 15 years for serious crimes including arson, assault and kidnapping. In retaliation, in January 2010, he threatened to secede Thembuland from South Africa unless the government apologised for his conviction and hand over more than £7million in compensation. The notion that Nelson Mandela's tribal homeland could become a separate state to South Africa was so laughable most people did not give it a second thought.

"I didn't even take it as something serious. I saw it as a joke from the very beginning," she says.

In the coming months, the king persisted with his threats and when I met Nokhakha, she and the other chiefs were growing concerned.

"People already get slaughtered in Thembuland for telling someone they are wrong. If the King was allowed to get away with his charges and be permitted to secede from South Africa there would be no justice at all in Thembuland. It would mean that it was a good thing to kill and kidnap. People could be killed like goats."

It was against this Shakespearean backdrop that Nokhaka's own drama began to escalate. She received personal threats from her husband's cousin, he intimidated her and threatened her with physical violence, and instead of supporting her, the King responded by ordering for her appointment to be withdrawn.

"He said in order for there to be stability in our community, a woman must not be in charge."

The conflict came to a head the previous December when the cousin and his men convened a meeting with the King in her kraal in Tabase village without her consent. They handed her a letter saying that she would rule only over dead bodies.

"They presented it in such a manner that they reminded me what happened to Lindiwe's mother," she says. "They want me out of that throne and they are not afraid of anything. I don't know where else to go now."

The tears she had been biting back begin spilling down her cheeks.

"At this stage I'm just tired of fighting. And I've said to myself, what God likes, that's what the solution will be, because I've tried."

Since December Nokhakha has been too afraid to sleep in her kraal. She works in Tabase village during the day, writing affidavits and reference letters for her subjects, but each night she journeys back to Mthatha to sleep in relative safety. She also worries for her son's future.

"He is 16 this year. By right he is supposed to take over when he is 21, but as long as I see that he is not ready for this ordeal, I may postpone it. My main aim is that he gets a proper education, that he doesn't depend completely and solely on the chieftainship because it is a hell of a challenge. It is not a sweet thing. At a distance, one might think to be a chief is honorable, a great thing, but it's not as great as that."

I ask Nokhakha if she blames democracy for her troubles. She shakes her head.

"In traditional leadership we always cry about justice or recognition, but not equality. We have our own challenges as women in rural areas. If you claim that we have to be equal to men, then we will have the challenges of digging graves. If we say we are equal, it means we must take the spades and go to the graves. As women in traditional communities, we are not so strong about equality, we only need justice."

But what shapes does justice take for unelected chiefs in a democracy? In these same months that I was travelling through the Transkei, elsewhere in South Africa rural communities were preparing to challenge the authority of the tribal councils in the Constitutional Court – the highest court in the land. The basis of their argument: that during apartheid, many of the old chiefs colluded with the white government in order to secure themselves more land and power. The complex and uncomfortable truth is that the tribal homelands, also known as Bantustans, of which there were ten – Venda, Qwa qwa, Kwazulu, Lebowa, Bophutatswana, Transkei, Ciskei, Gazankulu, Kangwane and Ndebele – were an integral part of the apartheid idea of separate development. The white government did not want black people settling permanently in white areas, so they shored up the country and created "independent homelands" where black people were permitted to self-govern. To make this work, the apartheid government needed the support of the main chiefs of these areas, and to this day, many chiefs are hated for the role they played in establishing the apartheid vision.

One community that was betrayed by its own people was the Makuleke in Mpumalanga in the north of the country. In 1969 the Makuleke were forcibly removed from their land and resettled under the authority of the Mhinga Tribal Authority to make way for part of the Kruger National Park. The Makuleke argue that this forced removal was the result of a deal between the Mhinga tribe and the apartheid government. Four decades later this remains a burning issue in South Africa and the fires were stoked in 2004 when the government passed the Communal Land Rights Act (CLARA). In principle the act meant well. It would enable people living on tribal lands to get title deeds to the land they have inhabited for generations, effectively ending a century of black land dispossession. However, the bodies entrusted with the power to distribute these title deeds were the tribal councils. The Makulele argued in front of the Constitutional Court that to give that kind of power to the tribal councils, in their case to the Mhinga tribal authority, would entrench apartheid's unjust land and power divisions forever.

"The real problem," Tembeka Ngcukaitobi, an attorney at Legal Resources Centre who argued the CLARA case on behalf of the Makulele, explained to me over the phone, "is the distance between the legislators and the people themselves. What happened is that the government basically listened to the powerful voices and ignored the voices of the people."

How could a post-apartheid government have done this? It boggles the mind, and yet dig deeper and you will find that the issue of tribal political power divided ANC leaders during the transition to democracy, and continues to rear its head at every national election. It is an issue so complex and so fraught with tension that it splits the head of everyone who tries to think about it. Some argue that the only truly democratic way forward is to eradicate the tribal system altogether, and shift all power to the ward councillors.

Tembeka Ngcukaitobi cautions against such a radical approach.

"Democracy does not provide fool-proofing against bad guys, it produces bad guys all the time, but the crucial thing about democracy is the ability to change the bad guy. There is an old African saying: *Inkosi enkosi ngabantu*, a chief is a chief by the grace of the people. It's a truly democratic saying. It says unless you come from the people, and unless you exercise your powers in a way that is consistent with the people's expectations, then you will be removed as a chief. It was the apartheid system that said that you could not be removed, that you were born a chief and that you would die a chief and that your son, not even your daughter, would take over. Whites didn't want to deal with many people, they wanted one person. The real issue is how you can salvage the good out of the customary law and dismiss the bad. This argument is not about the contrast between western and African ways of doing things, this argument is about democracy in its true and real sense."

So there was Nokhakha: a woman who does not fit in with apartheid-tinged tribal patriarchy, who is out of step with the modern democracy, and yet is a living, breathing cornerstone of rural society.

Her world and her story could not have been further from my own, and yet I felt a strange kinship with her. There she was, out of step with the past, out of step with the present, like so many of us, our personal lives fallen between the cracks of our country's transition, lost in transformation.

Chapter 11

············

Send in the cows

T AKE THE FIRST GRAVEL road after the Langani Forest turn-off. From there it's about three kilometres," Nokhakha had instructed me.

Nokhakha had invited us to the Great Place of the Jumba clan. The Great Place is the cornerstone of a rural community, the place where the locals air their grievances and settle disputes. Nokhakha invited me to observe this weekly Tuesday morning meeting, and meet her *isibonda* (advisors).

Her directions sounded easy enough but we were already lost. Head out of Mthatha in the direction of Elliot and within minutes the city vanishes and you are adrift in open fields, not a signpost in sight. Your only hope is to string together natural and manmade landmarks, but today the world is blanketed by low cloud and fine drizzle. It is as if the mists of time have descended to further cut off this part of South Africa.

We flag down a taxi driver and ask for directions to Tabase village. He waves us back the way we have come. We stop again to ask for directions outside the Zadasheni Superstore where a crowd of elderly men and women are gathered around a white armour-plated van, their small huddle being policed by men with machine guns. Pension day.

We jump down from the bakkie and approach the crowd. A kindly mama tugs me on the arm and instructs me to wait a moment. A few minutes later a strong, elderly man, who wears his years well, strides over and asks how he can be of help.

Aaron Kwelemitini spent his youth in Springs, the neighbouring town to Benoni. He worked first for a paper factory and then from 1979 to 2001 was a miner with Anglo American, one of the world's biggest mining companies. Now retired, he is back in his home village where he heads up the Ngqunge Farmers Association. I ask him what it is like to be back after all those years. He raises his eyebrows.

"I've tasted urban areas, I've tasted city life. For somebody of my age to come back here, I feel for the people. The new democracy has been there for 15 years, but what has it done in the rural areas? Zero."

"What needs to happen?" I ask.

"The only solution is to go back and till our lands. Agriculture is our only hope. If the government can give us the implements to do the business, then in the next five to ten years, we can live off our own land.""And could it happen?" I ask.

"No, here we have this problem with our chiefs fighting. You see these fields," he says pointing to empty mist-laden fields behind us. "Last April we planted these fields with canola. R1.7 million of crops. We would have been the first in the Transkei to produce canola, but in June the people let their cows into the field and they ate all the crops. All the work and organising we've done has gone down the drain."

"Who sent in the cows?" I ask.

"The people who follow her, Nokhakha. This project cost millions, it could have uplifted the lives of all the inhabitants of this area, but it was destroyed by cows. I tell you, something is wrong here. Something is very wrong."

I glance across at Marc. He raises his eyebrows.

From our first meeting we had pinned Nokhakha as a modern regent, someone who cares for her people and for progress, not someone who would authorise petty destruction. Unemployment statistics in this part of South Africa are off the scale. Rural development is crucial. Would she really have allowed personal politics to get in the way of rural development? Could she really have authorised this destruction?

We follow Aaron's directions on to the Great Place, a tin-roofed hut that sits bookended by two squat grey bungalows, behind a fence. Parked outside the fence are three bakkies and three saddles. Inside three horses help a handful of sheep to mow the lawn, while a lonely chicken wanders among their hooves. The hut is crowded with about thirty people, all men, except for an elderly woman, a young woman and Nokhakha, her head crowned with a black and white turban. On the verandah of one of the bungalows sit another eight people, seven men and one woman, waiting the council of the chief.

I approach the door of the hut and stand respectfully outside. The proceedings are in Xhosa. When people wish to speak, they raise their hands, and everyone addresses Nokhakha. She is the font through which all the discussion flows. I find out that, under discussion today, is the establishment of a joint agricultural co-operative. A few of them have already started smaller co-ops and now they are suggesting they should unite them. This is grassroots democracy in action – everyone's voice is considered, not just the voice of the majority.

After a few minutes one of her councillors notices me, stands up and waves me away to join the other subjects on the verandah. His instruction reminds me that this weekly council meeting is not a place for outsiders and interlopers, and my order of business is at the very bottom of a long list of more pressing issues.

I take a seat on the verandah and try to imagine what it must be like to live out here, among the mists, without access to electricity, the Internet, banking and all the mod-cons of the modern world. Where your prosperity is tied up in the land with which you do not have the tools to work. Life must feel very long and very slow.

A long hour passes, and finally Stanford Ncinca, one of Nokhakha's councillors comes over.

"We are finished. First the councillors want to talk to you. Then you can meet with Nokhakha," he says.

He unlocks the door of the bungalow and ushers me from the verandah into a living room with comfy sofas, the arms draped with crocheted doilies. A few minutes later, five other councillors, Mr Xentsa, Mr Jonga, Mr Duman, Mr Njeyana and Mr Mbiyo file into the room. They are all elderly men, some dressed as rural farmers in wellington boots and overalls, some in the cardigans of sedate grandfathers. These men would have spent their youths being subservient to white people. Their collective manner is cool.

Our conversation begins, as all these conversations begin, with my awkward introduction. I feel strangely comfortable explaining myself to a room of grandfathers, like a young child sharing their childlike curiosity for the world. My honesty, in turn, seems to relax them and they nod and smile as I speak, and I can feel them warming, ever so slightly, to me. Their ease in turn relaxes me and it makes it easier for me to ask the difficult question: did Nokhaka order the canola to be destroyed? My question is translated first into Xhosa and discussed.

Alfred Mbiyo eventually answers: "The first thing I knew about the canola was when I saw an airplane spraying our fields with chemicals. I phoned Chief Nokhakha and asked her what is going on, and she says she didn't know. Then we were worried. There are streams there that our sheep and goats use. We thought some guy is coming to kill us, or kill our livestock."

"Nokhakha called the department of agriculture and we found out that it was a rural development project. That a white man called Graham Casalis had met with the headman and that the headman had got all these people's approval. But this was not true. The other headman, he had pretended to the department of agriculture and to Casalis that he was the chief and he had organised all this without us knowing about it."

"But surely this was a good thing for the community, regardless of who was in charge of it?" I prod.

"Yes, as councillors we liked the project, it was going to bring employment, and we welcomed it, but when we met with Graham Casalis, he could not explain exactly how it would work. When Nokhakha asked for a working plan, Graham couldn't answer how long it would take to grow canola in the fields. He said after canola they would plant sunflowers, and after sunflowers it would be beans, and then he was going to build a factory, but he didn't explain any of this properly. Graham Casalis saw himself as coming to help the people, but the people don't want help, they want a partnership."

The penny began to drop. This was not about a lack of acceptance of women chiefs, it was not even about a conflict between rival chiefs, this was a much deeper, more ingrained problem: an entire mistrust of the motivations of a white man, of the motivations of the government, and a fear of losing control over the only thing that rural people actually have any power over: *land*. These rural people were not prepared to speculate in order to accumulate with their only asset. Aaron Kwelimitini who had spent the better part of a lifetime down a mine, making and taking educated risks, understood that in order for there to be rural progress, the people needed to take this risk, but out here, people feel so disempowered by the greater scheme of things that they are unwilling to move an inch on the ground beneath their feet.

"So the canola was destroyed on purpose," I say.

"Yes," he says. "I'd say the canola was destroyed on purpose because people want assurance and they failed to come with the assurance. To us, people with the land should be partners of the project. Graham failed to explain what were the benefits to us, so I'm not going to risk giving my fields to him. The boys let the cows into the fields because we don't know about that canola. If we had all the resources, we could be richer than the urban people because we could supply the urban people with food. But our incapacity to do this is down to the fact that we are not given the proper things to farm with. We need the government to know that."

The destruction of the canola was a spoiled vote, a protest vote. It was a red flag highlighting the lack of trust the people of Jumba have in the government, the rural development agency, and especially the white man.

"One of our biggest problems," confides Alfred, "is that the people who decided what should happen to us are people who are living in urban areas, people who don't care about us. We are trying to force the government to understand that our traditional leaders play a more major role than they think in our societies. In urban areas, to have councillors is quite correct, but in rural areas, we have traditional issues, for example sometimes there's a dispute about cows, and it is the traditional leader who understands that the most. It is real democracy, but it is aligned to our traditions. We should be having small conferences in the fields, wearing our boots, not talking in English and high grammar in the city and then writing some thick books about how their plan is going to follow. It's not working."

*

While I have been inside, the rain has moved on from a lazy drizzle to an energetic downpour. I leave the bungalow and spend a few minutes perched on the windowsill of the veranda, scribbling furiously into my notebook. A few minutes later I look up to find I am being watched by three twentysomethings: a young man with dreadlocks, a well-dressed guy in white trousers and a white shirt, not unlike a cricket player, and a young woman in a pink skirt holding a leopard print umbrella.

"Molweni," I say.

"Hello," says the young dreadlocked guy.

"Are you here to see the chief?" I ask.

He shakes his head. The three edge closer.

"We've come to see you," the guy with dreadlocks says.

"Me?" I say, surprised. I motion to them to take a seat. The guy with the dreadlocks takes a perch on the windowsill. The other two remain standing.

"I'm Khululekile," says the guy with dreadlocks, offering me his hand.

"Khulule..?" I say, shaking his hand, African style.

"Not easy for a white person," he says, laughing.

"Write it down. That'll make it easier," I say, offering him my notebook.

He scribbles it on the page and then introduces the other two. "And this is Lungelwa and this is Mpumzi."

"Howzit," I say.

They smile silently and nod.

"Why do you want to speak to me?" I ask.

Khululekile shrugs. "I don't know. We thought that maybe you can help us."

"I will if I can," I say. "How do you guys know each other?"

"We're in the youth league," Khululekile says.

"You mean the ANC youth league?" I ask, referring to the youth wing of the African National Congress which, at the time, had a firebrand reputation. In 2008 then youth league president Julius Malema threatened the country with violence if the corruption charges against ANC president Jacob Zuma were not dropped. "I don't want to say which league because then you will judge us," he says.

"Well what other youth league is there?" I say.

"We welcome everyone to join. We can only make change if we stand together," Khululekile says.

I nod in agreement. Fair point. "So who's who?" I ask.

"I'm the chairman, Mbumzi is the vice-secretary and Lungelwa is the general secretary," Khululekile says.

"And what do you do when you're not at the league?" I ask.

"I do nothing. I'm staying at home," Khululekile says. "I passed my matric in 1999, but I didn't have the money to go to the higher levels."

"So you've not worked since you left school?" I ask.

"I did go to Jo'burg, worked in Nandos being paid R1400 per month. Life in Jo'burg is good if you are working. But if you've got no money, it's much worse than here in the rural areas. Most of the time we know each other very well, so if I need something I can ask it from my neighbour. There you don't even know your neighbour and your neighbour doesn't even speak the same language, so it's not easy to live there even when you have no job."

"But it must be hard being out here, with nothing to do. You must get angry," I say.

He clicks his teeth. "We've got angry, and more angry, and more angry, it doesn't help. People just got tickets to get on the gravy train and then closed the door. They eat alone."

"So what's the youth league's plan? How are you going to change things?" I ask.

"We are having a meeting soon. We have 240 young people from the Jumba area in the league. We would have more but you have to pay R10 to join and not everyone can afford it."

"So why ask them to pay?" I ask. "Why do you need to pay to join a league?"

"Because you have to pay to get a card," he explains.

"But why do you need a card?" I ask.

"Because you have to have a card if you want to do any of the development things in the area. If there are opportunities for bursaries or development, you need to show your card," he explains.

Alarm bells flash in my head.

"Are you saying that in order to be eligible for any youth social development initiatives you have to be a card carrying member of the ANC youth league?" I ask.

He nods.

"That's not very democratic," I say.

Khululekile shrugs.

This, it seems, is not unusual. Around the same time, the Eastern Cape newspaper, *The Daily Dispatch*, ran a piece headlined "Only For Cadres". It reported a fracas in the town of Alice when ANC members attempted to stop local youth from signing up to take part in a government learnership programme.

"We are forced by these ANC people to join their youth wing to qualify for the learnerships," said Neliswa Baliso from Upper Gqumashe. She had decided to blow the whistle because many youth were being denied participation in an event that was supposed to be to the benefit of all, purely because they were not seen as being in the inner circles of the local ANC Youth League. The Dispatch journalist, Bongani Fuzile, had accompanied some youths who tried to sign up but an ANC representative had refused to sign them up for the programme "saying you must come with your money". She also refused to sign up two others saying: "these two must go, they are Cope (Congress of the People, a breakaway political party from the ANC) members". When the newspaper asked for comment, the ANC representative replied: "You are not ANC and I am not reporting to you. Whatever I do is not for you to write about."

I am curious to know what the ANC Youth League think of Nokhakha Jumba. Khululekile responds diplomatically.

"She is the bond between government and us. To talk to the government we must go to the chief, though the ward councillors seem to have taken the chief's jobs."

I look across at Lungelwa.

"Chiefs are the people who know our cultural things," Lungelwa says softly. "If people have a misunderstanding, then the chief is the easiest way to solve that. It's a way that uneducated, rural people can communicate with the ward councillors."

"But what about young, educated people, like yourselves, do you need a chief?" I ask.

Lungelwa shakes her head. "I do not like them. Here at this Great Place, there is conflict between these people and there is no way for it to be resolved. From 2007 up until today, they do not see eye -to eye. In the years to come, it would be easier to have no more chiefs because they use us for their interests, to fight against each other."

"Is the problem that she is a woman?" I ask.

Lungelwa nods. "If a woman is on a higher position, there will always be conflict because if someone doesn't like what she does, they will be negative to her. Women are mentally strong, but physically weak. You must expect conflict when a woman is in a higher position."

"What about you? You are a woman. You are in politics. What does the future hold for you?" I ask.

"I can't afford to study in a college because I have a single parent and they are unemployed. The biggest challenge for our community is the unemployment rate. So many people younger than 18 are getting pregnant because there is no hope for them, no hope. If I went to the tavern, I would not be like this. I would drink, then I wouldn't be in a sober mind, then I would have unprotected sex, then I'd get HIV/Aids or an untimely pregnancy," she says.

"Do you think the government has forgotten about you?" I ask.

"I don't think so, but I think the fraud and corruption in South Africa are the problem," she says. "If we could just get the Democratic Alliance (DA) in power. That would be right for me. If we could go back to European rule, maybe we'd have a better employment rate. I like white people to come here and rule this country because this situation would not be like this."

I looked at her stunned.

"How can you say that? After everything that has happened in this country?" I ask.

"Yes. I am a history student. I know what happened before. But I like white people because they bring job opportunities. The black government do not have the experience in how to lead a nation. There is too much fraud and corruption. They do not care about other people. You know one day I was in the Nelson Mandela Hospital and I saw an old woman who was very, very seriously ill. Then I saw the young lady who is the nurse there shout at the woman: 'I can't help you. I'm knocking off now. I can't help you. I will help you tomorrow.' That's supposed to be the best hospital here in the Eastern Cape!"

"Why do you think people don't want to help each other anymore?" I ask.

"We used to. I don't know. I want our people to develop. I don't want our people to suffer," she says, her shoulders heavy.

The rain is not letting up and nor is the mood. It feels like the sky is mourning this intractable tale. Marc walks over. "Are you done? I think we should head," he says pointing at his watch.

It is nearly 3.30pm. If we leave now, we can just about make it to my parent's home across the Natal border by nightfall. It is a good call. You do not want to be on these narrow, winding, unlit roads at night, where you are as likely to crash into a cow as a car.

Marc takes the first driving shift and I stare silently out the window. As the N2 climbs up to the higher altitude towns of Mount Frere and Mount Ayliff, a thick mist descends. It is as if the outside world is reflecting the interior of my mind. Three weeks ago, I was wholly ignorant – I had no idea of what I did not know. Now it is as if someone has dumped all the pieces of a jigsaw puzzle at my feet and forgotten to give me the picture.

We have not been driving long when a text beeps through from Khulelekile: *"Please sisi, I hate to ask this but I don't have anyone else to ask. I need money to get my driver's licence so I can get a job as a taxi driver. Please can you help me?"*

I feel that same flash of annoyance that I felt when Faith asked me for more money. Why does Khululekile automatically think that because I have a white skin, I can afford to help pay for his education? I am here as a writer, not as a charity worker. Was Faith speaking the truth when she said "whenever a black person sees a white person, they think there goes a millionaire"?

I read the text message out to Marc.

"Do you ever get texts like this after you've been out on a story?" I ask.

"All the time," he says.

"What do you do?" I ask.

"I say no. I don't have spare cash. It's hard making a living as a freelance photographer. There are no hand outs for me," Marc says.

Two economies, one country. A first world built on the precarious timbers of the third. Every day those who have walk past those who have not.

Every day those who have nothing watch those who have walk by.

As the road descends out of the mists, I remember a quote from John Bunyan, the English writer: "You have not lived until you do something for someone who can never repay you."

I stare morosely out of the window.

I came here because I felt homeless, disconnected, lost in the northlands. I felt that if I could just get close, something in me would shift, but now I feel even further away.

As a journalist the job is supposedly to tell the story as impartially as possible. The balanced view. All sides of the story. But all sides of this story included me too. I had fancied myself as a liberal-minded roving observer, but I was just a scared wee Benoni girl, ensnared by the past, trapped in a spin cycle of turbulent, entangled emotions, plagued by an inner monologue that was thick with years of prejudice and mistrust. Poor Khululekile. He was pitting me as a white knight with the power to save his soul, while I was still trying to save my own.

Chapter 12
....

The Promise

I SPEND A FEW DAYS at my parent's cottage. Well, we call it the cottage but it is actually a static caravan with a wooden deck that they reluctantly share with a troupe of monkeys. My parents have never been lucky with money. When my dad retired, they sold their house in Benoni and spent a year and a half travelling around South Africa in a caravan, trying to find their dream place to see out their days. By the time they had settled on the sub-tropical Natal south coast, the economy had boomed, house prices had trebled and they could no longer afford bricks and mortar, so a caravan it had to be. It is nice enough, though. The kitchen table is a booth and my mum never tires of saying: "It's like being on a train, isn't it?", as we sit down to our tea, which is not tea at all, but actually our dinner, served at 5.30pm, Yorkshire time, and usually involves some combination of mince and potatoes. To help spur the imagination, she has covered the walls with framed pictures of British steam locomotives.

Very little happens on this semi-tropical coastline, a hundred kilometres south of the port of Durban, and I soon grow bored. While many seaside towns have reinvented themselves since the end of apartheid, becoming trendy weekend retreats for busy urbanites, the south coast remains a coastal outpost of 1980s suburbia. The coastal land is divvied up between white and wealthy Indian families who have built holiday homes that they visit once or twice a year, while the black population lives in the hills set back from the sea, on the other side of the N2 motorway. The few amusements that are to be found are in uninspiring strip malls and the local pubs are mostly propped up by decaying ex-Rhodesians, who have been in Africa too long to call anywhere else home, but have been homeless ever since Rhodesia became Zimbabwe. From early morning to the wee hours, they gather under clouds of fag smoke and beery belches, nurturing their racism and reminiscing about the bad old good old days.

To keep themselves amused, my parents go on long beach walks, frequent the aforementioned pub (my dad for a beer, my mum for a lemonade), and wage a daily, embittered war with nature. My parents are the most unlikely Africans. While Africa grows its grasses long and wild, my parents prefer their garden with hospital corners. In Benoni, they fought a brave campaign to keep their home free from ants, spiders, ghekkos and flies, but this war became a blitzkrieg after they decamped to the sub-tropics. In summer, humidity levels frequently reach 98%, and their days are book-ended by rage against fungus that grows as soon as you turn your back, mosquitoes as black as the devil's heart, and monkeys that tap dance on your roof and plunder your fruit bowl. When they bought the cottage it had a beautiful giant tree growing through the deck. When I next visited it was gone.

"Why did you chop down that beautiful tree?" I asked.

"Those bloody monkeys, always watching you and making a noise" snarled my mother. "You'd be sitting reading your book and they'd be staring down at you. Bloody nuisances."

After a few days I continue on to Cape Town, and set up office in the back room of the flat my husband has rented in Seapoint, the old Jewish quarter overlooking the Atlantic Ocean. The neighbourhood went briefly down-market after apartheid when druglords and prostitutes moved in among the stalwart Jewish grannies, but it had been rescued from permanent ghettoization by the snowbirds from the northlands who quickly forgot their previous discomfort with racial inequality when they noted how cheap it was to buy beachfront apartments. It has worked out well enough though. Seapoint is now one of the few neighbourhoods in Cape Town that is a genuine melting pot of cultures, where Europeans can rub shoulders with immigrants from across the African continent. The same cannot be said of Cape Town's southern suburbs which remain mostly white-skinned enclaves.

I begin transcribing my interviews and pitch the story about the women chiefs to my editor at *Time*. No reply. Unbeknown to me, the global media empire that was *Time* magazine has begun to collapse. They have announced the closure of the London office, from which the European and African editions of the magazine are produced, and staff are being either fired or recalled to the New York office. The story pitches of a freelancer are at the bottom of a pile of priorities but as the days tick by with no response, the radio silence becomes easy fodder for the anxiety that has trailed me around the Transkei.

My constant obsession with my work starts to grate on my husband and our relationship begins to show strain. There had already been tensions before we left Scotland. He had not wanted me to accept the fellowship. He did not like the idea of me trundling alone in a bakkie down dusty roads. In his mind, his wife was doing her utmost to throw herself into danger. His attitude infuriated me. He had been a war correspondent, reporting on frontline fighting in the civil war in Lebanon, the first Iran-Iraq war, countless coup d'etats and uprisings including China's Tianamen Square, and the internecine conflict in the South African townships during the last days of apartheid. If he could do it, why not me? Besides, there is no war going on in the Transkei, I argued. No, he replied, which makes your situation worse. In a war, the journalists and storytellers have special status, they are protected by the military, the rebels, the establishment. A lone storyteller without a beat is an open target to all the ills of the world. His words do nothing to ease my anxiety. Nor do the words of *Time* magazine's South Africa correspondent, who I had met for a coffee when I first arrived in the country. I said I had hoped I would not stand on his toes. He said that he very much doubted it, that the Transkei was a horrible place, full of hideous poverty and corruption, and he avoided it as much as he could.

My remedy is to take long walks along "the Prom", the nickname for the three-kilometre stretch of paved promenade that runs along the seafront from Mouille Point to Bantry Bay. In the early morning and evening, this is where Jewish grandfathers take their constitutionals, where Muslim mothers push prams, and where athletes of every skin tone stride past, training for yet another of South Africa's many marathons and ultra-marathons. It is Cape Town's multiracial melting pot, overlooked by Table Mountain. On a clear day, you can just make out Robben Island, where Mandela spent eighteen of his twenty-seven years in prison. Standing there, I think back to the first time I ever visited the island. 11 September 2001. Who could forget where they were on that day – the day the Twin Towers fell?

I had come back to South Africa after being in London for two years. Abroad, I had assiduously avoided the South Africans who arrived on two-year work visas and drank their wages while watching rugby in overcrowded flats. I despised the way they stuck together, replicating boerewors and beer in west London pubs. I could not see the point. I wanted art, books, foreign boys, and had set up home in Brixton, then London's most black neighbourhood. Together with another South-African-in-flight, we joined forces with a gang of Swedes who lived above an all-night Bedouin-den, deep in south London, and who were fleeing the designer conformity of Scandinavian life.

At the time, the world was in the throes of the first internet boom and I had been hired as an assistant editor at online magazine to write about travel. The boss was an old punk who wore a smelly leather jacket and eyed me suspiciously. When he eventually warmed to me over a couple of beers, he sang me the chorus of this song:

"I've travelled this old world of ours from Barnsley to Peru
I've had sunshine in the Arctic and a swim in Timbuktu.
I've seen unicorns in Burma and a Yeti in Nepal
I've danced with ten-foot pygmies in a Montezuma hall
I've met the King of China and a working Yorkshire miner
But I've never met a nice South African
No he's never met a nice South African
And that's not bloody surprising man
'Cause we're a bunch of arrogant bastards
Who hate black people"

"Have you never heard it before?" he asked over a post-work beer.

"No I've never heard it before."

"Come on," he said. "Everyone knows this song."

"And does everyone think that all South Africans are a bunch of arrogant bastards who hate black people?" I asked.

He shrugged.

My close friend starts to change her accent, lengthening those South African glottal vowels. I follow suit. It is safer that way. Pretending you are not from there.

As the months go by and the novelty of London wears off, I grow mournful and find myself staring into people's homes from the top of the red double-decker buses. The little matchgirl, who has locked herself out.

I begin to pine for home, for the vast emptiness of the veld. I want to be in a place where being lost and alone is not a burden, where it is just a feeling, caught on a breeze, and so on a whim I buy a ticket on my credit card and I fly home. I surprise my parents and after a week in Benoni, I take the train to Cape Town.

At Jo'burg station, the platform is a microcosm of the new South Africa, with white, black, Indian and coloured elbows all banging into each other. The low-slung train stands patiently, awaiting the frenzy of faces waving tickets and goodbyes. Onboard it is a microcosm of old with white passengers tightly locked behind first-class carriage doors, black passengers bundled with all their luggage into the cheapest third-class seats, while the coloured passengers, who have a reputation for knowing how to enjoy life, are already "*making party*" and new friends in the bar.

I knock on my locked first-class door. No response. I try again. Silence. I fetch the train conductor and he uses his special key to unlock the door. My fellow passengers, a middle-aged Afrikaans woman and her ageing mother, regard us with suspicion and distaste.

"This young lady is going to be sharing this compartment," the train guard says.

Their faces crack into reluctant smiles and they half-heartedly remove their luggage from the old, blue leather seats.

I dial my mother on her mobile phone to tell her I am safely onboard. She had nervously dropped me at Jo'burg station. Towards the end of the Nineties, downtown Jo'burg had become a dangerous place. Drivers were frequently hijacked at traffic lights, their cars taken from them at gunpoint. My mother kept as far away from this world as she could.

Her phone rings out. I try again, still no reply. All down the train, the doors are slamming shut. The conductor blows hard on his whistle, and then the last door shuts, and with a gentle lurch the engine gathers together all its ducklings, and we set off, gingerly, through the inner-city suburbs of Jo'burg, for the great emptiness of the Karoo and the Mother City.

I love the faded architecture of Jo'burg. The tumbledown art deco buildings built from gold mining glory, now home to panel beaters, exhaust repairs and corner shops.

As this fond, familiar world of old rolls past, the supressed anguish in me spills over, and salty tears roll down my face. The Afrikaans ladies are too busy tucking into their lunchtime picnic to notice or care.

I try my mother again. Still no reply.

A fresh anxiety wells up and I need to walk it off. I stand and unlock the compartment door to leave.

"*Moenie* unlock the door," the old woman barks.

"If you lock it behind me, I'll knock three times when I get back so you know it's me," I reply.

I walk down the carriage, in the direction we are travelling. I stand on the metal grid that joins our carriage to the next, breathing in the rickety rhythms and the hot air billowing up from the tracks. The growing worry in my head is almost as loud as the clonks and clunks of the iron wheels and it feels good to deafen it.

I carry on to the dining carriage. The bar is open and some good-natured souls are already making themselves at home.

"Howzit!" says a coloured man, offering me his hand, while the other clings to a beer.

I shake his hand and then slip into an empty booth at the opposite end of the carriage. It is an hour since my mother dropped me off. I try her again, this time on the landline. After a few rings, she answers. Her voice was shaky and tearful.

"What happened?" I ask.

She had stopped at the traffic lights in downtown Jo'burg, and a man had dashed across the road in front of her car, smashed her window and snatched her mobile phone from her lap. She had driven home, covered in broken glass, a victim, for the first time, of a very South African crime.

"I'm fine," she reassures me. "It's just a phone. I just got a fright."

She is right. It was just a phone. But as the train gathered speed, leaving behind the inner-city and breaking out for the fields, I am angry with myself for putting my mother in danger. Those who live here have found a *modus vivendi* – a way of staying and living. I feel ashamed that I have come home only to wreck havoc with her carefully curated world.

I go back to my compartment and knock three times.

After a minute, the middle-aged woman slides back the door and I spill

116

out my tale of woe, and for the first time they offer me genuine smiles, and a biscuit. Before this moment, we had nothing in common. Now, we have something to share: the very South African story of fear and loss.

The train rumbles on. To Klerksdrop where they found gold, to Kimberley where they keep the diamonds.

I eat a simple dinner of hamburger and chips in the restaurant car and return at 8pm to find my bed already made up for the night. I climb to the top bunk and am rocked to sleep by the rickaticka-rickaticka of the metal steed. I wake to stillness at dawn. I slip out of my bunk, quietly slide back the compartment door so as not disturb the gentle lady snores of my fellow passengers, and make my way to the end of the carriage where the train door stands open, the conductor smoking a cigarette on the platform. I glance at the sign: Beaufort West. He stubs out his cigarette and marches off down the platform, and I breathe in for the first time, the sweet, still Karoo air, tinged with a hint of nicotine. The conductor slams shut the open doors, so I climb back aboard, tug the door shut behind me, and push down the window, as his whistle jerks the train into motion, I rest my head on my arms and stare at the vast emptiness of the Karoo.

The Karoo is not a sandy desert. It is more like the surface of the moon, peppered with a silvery-green afro that never grows more than waist-height. From Kimberley to Beaufort West the flat plains are dotted with strange shaped hills, but as you get closer to Matjiesfontein - a beautiful old watering station, a true colonial oasis that was founded by a Scotsman and which remains intact almost as a living museum - more of the ground begins to rise up, and by the time you reach the Hex River, the land has burst upwards and the train is forced into a series of tunnels, that bore eighteen kilometres through Table Mountain sandstone, leaving behind the emptiness and delivering you into the rich, fecund valleys of the Cape winelands.

I stand at that window for hours. Breathing in the emptiness. Smiling at the emptiness, until, eventually, after 27 hours, we screech and groan to a stop in the Mother City. Beautiful Cape Town.

I stay with a friend in Higgovale, an upmarket suburb on the slopes of Table Mountain. I spend whole days sitting in silence in his garden, mesmerized by this granite figurehead at the prow of Africa who has watched so silently, so sagely, as the storms of our country have raged. From her vantage, she has kept a forever eye on Robben Island and I decide to visit. I am the only South African on the trip out to the island – the rest are foreign tourists. A former inmate shows us around. We see the cell where Mandela lived, the guards room where all incoming and outgoing correspondence was censored, and the limestone quarry where the prisoners had toiled for thirteen years, their eyes and lungs scarring under the harsh conditions. I learn that here, during their lunch breaks, that they had instituted a regime of Each One Teach One. Each prisoner that was literate and educated had taught one that was not. They had been oppressed, divided, imprisoned, made to work in the dust, and they had turned that place into a place of learning.

I stand there, looking back towards Table Mountain and for the first time I do not see her as beautiful. I see her as an impenetrable wall, a barrier shielding the rest of South Africa from the eyes of the prisoners. Africa's Berlin Wall. Life goes on beyond, and you are not permitted to take part. We have cast you away from your homeland.

I walk back towards the bus that will return us to the boat, and as I am about to board, the guide takes my hand, pulls me aside and looks me in the eyes.

"Don't stay away forever. You must come home. You are needed here," he urges. "I.. I.. promise" I stutter, surprised, unsure, shaking his hand.

I am 24 and I have no idea how I could ever be of any use.

The boat deposits us at the V&A Waterfront and I walk and keep walking. I walk past the newly built glassy penthouse apartments. I cross the ever busy Buitengracht street, the main jumping-on point for the city's motorways, turn right at the lower part of Long Street and watch as the drab block-like apartheid architecture of the foreshore morphs into Cape Dutch arches and filigree Victorian balconies the closer you get to Kloof Nek. For as long as I have known it, the top of Long Street has been the home of bohemian Cape Town, lined with second-hand book shops, quirky antique shops and alternative fashion boutiques. A shop assistant buzzes me into one of the clothing stores. After a few minutes browsing I find something I like and head to the counter to pay.

"Have you heard?" says the shop assistant. "A plane has crashed into a building in New York."

"Oh my god. When?" I ask.

"Just now. Ag, but it's about time something kak happened to that country. It's always us that's got the kak going on," she replies, in her thick South African accent.

Her lack of compassion stuns me, though it probably shouldn't. I know this breed of white South African only too well. Incapable of feeling the pain of others. Maybe there was some truth in that song.

"Where is the nearest TV?" I ask.

"At the chicken takeaway across the road," she says, waving her hand.

I forget the T-shirt. I run across the street and arrive just in time to see the second plane crash into the second tower. Around me, people clutch their arms to themselves, their hands reach for their faces. We are white, black, coloured, Indian standing shoulder-to-shoulder in a fried chicken takeaway, looking on as another country's tragedy publicly unfolds.

As the towers fall, nobody says a word.

Tomorrow we will wake up to another world. It will be imperceptible at first. But bit by bit, that in which we had no part, will imprint itself on our ordinary lives.

Chapter 13

....

Back to Pondoland

THE PHONE RINGS. I am sitting at my desk in Cape Town, staring mindlessly out the window. It is John Costello.

"Good news," he announces. "I just had a call from the Queen of Pondoland's daughter. The Queen wants to talk to you. The local ANC have just tried to kill her."

It is good news. In an odd, journalistic sort of way.

Queen Sigcau of Pondoland is African royalty. She is the daughter of the King of Swaziland and was "deployed into marriage" (her own words) on the eve of Transkei's so-called independence in 1976 in a similar way to how European royalty of old married off its daughters to strengthen alliances and allegiances. But while her marriage may be old fashioned, her education is not. Queen Sigcau holds a Bachelor of Arts from New York University (NYU), a Masters in Library Science from Columbia, and (before marriage) worked as a documents analyst at the United Nations. In recent years, like Britain's Prince Charles, she has developed a reputation for being an environmentalist who is openly sceptical of proposals to develop roads, casinos and mining along the Pondoland coastline.

Look back through history, though, and you will find that the Pondoland royals were not always associated with the moral high ground. In the 1950s and 60s, the white government devised the so-called "Betterment Plans" which aimed to relocate rural villagers into closer-knit settlements, clearing the way for more white farm land. Pondo villagers fought back in a bloody revolt, burning down the homesteads of those chiefs who were seen to be colluding with the apartheid government. The revolt gained momentum, and a mass march was organised to burn down the Great Place of Botha Sigcau, the then king of Pondoland. The march was thwarted, but a later enquiry into the uprising found the people felt that the king had sold the Pondos and the country for his own ends.

In 1976, the king's daughter, Stella Sigcau, became a politician in the fledgling Transkei National Assembly, going on to become the Transkei's first and only female prime minister in 1987. She was deposed a few months later in a bloodless coup led by ANC activist, Bantu Holomisa, who suspended the constitution, insisting that a civilian Transkei government was just a puppet controlled by Pretoria. The fact that both Holomisa and Sigcau were later selected to be Cabinet ministers in Mandela's government is a testament not only to Mandela's commitment to peace and transformation, but also to the complex, tangled web of old allegiances and conflicts at the heart of South African politics.

I call Princess Wezizwe, the Queen of Pondoland's daughter. John, it turns out, has the inflated end of the stick. The Queen has only been threatened with guns by ANC supporters. Not quite the same as an attempted murder, but interesting nonetheless, and a few days later I board a dawn flight to Durban. It is a blue-sky day and within minutes the craggy granite peaks of the Hottentots Hollands mountains that buffer the Cape wines from the harsher, drier, hotter climate of the interior give way to the vastness of the Karoo, a nomad's paradise where silence is the strongest force. The throbbing engines track up the coast, skirting lonely valleys to the north of the better-known Garden Route, places with names only farmers know and only those with four-wheeled drives can discover. After an hour and a half of scorched earth, the land morphs into greener, rolling hills, pinpricked with microscopic thatched huts. The engines drop to a deeper baritone and we descend that bit closer to the earth, and spot terrain that has been split open by the movements of water long since run off to the sea. The Transkei from the air. I squint into deep crevasses and make out a river, following its curves and ox-bows to a place where the riverbed vanished and the water tumbled over itself, cascading into a hungry mouth below, swept away on a journey, not knowing where it will lead.

My parents pick me up from Durban airport and in her usual fashion, my mum chit-chats all the way home about the misfortunes of people I do not know, including this story that she has plucked out of the newspaper: A gang of men broke into a woman's home in the middle of the night. They tied her up, and threw her off a motorway bridge – "Maybe it was this one," my mum points – and into the deep ravine below. The woman landed in the river below and was found the next morning by people walking by the river, on their way to work. Miraculously she was still alive. This is the story my mother tells me before I head alone again back into the Transkei. These are the stories South Africans trade. The tales that keep us fearful, that keep us apart.

By midday I am behind the wheel of the bakkie and heading towards the old border. As I cross the wormhole bridge I feel a strange lightness of being. It is just after lunchtime and the schools are out. The dusty shoulders of Mzana road are buzzing with children in colourful uniforms, laden with heavy bags, laughing, pushing each other, eating sweets. I get stuck behind a school bus as it chugs out of town. Faces press up against the back window, waving and pulling tongues. The bus pauses again and again at invisible bus stops and the kids pile off to begin long, hot, slow walks home through the fields. It reminds me of the hot, slow journeys home from my primary school to our Crystal Park home amid the mielie fields.

Life thins out the further I drive from the village. The houses and huts become more dispersed, and just a few hundred metres from the side of the road are deep crevasses, giving way to villages that seem to live below the surface of the world. It is as if the road runs across the rooftops of hundreds of natural skyscrapers with the foundations in a secret world. Off the road, off the map, off the radar. A low-slung black Mercedes, the ANC politician's car of choice, overtakes me at speed.

Today I wave at a man on a horse, a little boy carrying a plastic bag filled with oranges and an elderly man, standing by the edge of the road, resting his weight on a cane. They all wave back. The road straightens up for a few kilometres to bring us into the tiny hamlet of Redoubt. I slow for a series of potholes that I know are coming, and as the road winds up to become hilly once more, I reflect on how familiar this landscape is becoming. I know where the trees thin out, where taxis will suddenly slow and stop in front of me, where children might emerge from the bushes, and where I can briefly take my eyes off the road to get a view of deep, vast, empty valleys. With this growing familiarity, the fear is thinning, the anxiety diminishing. I cast my eyes upwards, to the big, blue African sky and smile. This is what I had dreamt of when I applied for the fellowship. To wander solely, freely, hopefully through this part of South Africa. I tune my iPod to Johnny Clegg, and drive along with the window down, singing loudly and without shame: *"I'm searching for the spirit of the Great Heart, To hold and stand me by, I'm searching for the spirit of the Great Heart, Under African sky"*.

It is 4pm by the time I arrive in Lusikisiki, my bed for the night. I have reserved a room at Sips B&B, which as it turns out, is owned by a relation of Queen Sigcau. After a few moments chatting, I discover the owner's daughter has also been living in Scotland, working in the oil business. I have barely put down my bag when the owner dialled up her daughter and handed the phone to me; so I can have an awkward conversation with a daughter on the other side of the world about the smallness of the world.

It is a charming welcome and a world apart from over-the-phone snort I had received when I told Graham Casalis, the white farmer at the heart of the dispute in the Jumba tribal authority, that I would be staying at a B&B in Lusikisiki.

"Rather you than me," he said.

"Why? Should I be worried about something?" I pressed him.

"Ag no. It just might not be very clean," he jibed.

It is clean. In fact, there is a fountain in the garden and my en suite bathroom has a heart-shaped bath. Dinner is served in a conference-style dining room, and I am handed a plate of chicken, gravy and potatoes. There is one other table where three black women, who look like they have spent the day at a conference, eat and gossip and ignore me. *Isidingo*, the South African soap opera, is blaring down from a TV up high, and I settle down to watch it, feeling comfortably out of my comfort zone. The next morning I wake early to the sound of children laughing. My bathroom window overlooks a huddle of wooden and tin shacks and the sounds are from children getting ready for school. I put on my running shoes and head out for a jog before the sun gets too high in the sky. My run takes me down dirt roads lined with rectangular, 1970s-era bungalows, fronted with lawns and low walls made of pressed-cement. It looks exactly like the Crystal Park of my childhood, a South Africa of thirty years ago. There is not an electric fence or gate in sight. I feel myself relax, smile. I feel strangely at home, at ease. A misplaced nostalgia for another place, another time, another country.

I am expected at the Royal House of Pondoland at eleven o'clock. The main home is a pink bungalow, fringed with smaller squat buildings and a few traditional huts. The only thing that marks it apart from the other homesteads is the dusty white Mercedes parked in the driveway.

On the opposite side of the road, a large, grand thatched building is under construction. If this were a work of fiction, this would be where the Queen would hold court. Instead, in real life, we have to make do with the face-brick, apartheid-aesthetic rectangle which is the Royal Chambers. Like their fascist brethren in Europe, the National Party did not rely only on their policies to crush the nation's spirit, they added a bleak architectural aesthetic to the mix. Curiously this building does not seem old, possibly built in the last ten years. Another example of how the long tail of apartheid remains coiled around the country.

I am left alone to wait in a large room, furnished with a bar and rows of pale wooden armchairs upholstered in an orange, purple, red and green African pattern print. The only sound is the low buzz of neon lights. I check in with myself and notice I am somewhat nervous, a little excited and slightly star struck: I have never met royalty before.

The Royal Chambers may disappoint, but Queen Sigcau does not. She arrives late, chauffeur driven in the dusty white Mercedes from her pink bungalow, just a few hundred metres away. She is wearing an African print dress and a matching headscarf and gracefully ushers me into a council room, taking her rightful seat in the middle of three cowprint chairs. She bids me sit on one of the ordinary office chairs that are also pulled up to the table.

She begins by welcoming me to Pondoland and I comment on the land's natural beauty. She encourages me to visit the coast to the north of Lusikisiki.

"It is the most beautiful part of Pondoland. God decided to display His artistry there," she says.

I tell her about my journey so far and my bid to understand how democracy has affected the lives of people living in this *former* homeland, to which she smiles wryly and says, "*Not former*, life here still feels the same."

"What about the women chiefs?" I ask. "Isn't that progress?"

She shakes her head.

"King Faku was one of the most famous Pondoland kings. It was he who brought in the first missionaries and signed the first treaties with the British.

Before the colonial era he made his daughters chiefs. They were allocated land and did not have to marry."

"So do you have many women chiefs now?" I ask.

"We have 21 chiefs in eastern Pondoland, and a third of them are women. There are lots of conflicts in chieftainships but I have never heard of any clashes right now which are solely on gender."

"So what is behind the ANC's threat to kill you?" I ask.

She sighs.

"We are changing the way traditional councils are elected. Forty percent of traditional councils must now be elected. This has gone well in all the other traditional councils in Pondoland, but there is conflict here, in Qaukeni."

"Why?" I ask.

"Well, Qaukeni is the seat of the kingdom, the headquarters of Pondoland. If you control this traditional authority, then you control all of Pondoland. It means you have influence over all the people of Pondoland."

The power she speaks of is not absolute political power, but perhaps just as influential. In post-apartheid South Africa, every rural area in the former homelands is represented by both a government-appointed ward councillor and a traditional leader. The traditional leaders have to be consulted on all developments plans, and without their buy-in, nothing can happen.

The Queen explains the threat to her life came on election day. During the previous year each community had nominated a person from their own area whom they wanted to put forward for the traditional council. On the day these nominees and their supporters gathered to elect the new council, the official in charge suddenly changed the rules.

"He said he was the only person who had the right to nominate people and then put forward the names of people who weren't even from this area - they were from Kokstad," the Queen says. "I couldn't believe what he was saying. It was ridiculous."

The threat to the Queen's life came from the people who had been bussed in from Kokstad, Bizana and Flagstaff to support this about-turn in the electoral process.

"They pushed their way into the hall, wearing ANC T-shirts, singing slogans and carrying guns. They were threatening us," she says.

"So are you saying ANC people were using threatening tactics to try to claim seats on the traditional council?" I ask.

She nods.

"But why?"

"In the Lusikisiki municipality, they are shooting each other all the time. People have been dying. People have been crippled. Others go to hospitals holding their own intestines. Democracy is great, but I believe our traditional leadership system was very democratic and these political opportunists who are professing to be democrats, they realise democracy is really what they make it to be. They are politicians in the western sense, but they would rather be referred to as traditional leaders so they can use traditional power over people. Although," she adds ruefully "in traditional leadership there is very little chance for opportunism, but why not give it a try?"

This fracas starts to make more sense when you realise that Pondoland has been earmarked for controversial development projects including a titanium mine, an extension of the national highway from Cape Town, and the rerouting and damning of a major river. The Queen has a reputation of being cautious in her attitudes towards development. I ask her if it is true that she is opposed to mining.

"You know, Pondoland could easily be South Africa's bread basket. But it's very, very difficult to figure out what it is that's more important. I'm not exactly a conservationist and environmentalist in the strict sense. I believe in development, but I believe development shouldn't be done at the expense of the environment altogether. Our environment is something that you just can't find anywhere else in the world. I haven't been everywhere, but we have one of the best-kept wild coasts and to just throw in development without weighing what you are doing, I don't think it's worth it. It's just grabbing what you can get and not caring about what comes after you. With global warming and all of that happening so fast, you just wonder where we are all going to be in 2020, just ten years from now," she says.

"So do you think the mining is behind this electoral fracas?" I ask.

She softy shakes her head. "It can only be a part. There are so many things. There is land. There is the Umzimvubu River that they want to divert to Komga. There are huge portions of Pondoland without any water and no one has ever mentioned any of it. Then there is the land called Magwa. It used to produce the best tasting tea in the world. The soil is just right for tea. Everyone wants Magwa, and yet Magwa was land that the Pondos fought for, it used to be royal grazing land. In the 1960s the king gave it away for development because he wanted job creation, especially for women. Profits from Magwa built Magwa House, which is not even in Pondoland. The government said they couldn't build such a huge structure here in Lusikisiki, that it had to be built in Mthatha. You keep thinking, how are we ever going to develop?"

"Do you blame opportunism?" I ask.

"I do. Especially in our area. I think there's a lot of individualism and self-centredness. It's selfishness. It isn't as if people want to develop because they want to see progress in Pondoland. I don't think so. I think it's people who see an opportunity to grab something and line their pockets as fast as possible. It's opportunism. Maybe it's typical of Africa." She laughs.

"Why do you say that?" I ask.

"Nepotism, I think, does have some traditional roots. It comes exactly from African families taking care of their extended families. It has riddled all these municipalities right now. That's why this corruption is in the tender system, because I want to take care of my brothers, my uncles, and with that comes kickbacks, bribes.

"And you think it's ingrained?" I ask.

"I think so, really. I think it has traditional roots. By the way, I believe in it too. I come from a very large family. But I wouldn't carry it to that extent. I mean, that idea or custom of extended family ties and feeling of responsibility was something that you take care of at home, you don't drag it to the offices," she says.

"So do you think it's okay to give your brother a tender to build a road?" I ask.

She nods. "I guess it's okay if I give my brother a tender to build a road, as long as he built the road. But here, it's: 'I'll give you the tender provided I get a cut'. 'I'll give you the tender, but it doesn't really matter to me if you build the road or not, as long as you get 50% and I get 50%'. You know, the road to this Great Place has been tendered 10 times, and still the road is not fixed. That's why the roads are ruined. No one seems to care. There is no follow-up on tenders. The money will disappear and the roads will never be done. And the roads are just one thing, everything has fallen apart."

I mention how surprised I was that in Mthatha the streets are still called by their colonial names, while in Johannesburg, important streets have been changed to the names of struggle leaders. It's as if Mthatha has been abandoned, everybody has fled on the *Mary Celeste*.

"Honestly, to tell you the truth, I wouldn't care if the streets were called Queen Elizabeth II, if there were roads. If they were maintained properly," Queen Sigcau says. "What are we going to do with name changes if we are not doing anything about the physical structure? They are falling apart. We thought it was going to be better after apartheid, but whatever existed before has crumbled to nothing."

"But as Queen of Pondoland, do you not have any power to change this?" I ask.

She laughs uproariously.

"Oh no, no, no, no. That's political power. Even a king doesn't have political power. It's democracy. It's called democracy."

"So what could change things?" I ask.

"I wish I knew. I honestly wish I knew. I think it will be very difficult because there is a lot of politics involved in this. It will mean a change of heart amongst politicians. I really don't know."

"Do you have hope?" I ask.

"I'm not hopeful at all for our areas. I honestly wish I could say I see a glimmer of hope, but I don't. I just see deterioration getting worse. The ANC has already enjoyed the majority in Pondoland, so the conflicts are within the ANC. I honestly don't know how many factions the ANC locally has right now. I don't think anyone does. All the money that they are fighting over is within the municipality, there is nothing else they can fight over except control of the cash."

To be fair, it is an issue that the ANC and its partners in the Tripartite Alliance – the South African Communist Party (SACP) and Congress of South African Trade Unions (Cosatu) – are gravely aware of. At the end of 2010, the Cosatu Central Executive Committee were so concerned they issued a statement: *"If we, as the broad liberation movement, don't act decisively, we are heading rapidly in the direction of a full-blown predator state in which a powerful, corrupt and demagogic elite of political hyenas increasingly control the state as a vehicle for accumulation."*

In the same year, Cosatu published a discussion document titled "The Alliance at a Crossroads – the battle against the predatory elite and political paralysis" in which they warned that unless the ANC tackled the tendency towards corruption, South Africa would go the way of the rest of the Continent.

"Africa itself, as well as revolutions elsewhere, has seen too many liberation movements with noble ideals hijacked by corrupt individuals, predatory classes and foreign interests for us to close our eyes to that danger now. Our liberation movement and our struggle will never be up for sale. It is the working class, and the poorest of the poor, who always end up the worst victims of these failed revolutions. While the rich have the resources to cushion themselves, a predator state will ultimately eat away and consume the whole of society. No one is immune."

As I bid farewell to the Queen of Pondoland, I feel the weight of our collective history. This country has been eaten alive from the inside since colonial times, and this rapacious march for more was continuing, unabated. Would the day ever come when we stopped helping ourselves and started helping each other? I started to wonder about our collective morality as a nation. Do we even have one?

Chapter 14

....

The state we are in

TURN LEFT AFTER LUSIKISIKI and the tarred road soon degenerates into a scarred rut that winds its way down to Mbotyi, a village set with its back against mossy cliffs, and its feet in a turbulent ocean. Mbotyi is a microcosm of old South Africa. The land, closest to the sea, belongs to white-owned holiday cottages and a guest lodge, both served by electricity mains, while the homes of local families are still without power. I am here to meet Graham Casalis, the farmer at the heart of the conflict with Nokhakha Jumba and to visit another agricultural project that he is co-developing. The rain, however, has put a stop to our plans – once again the roads are impassable – so instead I check into the guest lodge and ask Simphiwe the local hiking guide if he will show me around. He agrees.

We head first to the new clinic, built on the edge of the sea. The building work is finished but it remains closed because there is no electricity nor equipment. Simphiwe just sighs.He points out a murky stream from where water trickles towards the sea.

"This is the river we use, where we get water," he says, with disgust.

He takes me to the local school, Mbotyi Junior Secondary. We pop our heads round a classroom door. The classroom is full of teenagers bursting uncomfortably out of wooden desks built for children half their age.

The teachers greet us with a narrow-eyed suspicion and it takes a few minutes of persuasion before one teacher agrees to talk.

"Come," she says. "I want to show you something."

She leads me to the end of the long, narrow school building.

"This is the Grade 8 classroom," she says, pointing at a patch of grass. "We lean the blackboard against this tree. We have 7 classes but only 6 classrooms. We are still living in the past. There have been no changes at all. It's just like before," she says.

"What happens if it's raining?" I ask.

"If it is raining, like today, the Grade 1s do not come to school so that the Grade 8s can have their classroom."

That explains the tiny desks.

"We have no electricity so we have no photocopiers to prepare handouts for the learners and we have no computers," she says.

As we stand outside, we are joined by two other teachers. Buoyed by the one teacher's honesty, they pitch in.

"We are not paid according to our worth," says one. "There are so many things we are promised, and we don't get. It's not that we like going on strike, it's because we don't see any other alternatives to force the government to do it."

"It's all empty promises. We are just the step ladders to get them into power," says another. "They always blame the apartheid era. They put the blame on others, but it is them."

I ask them for their names, so I can attribute their quotes, and all of them refuse. Not one is prepared to be identified with their opinions.

"Why?" I ask. "You have such strong views, why don't you want your voices to be heard?

They shake their heads, and refuse to tell me why.

"Are you afraid of something?" I ask. "Are you afraid you will lose your jobs if you speak out?"

Still they won't answer. I push again. And again.

"You journalists," says one with a glint in her eye. "You are always digging."

"But why? Explain it to me," I say, exasperated.

"We are afraid of the unknown," says one, finally.

That's all she will say.

I leave the school feeling unsettled. I had been looking for insights into the state of education, and I ended up with an even more troubling insight into a state of mind. These teachers were openly critical of the way the government was managing the education system, and although our constitution protects the right to freedom of speech, they did not feel safe to speak freely. Was this a hangover from apartheid? An inbuilt self-censorship from a time when criticising the establishment could have brought trouble to your doorstep? Or did this have nothing to do with the past and everything to do with the present?

In 2010 the government introduced the Protection of Information Bill, nicknamed the "Secrecy Bill", and later renamed the Protection of State Information Bill. The bill was supposed to replace an outdated piece of apartheid legislation, but was viewed by critics as even more draconian than its predecessor because it proposed harsh penalties – up to 25 years in prison – for journalists and citizens to be found in possession of classified documents and harbouring state secrets. Critics, including the Public Prosecutor, Thuli Madonsela, argued that the definition of what constitutes a state secret is too broad. Because there is no clause that excludes documents that might be "in the public interest", if enacted, this law would put her and many journalists in danger of being arrested on a daily basis simply for doing their jobs. The only way this draft bill allowed individuals to avoid prosecution if they came into contact with classified documents was to hand them over to the police while they submitted a request for declassification. The worry was that this would enable the malicious prosecution of whistle-blowers, activists or journalists seeking to do nothing more than to expose crime and corruption.

Commenting on this bill in Martin Plaut and Paul Holden's exhaustive 2012 book *Who Rules South Africa Now?* ex-Mail & Guardian editor Nic Dawes, says: "*It does at times feel as if the ANC tries to run the country as if it were an exiled liberation movement operating out of a flat in London. There is a pervasive feeling amongst those people that you subsist in a world of enemies and that you are to understand negative press coverage in terms of a conspiracy of some kind to bring down the movement and as the product of the machinations of the forces opposed to change... There is an intelligence focus and paranoiac attitude that developed out of the world of exile.... There is an ANC of fear that believes you deal with challenges by identifying the conspirators and nailing them. The reaction to the ANC of fear is to seek mechanisms of enhanced control and the natural response is through a security apparatus style intervention.*"

This unease with criticism intrigues me because it is not just a malaise that permeates the highest levels of government. Try to have an honest, thoughtful discussion about apartheid and how it impacted us as individuals at most white South African dinner tables. You may be allowed to speak about it for half an hour, an hour at most, but then someone will inevitability say: "Jeez man, can't we just get over it?" and the topic will be dropped. Try and bring it up again and you will not be invited back. People will happily discuss the symptoms: crime, corruption, poor services, but the disease itself, apartheid and its ongoing economic and racial divisions are an inconvenient truth that most white South Africans do not want to talk about.

Perhaps it is not surprising. For the twelve long years that we trudged through the apartheid school system, we were never encouraged to question. Until the end of secondary school, we were taught "facts" through rote-learning, no opinions required. The ability to think, question, use our minds, is a treasure with which most healthy humans are born and which the apartheid government did its best to suppress, and which continues to be supressed by the current government's paranoid fear of criticism, by their lack of investment in education, and by the use of the label racist to silence any unwanted debate. It struck me that the fearful silence of those Mbotyi Secondary School teachers was like the canary in the mine, a disquieting sign of a foul, Verwoerdian poison that still lingers over South Africa, threatening the health of our democracy and our freedom of thought and speech.

The rain is getting heavier, as is Simphiwe's mood. We continue on up the road that is not a road, trying to find the patches where our boots will not disappear into sludgy, sticky mud. To lighten the mood I glance up at the distant, mossy cliffs and repeat what the Queen of Pondoland said - about this being where God shows his mastery. Simphiwe shakes his head.

"You know I don't see the beautiful," he says. "The things we need, we don't get. No running water. No electricity. No TV. We only listen to the radio and even then we lose the signal when an airplane passes. The life as I know it is worse. Instead of getting better, it's worse. But the people who make the life worse are the black people. I can say it's the black people. They understand where we are now, where we've been. So why are they not making the life better for us. *Why*?" he demands.

I shake my head. My inner monologue answers. *Because this is what always happens in Africa.*

This time, I don't keep it to myself.

"I don't know Simphiwe," I say gently. "But it seems to happen a lot in Africa."

"But why?" he sighs.

It is question to which many people have sought an answer. Jonathan Hyslop, director of the Wits Institute for Social and Economic Research makes a stab at it in his paper "Political Corruption: Before and After Apartheid[4]". Hyslop looks back over the previous century of economic

4 Journal of South African Studies, 2005

development in South Africa, analysing the levels of corruption in the Boer, British, Afrikaner Nationalist and ANC governments, and deducing that the current corruption is a legacy of the previous political and administrative practices. The Transkei is a classic case.

As a puppet state of the Afrikaner Nationalist idea of separate development, the white government in Pretoria ploughed billions of rands into supporting the traditional chiefs and recruiting black civil servants to staff the old Transkei bureaucracy. Because of this funding, a social strata of black bureaucrats and political brokers emerged who, to some extent, shared the apartheid government's philosophy of separate development in so far as it served their own ends. They were opportunists who sought to make personal good out of political bad. The result, says Hyslop, is that already during apartheid, the Transkei and other homeland governments became a by-word for corruption and incompetence, official extortion in relation to everything from the issue of trading permits upwards was rife, and homeland leaders presided over massive patronage networks with friends and families to the exclusion of others. Hyslop concludes that the same people who presided over those networks, in the case of the Transkei, are now running the Eastern Cape civil service.

Later that evening, sitting on the wooden deck at the lodge, watching the Indian ocean churn up the shore, I find my mind drifting back to what the Queen had said: that nepotism has African roots, that it is customary in this part of South Africa to help care for the enlarged family, to attend to the needs of your uncle, and your uncle's uncle, and your uncle's uncle's brother's uncle. I found myself wondering: are there irreconcilable differences between the normative ethics of democracy and of African family life? Between what you should do in a democracy versus what you should do in Pondoland? That the greater good was being sacrificed in favour of African customs?

My mind drifts further back, to my university philosophy class. For centuries philosophers have tried to determine what makes an action morally good. Utilitarians, for instance, believe an action is moral if its consequences benefit the good of the greatest number of people. Others argue it is not just the consequences that matter, but our motives. We may do something that does not have any obvious benefit to our greater community, but we do it because we have made a promise to one person, or because we are bound by duty to help a family member or to do our job. Sometimes the consequences of those duties and promises are unpalatable and can seem immoral. For example, soldiers are bound by duty to kill. But we cannot judge soldiers on their actions, we have to judge them on the normative morals of the army.

I thought about some Irish charity workers I had met in a bar the previous day. They told me that they came every year to Pondoland "to help" because in Europe "we have lost our way" and being here "made them feel good". Put like that, were their motives not also selfish, driven by a desire to improve their own lives? And so, I wondered, were the municipal officers any different? Were any of us? Are we not all motivated by a desire to survive, and to improve our lot in life – and the lives of those close to us? That is not an African custom, it is a human custom. Patronage networks exist in every country in the world. Catholics in Scotland help the other Catholics. The Jews in Glasgow help the other Jews. It is a tribal world.

But we do not judge each other solely on our motives, we cannot, because our motives are as hidden as our hearts. What we can – and do – judge people on, is their actions, and the consequences of those actions.

When the municipal councillors take office in a democratic country, they take on a duty to their constituents. They promise to manage the building of infrastructure and jobs in their communities. They assign government tenders to companies that not only promise to build roads and supply essential healthcare equipment – but who actually do it. As civil servants of the democratic ideal, it is their duty and responsibility to ensure that equal opportunities are delivered to everyone. They agree to work according to the principle of democracy – to treat everyone equally, to strive to give everyone access to equal opportunities, to improve society not just for the good of themselves and those close to them, but for the greater good. In a democracy, the good of the greatest numbers trumps the good of the few.

How then do we judge these municipal officers? We judge them on the roads, we judge them on the healthcare services. We judge them on whether they have fulfilled their obligations to the collective good. We judge them on the consequences of their actions. Every time a road is not built or a hospital does not receive its supplies, those democratically appointed officials have failed in their duty to improve the collective good of this country. They have stolen from the collective good. Just like apartheid did.

Chapter 15

....

The Red Dust

I AM BECOMING TIRED. FAMILIARITY has thinned my fear, but frustration and anxiety have grown in its place. I pitch stories to the features editors of newspapers and magazines but it is 2010, the cameras are on the football stadia, and nobody wants to hear about the complexity and conflicts of unknown villages of unknown tribes in an unknown part of an unknown province. I begin to feel as voiceless as the people I am interviewing and despondency sets in. It starts to affect me physically. The mornings are worse. I wake with first light, at about 4.30am, with a wrenching pain across my chest. Lying still only makes it worse. By 5am I am up, pacing up and down, feeling like the whole of the Transkei is swirling around in my head.

I need to find a different voice. I am craving the voice of someone noble and good who is actively fighting back against this tide of despondency. My search leads me to Nonhle Mbuthuma. She agrees to meet me at the Nando's in Port Edward, a chicken restaurant a stone's throw from the Transkei border and a short drive from my parent's caravan.

From 1998 to 2003, Nonhle, a beautiful, fine-boned Pondo woman, worked as a tourist guide for Amadiba Adventures, an EU-sponsored hiking and horse-trekking outfit along the Pondoland coastline. At that time it employed 60 permanent staff. But it did not last. Stories of ventures started by foreign investors, only to be run into the ground by the people they were intended to benefit are not uncommon in Africa. I had already heard about the demise of this horse-trekking business from John Costello.

"They didn't feed the horses," he said. "The poor things died."

His version had sounded like a cut and dried case of mismanagement. The story Nonhle tells me when we meet in Port Edward was one of calculated sabotage.

The Pondoland coastline is a wild, windswept place. Dramatic cliffs and waterfalls tumble into the sea, silver oak trees, palms and long grasses push up through the sands, and close to the village of Xolobeni is a place of natural wonder: the *empepetweni*, or the red dunes. For centuries, these dunes that fringe the Indian Ocean had been little more than a playground for cows and children and a source of frustration for houseproud Pondo women.

"I live ten kilometres from the dunes, and you can tell which way the wind is blowing by the amount of dust that lands in your house," Nonhle says.

In 2004, an Australian mining company saw in them a much more tangible, economic beauty: titanium.

"The same people who were directors of Amadiba Adventures became the directors of Xolco, a Black Economic Empowerment (BEE) outfit that represented the mining company. It was the directors that had been sabotaging Amadiba Adventures. They wanted to make sure nothing was happening in the area," she says.

Pondoland has one of the highest unemployment rates in the Eastern Cape. Amadiba Adventures had changed that. Now to grasp at an even shinier carrot, they had to show that there was no other economically viable business in the area.

When the community first realised what was going on, they bandied together to protest.

"There are 4000 people in this area and 88% of them are against the mining. Our headman said it would never happen while he was alive. We complained to our local municipality, but they said they knew nothing about it, although it is on the Reconstruction and Development Programme (RDP) in Mbizana. Then on the day the mining rights were announced, people were bussed in from Flagstaff and Lusikisiki to celebrate, and our headman was suddenly standing with the people from Xolco," Nonhle says.

The headman's words were prophetic. That afternoon, three people from the community beat him for his betrayal and he died shortly after.

Since the conflict began, three others have died. One was the first man who spoke out against the mining.

"A car drove up to his house and somebody shot him," she says.

The second was Scorpion Dimane of the Amadiba Crisis Committee. He was poisoned by African *muthi*.

"First his eyes went strange, then he lost his mind, then three days later he was dead," she says.

The third died of a heart attack after hearing about the mining licence.

"He couldn't believe his government could betray him like that," she says. "You know, it's very strange to see this happening. We thought this was a democratic government where everybody had the right to speak, but it doesn't seem so. They say all the resources underground belong to the government. But on top are the community. You can't just go underneath and bypass the people on top."

Nonhle and I agree to meet again the following week to meet those who live on the edge of the *empepetweni*. Before I leave I offer her money for her transport.

"Why do you offer me money?" she says, offended.

I am embarrassed and stammer out an apology.

"It's just that a lot of people are always asking for money and I didn't want you to have to ask. You've taken the time out of your day to come here and meet me," I say.

"I don't need your money," she says. "I'm not doing this for money. I'm doing this for my children."

A week later I set off before dawn to meet Nonhle. I am not alone. In Cape Town I met Linda Nordling, a Swedish journalist who is living in South Africa and writing about the development of science across the continent. We formed a fast, tight friendship and she offered to be Thelma to my Louise on my next Transkei tour. I accepted with relief, it was good to have a companion, though I made it clear that I was Thelma. In the end we compromised. We could both be Thelma.

We pick up Nonhle just after sunrise and it is not long before we leave behind the tarred road for a dirt track that crumbles away until it is no better than a riverbed. It bounces us over and around hills, and although the sea is always in sight, it seems never to get closer. Outside it is a quiet morning. We pass the occasional bakkie and bicycle, but the only real noise is from the wind darting between clusters of gum trees and thatched homesteads, the huts far enough apart to make a stroll to your neighbour a morning's outing. I comment on the vastness of the land, the ample land for farming and cattle, and Nonhle smiles with a hint of pride.

"Our people fought for that. In the 1960s they tried to squash us together. They called it the Betterment Plan, but it would have made our lives worse. It's not too different from what they are trying to do to us now. Except now it's our own government," she says.

We arrive at Mrs Mthwa's homestead, three white thatched huts, set on a windswept open plain. The garden is alive with chickens, six small children, and dogs stretched out in the morning sun. They growl at us as we approach, but are not concerned enough to get up. Mrs Mthwa is wearing a red and white floral turban, a brown shweshwe dress and a blue apron. She is on her knees, scrubbing the floor of her home with a brown paste, and smiles and waves her dirty hands apologetically as we approach.

"That's *udaka lwenkomo*," explains Nonhle, pointing at the bucket of brown paste. "Cow dung. That's our polish. You have to do it every Friday to keep your house from getting dusty."

While I wait for Mrs Mthwa to finish her Friday morning ritual, I wander around the back of the house where long grass for thatching is drying in the morning sun. Here the high plateau on which the huts are built folds away into a deep rocky gorge that ends in a river on its way to the sea. As the crow flies, we are less than a hundred kilometres from the brightly lit tourist resorts of the Natal south coast, and yet it feels like we have stepped back in time by a hundred years. I glance past her homestead, towards a cluster of tall gum trees, and spot three local women walking slowly, their heads stacked with pile of firewood. I remember something Nonhle had said earlier.

"The locals were told if they wanted electricity, they would have to move closer together, so they said forget about it. They would rather continue to live the way they do and use wood to light their fires."

At that moment Nonhle calls us, and we walk around to shake Mrs Mthwa's now clean hands, and be invited into her home. She cannot speak English, but her eyes are warm and I know we are welcome here. It is a tidy, pretty room, a woman's room. Her family's clothes, blankets and beddings are suspended from a rope, and a tapestry suitcase hangs from a nail on the wall. Against the far wall is a table covered with a red and green plastic floral tablecloth on which she stores all her groceries, and to the right is her bed, a single bed with a burgundy fabric headboard and a blue and black bed patterned throw. Alongside it on the table are the same things alongside women's beds the world over: hand cream, face cream, a candle and some matches. The only picture on the wall is a 2010 calendar of one of her sons in his school uniform.

Nonhle, Linda and I are offered chairs to the right of the door, while Mrs Mthwa makes herself comfortable on a reed mat on the floor, two small children at her feet. A soft morning light filters through the door and the only sound is the swishing of the wind through long grass outside. I start by explaining who I am, where I come from, why I am here, and then ask her to tell me about the threat of the mining, and how it would change her life if it went ahead. The smile leaves her face and she nods pensively. Nonhle translates.

"As you can see me, I am not educated, I've never been at school, but I have all these kids and support them off this land, and grow everything for them. I've never been in church but I believe in ancestors and God as well. My parents are lying on this land. Before I do anything, I go to speak to my ancestors. If in my garden, I see something is not growing, I go and speak to them, or if my kids are not feeling well, I'm always speaking with them. They are the people who are very close to me. That's why the graves are very important to me. They will be disturbed if the mining is going to happen. How can I leave this place and take all these kids and all these graves?"

I tell her that there are people in Xolobeni that support the mining. Why do they think differently to her? She shakes her head. "Those who want the mining it's just because they think that money is going to last forever. That's why they keep pushing that mining. They don't know that after that money is finished, their life is finished. They don't care about their lives, they just think about the money. Look outside, you see I have cows and grass. Those cows eat the grass and come back and bring the kraal manure, which we use to plant our mealies with which we feed our children. If you take away all the grasses and trees, we can't survive as human beings, but if you leave the grasses and trees but you take us out, those grasses and trees can survive."

For a moment we fall silent, her words floating in the air. We look out the doorway across to the cluster of gum trees where another woman is now collecting firewood. This uneducated woman who cares for her children at the edge of the sea speaks with the insights the west has become accustomed to hearing from spiritual ecologists. I comment that it must be a hard life here. Gathering firewood, collecting water from the streams, growing your own food. She smiles.

"This life is a very good life, I enjoy it because the water from the stream is for free. You can collect the firewood from wherever, there are no boundaries, you do not need a permit. As a woman the work keeps my dignity."

Dignity. The word resonates in my ears. Politically, the anti-apartheid movement was a struggle for freedom from oppression and for democracy, but at a basic human level, where each of us live every day, it was a struggle for dignity. For the right to be heard, respected, valued, and allowed to live on your land – not driven away by those with more power and more voracious economic appetites.

I ask Mrs Mthwa if this conflict has changed her feelings about democracy. She nods. "The first time we went to vote for our government, we were thinking that we were going to see a big change, but we are just crying for our vote, because instead of seeing a change, we see more oppression in ourselves."

I imagine myself in Mrs Mthwa's shoes. A woman with six children, no husband, living a quiet life on land I inherited from my parents, facing my entire world being turned upside down. "How do you cope?" I ask.

She looks sad.

"Sometimes when you wake up in the morning it's difficult to go to the garden, you feel down because we have no direction because of this thing. We don't know how we can stop this mining. The councillors always told us the mining is going to happen whether we like it or not. If we just look and wait and see, it's us that will suffer as women, not anybody else."

We say goodbye to Mrs Mthwa and we drive down to the *empepetweni*. They are wild, windswept dunes impossible to access even by 4x4. Those in favour of the mining argue that there is no cattle grazing here, but the dunes are peppered with long grasses, and as we stand there, a young man walks past, herding his cattle.

We continue on to the nearby Kwynyana River, and sit on its banks and eat our picnic lunch. As we eat, Nonhle remembers how her grandfather, Zibula Dlamini, who was an advisor to the headman of Xolobeni village, defended his people during the times of the Betterment Plan.

"KD Mantanzima, the premier of the Transkei, called them to Mthatha and he invited the white people to try and bribe the Pondos to give up their land. They put a bag of money and a bag of sand in front of my grandfather and told him to choose. My grandfather chose the sand. He said: 'I choose this sand because it is life. Money, I don't know where it comes from, but I come from this land, so I choose this land. If the money is finished and I don't have the land, how is my life going to be?'"

Nonhle stares wistfully at the water flowing past.

"I wish he was still alive," she says. "If you talk to the politicians they will tell you that Nonhle does not care about people, she just cares about trees and butterflies. Do you know what the minister said the first time we met with her? She said she knows why we are protesting, and it's because of the white men. Can you imagine, as if environmentalism is a white man's thing. Don't we think as human beings like the other people? They say we buried apartheid, but we as black people are pushing people back to apartheid again."

(FOOTNOTE: In the months after I left the Eastern Cape, this situation took a turn for the worse. In July 2010, President Jacob Zuma deposed the Queen of Pondoland's husband, King Mpondombini Sigcau and replaced him with a new king, King Zanozuko Sigcau who declared strong support for the proposed N2 Wild Coast Toll Road from Durban to East London, and backed plans for the mining. Mpondombini Sigcau filed a case against Zuma in the Constitutional Court, and in June 2013 the court ruled that he had been unconstitutionally deposed. The verdict came too late for Mpondinisi who

died in March 2013, but the power has shifted back to the Pondo royals who in post-apartheid South Africa favour environmentalism over opportunism, and for the time being, the mining plans have been shelved. Though for how long Mrs Mthwa's dunes will remain safe, is anybody's guess.)

We drop Nonhle off close to Port Edward, and Linda and I continue on to Port St Johns. Half an hour into the journey I have to ask her to take over the driving. I am so exhausted I can barely focus my eyes on the roads. I rest my head against the passenger window, and gaze through half-closed eyelids at the hills and villages.

"What was it all for?" the inner voice sighs.

The white tribe had been ousted from power in the name of freedom and democracy. The policy of white minority rule was out of step with modernity and the global community would no longer, could no longer, sanction the oppression of one tribe by another. At least, not officially. And so we had cheered in a new world, a more equal world, and we had believed that this world of black majority rule would necessarily have a better moral compass. But democracy does not necessarily turn people into good guys. Or even define what or who is the good guy.

I thought back to the meeting I had had with Senior Chief Noitaly Mtirara, another Thembuland woman chief who had had her life threatened.

I had asked her why we still needed chiefs in a democratic society.

"There must be somebody who is going to take a leadership or control," she said. "If we leave it to democracy, we'll see everyone just doing as he feels because he will say that is his right because he is in a democratic world. Even if it's democratic, there must be someone who says its right. Even if it's a democracy there must be nobody who suffers at the end. Everybody must benefit."

Her view had confused me at the time. But after talking with the Queen and hearing so many tales of corruption, I started to understand what she meant. Democracy does not come with an inbuilt moral code or compass that informs a society how best to live, how best to prosper. Its basic promise is not to society, but to the individual: you have the right to participate freely, and then it trusts, perhaps naively, that if all citizens participate freely, the good will out itself. Democracy is just the framework, a bare scaffolding on which we then have to build and act.

When Archbishop Desmond Tutu addressed global leaders at the Rights and Humanity Emergency Congress in 2009 he said something poignant. "Human development and human rights are enshrined in the SA constitution but have not yet become the core values of our economy. It is up to our institutions, corporations and governments to fix the problems we face, but these institutions have no life of their own, they are only groups of people, they are people, like you and me, making choices, deciding to become God's partner or not."

We live in a country that might espouse Ubuntu as its core philosophy, I am because you are, but is it that we are still really living according to the apartheid maxim: I am because you aren't?

I feel hot tears prick at my ears. Our beloved country, trying to get better, trying to heal, and just getting more hurt on the way.

Chapter 16

....

Jimmy's Hope

LINDA AND I CHECK in to Thea's wooden hideaway in Port St Johns. In the open-aired kitchen where I began my journey, I try to chat with Thea about the thoughts swirling around in my head, but the warm welcome that she once offered me is gone. She dismisses my ponderings with a busy hand, she knows these things first-hand, but has already made her peace, in her own maverick style. The things on her mind are the everyday concerns of ordinary people: her children, her business, her loneliness.

I try again, this time with Jimmy Selani. He agrees to meet us for lunch in Port St Johns. It is a warm afternoon, distant thunder is rumbling. Jimmy eats fish and chips. I have a cheese and tomato toasted sandwich. Linda has a cheese scone. I confess to him that I am starting to wonder whether this whole journey was pointless. All I am doing is talking to people, dredging up uncomfortable emotions, swilling around in the swamp mud, uncovering depressing stories that no one cares about. Jimmy shakes his head.

"For this country to go forward we must stop saying "I". We must stop thinking about ourselves. We must think what we want this country to be like for our children. Sometimes when I go out from my house, I don't feel like hiking to Coffee Bay. But then I think, if I stay here, my children are going to suffer. So if we can act like that, to try make this country better for our children, I think things can change. Nobody said life is going to be easy."

I stare wordlessly back at him over my sandwich.

"Talking to people does make a difference," he counsels. "This is one of the poorest areas in the Transkei, you've seen that. It does happen sometimes that you wake in the morning having great energy, having hope that you are ready for the world, and then you see just a few things, you see the poor people, and then you get depressed and you lose hope. But it's by talking to people that you get new ideas and you get that hope back. The most difficult challenge for a person is to venture to the unknown," he says.

I nod.

"What do you think is the biggest thing that still stands between black and white people in our society?" I ask him.

"It's fear, it's fear. There is still that mistrust. We've got that mistrust and we don't want to open our hearts. We are still suspicious of each other. But you must open your ears and your eyes and your mind. You must never be scared of failing. You must keep on focusing on what you want. Don't give up," he says.

That afternoon Linda and I take a canoe down to the mouth of the Mzimvubu river. We drag our canoe onto a sandbank and lie in the shallow pools carved into the sand by the retreating of the tide. As I lie there, basking like a beached whale, Jimmy's words echo in my head: You must open your ears and your eyes and your mind. You must keep on focusing on what you want.

What is it that I want?

I want to understand this country.

I want to know how it was broken so I can help fix it.

I want to know how I am broken, so I can help fix me.

I want to be able to tell people that I grew up in Benoni and not to have them look at me with embarrassment and pity.

I want to be able to say I am South African, and for it not be something to apologise for.

I want my scars to be part of me, but not be me.

I want to *not* be disliked, feared and mistrusted, and vice versa, because I was a pawn in a political masterstroke.

I want to pull down the walls. I want to stop hiding.

I want to walk through Khayelitsha and not to be looked at strangely. I want to walk through Soweto and for it not to be a novelty.

I want to belong here because I am afraid I will never belong anywhere else.

I remember a conversation I had with my husband in Glasgow.

"It doesn't matter how long you live here, you can never be Scottish," he said, not unkindly.

"What if we have children?"

"Well, they will be Scottish. But not you."

Scotland is an exclusive club. Its members are not parochial. Following in the footsteps of Dr Livingstone, the Scots are world travellers: inventors, statesman, musicians, writers and actors who have forged paths – literally in the case of the engineers who have built some of the world's most famous mountain passes, railroads, bridges and lighthouses – in the most remote corners of the globe. The Scots' influence extends far, far beyond their rough, green hills, and yet while the Scots have ingratiated themselves everywhere, they are only willing to have you as a guest. A long-term, long-paying guest, but never one of them.

Glasgow is a perfect example. Stay in London long enough and you can – and will – become a Londoner. You can never become a Glaswegian. The rhythm of Glasgow comes from the sky: the rain. The water has seeped into the core of its children and created a damp patch on their souls. To thrive in this low light, Glaswegians have learnt to wear their despondency lightly. The most skilled Glaswegian is one who can hold up the ugliest, murkiest part of himself, to friends, and complete strangers, and mock it for the benefit of everyone else. Public deprecation is admired, respected and required. The only way to stop the pissing rain is to take the piss out of it. This gives Glaswegians the reputation for being hilarious. For being open and friendly. In any other place on earth, only your closest friends would tear you apart for your ridiculous hat. In Glasgow, the taxi driver sees it as part of the service. A long-term resident can learn this banter. Over time you can become fluent, and it will be easier for you to have conversations with shop keepers and strangers, but though you may learn how to survive under these dark skies, you will never become Glaswegian. Your soul is just not damp enough.

I sit back up and look out at the Indian Ocean. Something Jimmy said to me at the start of this journey pops into my head.

"In the veld you see the birds, and they give you hope singing to you. You listen to the water, making its own music. That keeps you going, that gives you hope. From nature you get the sense that these things are temporary."

Chapter 17

....

The Mission Station

I FOUND MYSELF THINKING ABOUT God. God had never been too
far away in South Africa. As a child, every school day would start,
religiously, with the Lord's Prayer, muttered in unison from Monday
to Thursday and sung dispiritedly at the weekly Friday assembly. In those
days it was the Christian God who we turned to for our moral code. Thou
shalt not. Ten commandments passed down to Moses and handed on to us
through the government's policy of Christian higher education.

As I ploughed deeper into the Transkei, I was struck by the number
of mission stations that peppered the map. During the colonial and
apartheid eras, it was missionaries who had often delivered basic
services and infrastructure to this pastoral landscape. All this changed
after 1994 when the control of these key services was removed from
church leadership and put under government control, and now I
found myself wondering how God almighty was getting on under our
democracy, and whether His Transkei representatives could offer me
any succour.

I scoured the map and one mission station caught my eye, more for
its location: on the eastern flank of the Transkei, in the foothills of the
Drakensberg mountains, close to the border of Lesotho, a part of South

Africa I had never visited. I typed "Mariazell Mission" into Google. The result read like an African version of Umberto Eco's *In The Name of The Rose*.

"The Mourning of Father Ernest"
(The Witness)
by Matthew Le Cordeur

MONDAY mornings normally start quietly for me in Hilton. I stumble through to the kitchen where I read the newspaper over a prolonged cup of filtered coffee. It's a good start to the week. Several weeks ago, however, my routine was broken by a phone call. "Father Ernest has been murdered," my mother said, her holiday spirit clearly broken. "We're coming home early so we can go to the funeral."

Father Ernest. Murdered. Life just stopped for a second. Then, it broke back into action. I scrolled through my cellphone. Sister Irene. I dialled. "Sister, what has happened," I asked. "Oh, I was just about to call you. They have murdered Father Ernest," she said, her voice weak. "Who?" I asked.
"Robbers, I think. They wanted the money for salaries, but he had already paid everyone," she replied.

Father Ernest — murdered for money. The man I ate breakfast, lunch and dinner with when I was just four. The man who let my family live on the mission station for five years. The man at the centre of my childhood kingdom. And now, he is dead."

My internal monologue didn't even bother to bat an eyelid. I picked up the phone and called Matthew Le Cordeur, a journalist at *The Witness*, a Natal newspaper. Matthew explained that since the article was published, police had arrested Lehlohonolo Matabane, the master of the boarding school. "Matabane was a man whom Father Ernest had trusted, a man he treated like a son," Matthew said, his voice still thick with disbelief. I asked if he would be interested in accompanying me to the mission station. He readily agreed and we arranged to travel together on the Easter weekend.

Linda and I drive from Thea's place to Kokstad on Good Friday. It is one of those days when the world is utterly still and a high-pressure system has painted the sky with featherlike, whimsical clouds. All along the route people are on the move, dressed in their finest churchgoing clothes, colourful scarves and hats. We see ten men in suits on horseback. We spot a nun in her black and white cassock, a heavy gold cross around her neck, boarding a taxi. On the only piece of flat ground for miles around, we see a crowd dispersing after a football match, the field filled with children throwing balls into the air. We see a congregation dressed in indigo blue robes, trailing cheerfully behind a bishop in a blue-pointed hat, a staff in his hand. I slow to let them cross the road and the bishop opens his arms widely to thank and bless us.

We spend the night at Willowdale Lodge, a beautiful old family farmhouse run as a B&B outside Kokstad and the following morning Matthew picks us up and we head to the foothills, driving past enormous fields of purple, pink and white Cosmos, the delicate yet hardy South African wildflowers. Matthew is a friendly, kind-hearted soul who laughs easily and can readily see the beauty in the world. As we drive, he tells us about his childhood, which could not have been more different from mine. In 1985 when Matthew was three, his father, an anti-apartheid activist, upped his wife and three children from their picket-fence lifestyle in Cape Town's Hout Bay, and moved them to Marialinden, a smaller Catholic mission station just a few kilometres from Mariazell. His father spent the next four years engaged in grassroots development in the Lesotho foothills as apartheid gasped its last breaths.

"For us it was an idyllic childhood," Matthew remembers as we bump along the road towards the tiny picture postcard hamlet of Marialinden, with its white-painted stone church framed by the distant backdrop of the Drakensberg mountains.

"You can see that Marialinden is tiny, but when I lived here it was the biggest thing in the world. Now it's dry and nothing is working and all the farmlands have gone, but back then it had an orchard with plum trees, apple trees, pears, grapes. The garden was full of carrots and tomatoes and I'd just walk around eating all day long. That's all I did, walk around and eat raw fruit and vegetables. The fields were filled with maize, the cows were always grazing and there were pigs and sheep all around. I was one of those children who went around hugging everybody. I'd go missing for hours and my mom would find me in some mama's kitchen drinking tea," he says.

As we enter the village, Matthew veers off the dirt road and steers the car into the long grass.

"I want to show you something," he says.

He brings the car to a halt on the banks of a small river. As we climb out we are greeted by the soft babbling of water and the gentle heat of a summer morning.

"Right here is where my father fasted for a week," he says. "He was praying for the end of the reign of terror."

Matthew explains how in 1988, 18 people were murdered in the area, including a child from the village who was reported to have been ritually killed on the banks of this river. This period became known to the local people as the Terror of the Black Bull.

"Who or what was behind it?" I ask.

"People blamed the chief, who was a woman, who still lives in the village. It was partly for the *muthi*, but partly to keep control. To keep fear. Rule by fear. But my dad prayed and it worked. It stopped it. Pretty much the whole community said enough was enough."

"Do you remember being afraid?" I ask.

"Only when people marched past, dressed in capes and ululating. They were probably part of a Christian rally but I thought they were witchdoctors and my two older brothers told me I was going to get chopped up and sold. That was the only time I felt fear," he laughs.

"I wonder if people still pray on this riverbank," I ask wistfully.

"Naah," Matthew says. "It's where the local guys come to wash their cars."

We continue on to St Matthews church in the heart of Marialinden, to meet Father Tsepo Tsalong who has been the minister here since 2008. Standing well over six foot tall, and impeccably dressed in long red robes, a rosary dangling from his neck, Father Tsalong is an imposing figure with a gentle handshake who invites us to join him for tea and biscuits. I ask him what the mission means to the people of this area, and whether its role has changed over the years.

"Ours is mainly a spiritual role," he says quietly. "We used to have care-givers, volunteers from the church who would look after the sick, but now there are government programmes that have renumeration for care-givers. Now people think that if they are not paid, they cannot do this job. People don't want to care for free. Money comes first and the church doesn't pay."

"It sounds like the church has lost some of its soul," I remark.

He nods. "It's as if we are a funeral parlour, you come to bury, instead of coming to save the soul of that person."

I mention that Matthew told me the old story of the woman chief sacrificing a child for *muthi*.

"Does it still happen?" I ask, not sure if I want to know the answer.

"Sometimes," he replies. "Sometimes they believe one will get rich, or he or she believes they will get dignity. There are many reasons why people do this."

"And who do they kill?"

"It depends on the prescription of the witchdoctor."

"Could it be a white person?" I ask gingerly.

"It could be. Depending on the prescription of the witchdoctor," he repeats.

My stomach knots. Here we are on our way up to an old monastery in the hills, where there is no mobile phone reception, and where the bones of its former Father are not yet cold in the ground. Thea's parting words echo in my head. "I wouldn't go up there. You are a braver woman than I am."

A more stupid woman, I wonder.

"What is the church's view on witchdoctors?" I ask.

"Murdering people is wrong, and we are vocal on that. But I still believe in traditional medicine. Last year I got injured, I missed the step and I fell. I was in a cast, but it did not get totally better. Then my brother cut me, put some traditional medicine and now it's better, so I cannot condemn that. Even now, there are some psychologists who feel that the beliefs of the Africans should be protected, because if they don't believe totally in this, they can end up not having an identity. This kind of medicine is really working for them and if the Africans do not believe in this, their lives will end up being mad."

As we finish our tea I ask Father Tsalong one last question.

"Who is safe out here?"

"No one," he says. "You end up not trusting anyone. Even when you came. I didn't trust you."

It is getting late and we are expected at Mariazell before teatime. As we leave the village Matthew points out the house of the feared woman chief. It is a modern bungalow with a fallen-down tree and an abandoned caravan in the garden, fenced off with a gate.

"Do you think I should pop in and see if she'll talk to me," I say, half-jokingly.

"I dare you," he says, braking at the bottom of her driveway.

On the wall of the house is a plaque that reads 'Tyrannous Apostelic Church'. Church of the Tyrant? Brazened by my back-up, I climb out the car, walk up the driveway, and knock on the door. No one answers. I knock again. I feel like a child playing tok-tokkie, the South African childhood game where you knock on the doors of strangers and run away just before they answer. I am just about to walk away when three young girls wearing matching summer dresses with a palm-tree print appear from behind the house.

"Is anyone home?" I ask.

One of them nods.

I knock again.

I hear footsteps and the door swings open. A woman in her mid-40s, her eyes diseased so they appear only as sockets of milky white, without pupils or iris, greets me with a visage of drunken distaste. Her hair is a mess of small, unfinished plaits, sticking out all around her head. An African Medusa. I feel the old fear ignite and my legs turn to stone.

"Is, is, the woman chief here?" I stammer.

Medusa's white eyes stare over my shoulder and into the near distance.

"She's not here. Tomorrow," Medusa replies.

"Can I, can I come back then?" I say, after a lame attempt to explain why I am here, on her doorstep.

"Yes. Tomorrow," she says, her face unsmiling, her eyes still looking beyond my shoulder.

I turn on my heel, walk hurriedly past the girls, through the gate, and jump into the back seat as Linda and Matthew roar with laughter.

"Drive. Oh my god, drive and don't look back," I say.

Mariazell lies at the end of a valley overlooked by dramatic peaks and a giant cross that has been tethered to a nearby clifftop. It is home to a family of Trappist Brothers and Precious Blood Sisters, and a boarding school where many of the anti-apartheid struggle leaders including Albertina Sisulu, the wife of Walter Sisulu, and Terror Lekota (named for his prowess on the football field) were educated. When we arrive at three o'clock on a Saturday afternoon there is not a soul about.

"It's rest hour. This place runs like clockwork," Matthew says, looking up at the Swiss-made clock on the top of the church steeple. We sit down in the shade to wait. The mission station and farm was first started by Austrian Trappists in 1894 and although deep within Africa, it has an Austrian sense of time keeping. As if to prove his point, an hour later, Brother Berthold strides past us, without even acknowledging us, and heads into the clock tower to wind the clock. Only once this daily chore is complete does he come over to greet us and show us to our rooms within the Brothers' quarters. Linda and I are spooked to discover our rooms do not have locks. I drag my mattress into Linda's room and make up my bed on her floor. There is no way we are sleeping alone.

We have a few hours before the Easter Vigil, the service held after sunset on the night before Holy Sunday in the Catholic calendar, and we are introduced to Father Clements, a curmudgeonly old German monk.

"Write whatever you like, just like Zuma does," he says, as I ask his permission to write about his views on how the role of the mission is changing. He explains how difficult it is nowadays to get young men to become Trappist monks. The monks take vows of poverty, chastity and obedience.

"Before they didn't think enough, now they think too much," he says. "The idea that you don't have children means to them that you are not a man. It goes against the grain. When you are very poor, you cannot take the vow of poverty."

"Are you sad that this is ending?" I ask.

"We don't care," he says. "If you start thinking these things, you go crazy."

That evening, the Easter Vigil begins outside Mariazell's red Sandstone church. A fire is lit in a brazier, and the faithful from the nearby villages and *kraals*, including young veiled women, teenage brides of Christ, gather around, gossiping and giggling. On cue Father Bernard, the mild-mannered Kenyan priest who replaced the murdered Father Ernest, arrives wearing a floor-length white cassock, the yoke embroidered with a pattern of African thatched huts, a camping torch strapped to his head. He is trailed by three altar boys, also in white, carrying the three-foot-high Pascal candle and waving incense.

As the clock strikes 8 o'clock, Father Bernard lights the Pascal candle from the brazier, and begins to read from the Bible in Sesotho while the congregants surge gently forward, one by one, lighting their own small candles from this single Christ flame. Once everyone is holding a flickering candle Father Bernard turns and silently leads the congregation into the darkened church.

We stand at the back, observers rather than congregants. The theatre of the Catholic Church had never brought me close to God. Even in my teenage years, when I flirted with religious fervour, agreeing to be Born Again at a Christian camp that I had gone on more for its slumber party potential, my idea of God was of a distant father whom I could have informal, questioning chats with while I lay in bed at night, listening to my own father drinking and slamming doors. But out here, in the foothills of mountains, where people have so little, I could see why God would be so much more appealing if He arrived in the form of a double-bill West End show, with lights, music and a fabulous building.

The service is punctuated with Biblical canticles sung in Sesotho.

"Bolela moya,moya wa hao, Morena u nchafatse, u nchafatse sebopeho, sebopeho sa lefetshe

Send Forth your spirit, Oh Lord, to renew the nature, the nature of the world."

The rising chorus of the African choir fills the stone church, rising from the wooden pews to darkened rafters, lifting our souls higher with every incantation. Even the most dedicated atheist might have felt the hairs on the back of their neck rise in unwitting benediction.

When the service is over, we feel exhilarated, hours from sleep. Matthew knows a secret way onto the rooftop of the mission station, and we head up there with burning liturgical candles and a bottle of wine. The moon is full above the church steeple and the conversation drifts back to Matthew's childhood.

"Everything changed when I was eight," he says.

His father decided he wanted to enter the priesthood and moved the family away from this wildflower valley to a multiracial ecclesiastical centre in Imbali, a black township just outside of Pietermaritzburg.

"It was the dream of South Africa but it didn't work. It was a disaster," Matthew says.

The Le Cordeurs arrived in Imbali shortly after the seven-day war which began when UDF (United Democratic Front) and ANC supporters attacked Inkhatha Freedom Party (IFP) members who were on their way home from a political rally in Durban. The IFP retaliated by killing 200 people and forcing 20,000 to flee their homes.

"The people in Imbali hated white people," Matthew says. "I was brought up in a world where everyone was loving and giving and I went to a world where everything was ugly and where I was mentally bullied. It stressed me very much and I ended up with childhood epilepsy."

But although Matthew's world had flipped over, the fact remains that he spent nearly his whole childhood living cheek to cheek with black people, while so many white children were kept apart.

"How do you think that affected the kind of South African you have become?" I ask.

Matthew takes a sip of his wine and thinks it over.

"I feel the barrier between black and white South Africans is a fear and a mistrust, but I don't have that mistrust, I don't think so. I am more intrigued, more interested to learn and understand. Perhaps it also comes from working in a newspaper world where everyone is Indian, black, and white together. We debate a lot."

"And do you talk a lot about difficult issues in the newsroom?" I ask.

He pauses.

"Not always. A lot of the young black journalists like to be controversial. They say we deserve to take everything away from you white people, or a lot of my black friends will say jokingly that I am a racist, just because they can. If we are having an argument, they'll just quickly say 'Oh you racist!' and then you can't say anything else. You ask how is that racist, and they just say, 'Oh it's just racist!'"

We laugh at this uncomfortable truth. Matthew is not alone in being casually branded a racist. The race card has become the ultimate South African trump card, used in seriousness and in jest, in all walks of life, from the corridors of power to the school playground. It is the punctuation mark at the end of an unwanted debate. The modern South African version of being bound and gagged. I have often wondered what would happen if we accepted that a shared racial prejudice is as common as the air we breathe? That the very thing which divides us, is the thing that unites us? The truth is, every person that lived through apartheid, lived under the fist of racism. It seeped into our hearts and minds in insidious ways. It was like living in a house with parents who hate the colour black. The children of that house would be forbidden to wear black clothes. Most would acquiesce to please the parents, one would rebel and wear nothing but black to spite the parents, but that is not the point. The point is that our behaviour is not our own, it is reactionary, counter-pointed against the rules laid down by an authority figure. Still today, South Africans are a bit like children with domineering, racist parents – we are not sure where their views end and our own begin. We are still learning to think for ourselves outside of that oppressive home. We are still caught in the vice of apartheid's mental oppression.

In his book, *Unpopular Essays,* the philosopher Bertrand Russell writes: "The essence of the liberal outlook lies not in what opinions are held, but in how they are held: instead of being held dogmatically, they are held tentatively and with a consciousness that new evidence may at any moment lead to their abandonment."

It strikes me that a nation of liberal racists, always open to debate and to question their preconceived ideas, would be better than a nation of colour-blind conservatives.

"How do you handle the racist slurs?" I ask Matthew.

"I'm very open with everyone and I think that helps them become open to me. I've always given my black friends that platform to nail me, and I just accept it."

"And do you think there are lot of genuine racists still in South Africa?" I ask.

"I think that most people in South Africa have racist tendencies. There are some people in this country who were lucky enough to have been brought up in a slightly different way, but I don't think any of us were brought up in a non-racialised society. Even me, from the age of eight, when we left Mariazell, I was brought up in a racist society. But I think on both sides. Can you really blame black people for being racist? You can't. Especially if you are poor in the townships today and you see these *wit ous* (white guys) driving around, acting all cool, being rich, living it up. It's unfair and you feel angry. It's a long road to walk."

Matthew sighs.

"It's quite hard sometimes. It's quite hard being someone who is trying to be open. I think it's very difficult to actually be a liberal, open-minded, non-racial, truly democratic person. I think it's much easier being racist, sexist, being bigoted because you just get to box everything up in a very neat little package. You stay in your very secure comfort zone and you block the world out."

"Or you leave the country," I say.

We stare up at the moon.

"Do you think it's worth it?" I ask. "Do you think it's worth building a life here, or do you think white South Africans will just end up getting thrown out of this country one day?

"I think you have to be honest with yourself," Matthew says. "It doesn't matter which country you live in, you should try to live to a standard of non-racism and non-sexism, you should strive towards being as inclusive as possible wherever you are. But that doesn't necessarily give you the privilege of being safe and secure. It doesn't entitle you to a happy life, to a first-world life. You might experience pain. You might not get what you feel you deserve. You might be the best South African, the truest South African and get raped and murdered. You have to make the decision, do you want to live in South Africa with all its beauty and all its pain and suffering? And all its ugliness. You have to make that decision."

"So why do you stay?" I ask.

"It's one of the last places on this planet where you can be truly free and you don't feel trapped by consumerism and by the west's grip on society. In Europe everything is perfect and clean but your soul is often trapped. So you do have that blessing in South Africa. Here you live in the wild west, you have to play by their rules. And you live and die by their rules."

That night as I lie on my mattress on the floor of Linda's room, I turn Matthew's words over in my head. Their rules? Whose rules? Are rape, murder and corruption really African rules? Or are they Europe's old rules, from when they used to play abroad? Who brought the guns to Africa? Who stole the land? Who first put women and children in concentration camps? Who dehumanized others so they could take home the spoils of gold and diamonds? Who systematically tortured and murdered those who opposed minority white rule?

Those lily white hands, stained with blood.

Chapter 18

....

Easter Sunday

I WAKE EARLY TO THE pealing of bells. Chinks of yellow morning light are spilling around the edges of the curtains and I am fizzing with a giddy energy. I lie there for a while, listening to Linda's breath, trying to coax myself back to sleep, but my restlessness only grows. I turn back the duvet, pick up a jumper and a pair of walking boots, and as quietly as I can, open my door and pad down the corridor and out the blue side-door.

A cool mountain air greets my sleep-warmed cheeks. I stoop to put on my shoes. I can hear faint sounds from the kitchen close to the nun's quarters and turn and walk in the opposite direction. I do not want to see or talk to anyone. I just want to feel what it is like to be here. And what it is like to walk alone, unseen, before the mission wakes up, on a mission of your own.

I walk the length of the Brothers' quarters and stop at the dirt track which continues up past the church to Father Ernest's house. I stop still and listen. A bird. A breeze. Nobody to hear you. Nobody to watch you. I turn in the opposite direction and head down the driveway past a low-ceilinged stone building. I veer off the track and go to peer inside its small windows. As I get closer I hear squealing. My heart lurches.

"It's just pigs, little pigs," I say to myself.

I turn on my heel and run towards the open veld, the cosmos fields, the big skies. I run away from the red sandstone buildings that looked on while one of God's deputies was murdered by his deputy, by someone he knew, someone he trusted. I take a deep breath and feel my tension ebb away. In the veld, I feel safe. In the veld, I am at home.

I close my eyes and imagine myself back in the mielie field next to my childhood home. Blackjacks brush up against my knees and my nostrils fizz with the scent of the dry, sweet earth. A happiness and a sadness wash over me. I am happy because for a moment, I am standing inside memory. And I am sad because it is just that, memory, distant, a fleeting moment from decades before when the world seemed safer, simpler.

A faint rumble catches my attention. At first it sounds like distant thunder, and I look up at the blue skies, scouring the heavens for a trace of a cloud, and then I spot him, in the distance, galloping through the cosmos, an African cowboy in a wide-brimmed hat, riding bareback on a chestnut horse. I raise my hand in a wave and he waves back. Morning rush hour in the foothills of Lesotho.

I glance back at Mariazell. The clock on the church tower reads two minutes to seven, two minutes to breakfast.

"Don't be late," Matthew had warned. "It might be in South Africa, but Mariazell runs on German time."

I turn on my heel and jog back, away from the veld, away from memory.

I open the dining room door to find a room that smells of old wood and cabbage. All the pupils are away on school holidays. Just one table is set in the far corner. Matthew, the German Brothers and Father Bernard are already sitting silently, eating their porridge. Bernard smiles a cheery good morning. The Brothers just nod. Matthew looks at me with wide eyes.

"Have you heard the news?" he asks.

"No," I say.

"Eugene Terreblanche. He is dead. He was hacked to death," he says.

I feel a chill, as if someone had just opened the door and let in a rush of cool mountain air.

Eugene Terreblanche, leader and icon of the Afrikaner far right, dead. The man who spearheaded a bloody campaign to wreck the transition to democracy, murdered.

Even during apartheid, when centrist politics were unequivocally racist, Terreblanche was to the right of centre. In this post-apartheid world, his politics were so far right, they had fallen off the political map.

"Who? Why?" I ask.

"No one knows yet. He was found in his bed."

"Live by the sword, die by the sword," mutters one of the old German brothers.

He is right, but his comment does not ease my immediate sense of foreboding. If right-wing Boers retaliated, could this be the opening shot in all-out civil war? Could this be the blue-touch paper that will ignite white-on-black violence? How would us soft, pseudo-liberal middle-class whiteys fare in the middle?

Father Bernard stands up: "I almost forgot".

He hands us each a bar of Cadbury's Top Deck. It's a two-tone bar of chocolate available only in South Africa, brown on the bottom, white on top.

"Happy Easter," he says.

Sister Patricia, one of the Precious Blood nuns, is on her way to the nearby village to pay an Easter Sunday visit to the elderly and infirm. I ask if I can join her, I want to chat to her about Father Ernest's murder, and so we head out across the fields on a gnarled footpath, scrambling down into a small river bed and up the side of a steep hillside to the village perched on top.

"I would have thought somewhere like this, a religious place in the mountains, would have been safe," I say, breathing heavily. Sister Patricia does not walk slowly.

"We are not safe, we are not safe, we are not safe," Sister Patricia mutters. "Did you hear about Terreblanche?"

I nod.

"I wonder if it was politically motivated," I say. "Julius Malema [then leader of the ANC youth league] keeps singing *Kill the Boer, Kill the Farmer*."

Sister Patricia clicks her tongue in annoyance.

"Eish. Why is he saying that? To kill the Boers, for what? They don't even remember the words of Mandela. You should forget what was happening yesterday, you should think about what is happening today. This freedom we have. We should enjoy the freedom."

A distant grumble interrupts our talking. We look at the sky. Black clouds are brewing over the mountains.

"Come. We must get there before those clouds get here," she says.

We push on and have just time to pay a few house calls before giant splats of rain start pummelling our backs. We make a dash for the home of the person Sister Patricia most wants to visit: Father Ernst's former cleaning lady.

The woman collapsed in nervous exhaustion after discovering his body and has not been able to get out of bed since. We slip inside just before the raindrops turn into torrents. The woman is resting on a double bed in the corner of the room that doubles as a bedroom and living room. Her two small daughters smile shyly at us, and she instructs them to bring some chairs out of the kitchen. The children are busy cutting pictures out of magazines, arranging the pictures at their mother's feet. The rain batters and bangs on the tin roof, with all the fury of a teenager let loose on a drum kit, so that we can barely hear each other talk. Sister Patricia and I look at each other in mock horror. Not only do we not have a raincoat or umbrella between us, Sister Patricia is wearing a white dress. Our journey home is going to put a whole new spin to the notion of nuns on the run.

We stay for half an hour chatting politely, carefully avoiding the talk of the murder so as not to churn up the woman's fragile emotions, and when the rain eases off, we decide to make a dash for it. The wild downpour has turned the footpath into a river and we slip and slide our way home, skidding down the steeper paths until every part of our bodies, from our faces to our feet is splattered with mud.

As we near the school buildings the heavens open once more. We stand for a minute under the metal awning of a classroom, but our clothes are so wet it is as if they have merged with our skin, and our shoes are like garden ponds. The only sensible thing to do is to make a final run for home and a hot shower.

Sister Patricia dashes for the nun's quarters. I fling open the door of the Brothers quarters, and tip-toe to my room, trying not to leave a puddle in my wake. I have barely shut the door on my room when there is a knock.

I open it and Father Bernard is standing there.

"There are people here to see you," he says.

"Really?" I say, surprised. "I need to get out of these clothes first."

"They have been waiting a long time. Come," he instructs.

I squelch behind him back down the corridor and into the Brothers' library, a room with tables, chairs and a single wall of shelves displaying a paltry number of books. Inside are three men, all in black leather jackets, sitting around the table, their arms folded. As I stand in the doorway, all three look me up and down with cold, sardonic grins, while the one nearest demands: "Where have you been? We've been waiting for you all afternoon."

It is more than a rain-soaked chill that runs down my spine.

"Where are Matthew and Linda?" I turn to ask Father Bernard.

"I don't know. I haven't seen them all afternoon," Father Bernard replies.

"We saw them earlier," my leather-clad guest says, turning his gaze from me, to the window. "They are somewhere out in the fields."

My belly turns cold.

Father Bernard makes to leave.

"Are… are you going out?" I ask, pleading with my eyes for him to stay.

"Yes, I have to go and speak to Sister Irene."

Then turning to the three strangers, he nods farewell and turns swiftly on his heel and leaves, the door banging behind him.

I shiver.

"What did you say your name was?" I say, turning back to the first man.

"Tebogo Makoro. And these are my brothers," he says.

"Were… were we supposed to be meeting?" I ask.

"I heard a journalist was here investigating the murder. I thought we should talk," he replies.

There may not be a mobile phone signal in these parts, but news certainly travels fast. I look back at them pensively. I need to gather my wits. And to do that, my body, at least, needs to be dry.

"I need a few minutes. I'm soaked to the bone," I say.

Makoro shrugs and turns to look out the window.

I squeak back down the corridor and fling open Matthew's and Linda's doors on the way past. No one. I head into my own room and peel my clothes off. It is like removing a sodden wetsuit. I briskly towel myself down and change into a pair of jeans and a T-shirt. I grab my notebook and my Dictaphone, slip on a pair of flip-flops, and hurry back to the library.

I choose the chair closest to the door, the opposite side of the table from Makoro.

"What is it you'd like to discuss?" I ask.

"What is it you'd like to know?" Makoro replies, meeting my gaze.

I look him in the eyes. There is no warmth, no friendliness. Has he come here to warn me off asking about the murder? And if he has, it is working. I feel uneasy, threatened. I change tack. I tell him that my prime motive is to investigate what democracy has brought to the old Transkei. Makoro considers this.

"There is a side effect to every tablet that we take," he replies.

"By which you mean…"

"Some people have better families and better lives due to the education that they got here. But there are others who misunderstood the message of the church. They thought the church was there to provide, not to empower them. I think the alleged murderer, if at all he might have committed this thing, will be an example of those who have misunderstood, who have in them a sense of entitlement. If the church came to you as a father, you feel that you are entitled to everything, even to your father's life."

"That's a very strange idea. I don't see how anyone could think that," I reply.

Makoro considers for a minute.

"The church came to people as a mother and a father, providing all the resources to make them become better people. Now they think the church *has* to do this and that for them."

Over the next few minutes he extrapolates his theory that the historic paternalism of the church has unwittingly created an inflated and incurable sense of entitlement among the local people. He offers an example.

"There was an orchard at Marialinden. We had to be cut it down because the kids were coming in, thinking they were entitled to fruit there."

I stare at Makoro, aghast. There is probably not an orchard in the world from which children have not stolen juicy apples. That is what growing, hungry, adventurous children do. The idea that someone would destroy an orchard in a bid to stop children stealing is even more bizarre and twisted thinking. It is the action of a cruel, tyrannical father.

"What is your role in the church?" I ask Makoro, finally finding my courage in the wake of this twisted tale.

"I am *Father* Makoro. Matthew has told you who I am," he says, irritated at my ignorance.

Suddenly the penny drops. This dark-eyed man with the cold demeanour is Matthew's boyhood friend who he had grown up alongside at Marialinden, the man he talks about with so much love and fondness, and who is now head of a nearby church. The image I had conjured in my head could not be more different from the figure sitting across the table.

I nod in assent and relax slightly, but his attitude makes me no less comfortable.

"People are very religious in South Africa," I venture. "Surely using the church to help people develop is a good thing? The church seems to be very close to people's hearts."

Father Makoro leans forward and taps his index finger on the table.

"It's a religious country by name, but it does not have the true spirit of a Christian country. A Christian country has martyrs, people who have sacrificed their lives for faith. I believe people are very casual with their own religion. At the centre of South Africa is politics, that's where people shed their blood."

"And you think South Africa would be different if people valued their faith above politics?" I ask.

"If South Africa was a true religious country, we would get a principled society. A society that is prepared to die for principles instead of... what? People are not committed to anything. The present president, Zuma, if it was a true religious country, he may not even have made it to the presidency. When we are very casual, choosing personalities instead of timeless, changeless principles that will bring a strong backbone to our country, we are in danger because we'll build a society where we just do as we please."

I cast my mind to the wild west corruption, opportunism and ANC infighting that the Queen of Pondoland described in Lusikisiki. Makoro has a point. There is a huge disjuncture between the idea of the noble anti-apartheid activist who was willing to risk all for freedom, and the deeply ignoble, self-servicing municipal official whose only motivation is to line his own pockets with gold.

"What about those who fought in the struggle? Don't you think they had principles?" I ask.

"It's very complicated," replies Makoro. "In the South African struggle there were two things happening at the same time. There were those who appeared to be struggling while also developing their own family and own international relationships. That's where South African politics got complicated for us. They were building their own wings so when 1994 came, they were flying. Now others are trying to do the same, at the end of the day, corrupting the nation."

"And a religious backbone would change that?" I ask.

"If South Africa had the opportunity of one person who would lay down his own life, if they just died for principles, and their own families never benefitted a thing, if it was pure self-sacrifice for a better cause, then I think things could be better. But this so-called struggle, we were fooled. When people came back we realised they had a lot of money, contacts and could use their financial resources to be in better positions. And so like in Animal Farm, we realise that some animals are more equal than others."

Makoro's outlook is dark and heavy. It's the outlook of someone who has been deeply and irrevocably disappointed by someone they trusted and admired. As I sit there, I feel like Makoro and I are staring at each other from opposite sides of a deep chasm. We are both children of apartheid. We are of a similar age and level of education. But we have emerged very different Phoenixes from the smoking rubble of the old order.

When my childhood bubble burst at university, it was exposed for what it was: a whites-only fairy tale built on a festering sore. My distaste for what I saw freed me to want to build a fresh worldview. But Makoro's childhood bubble was nobler than mine. It held within it a vision for a multiracial society, built on equality. But when he saw his political heroes return home from exile and use their power and influence to improve their own status in life, rather than the lives of all, his childhood bubble imploded, taking with it his hope for an equal world.

Makoro's worldview reminds me of that of the 16th century political philosopher Thomas Hobbes. Hobbes wrote that life is "nasty, brutish and short", that people are motivated only by their own self-preservation. The only way to stop people bulldozing each other is to get everyone to submit to a central authority. For Hobbes, that despot was mortal. For Makoro, that despot is God.

As I am contemplating Makoro's outlook, the front door bursts open and a whirlwind of laughter spills through. Matthew and Linda poke their heads around the library door.

"Hiya!" sings Matthew, striding across the room to embrace Tebogo

Makoro with a damp hug. The warmth seems to be one-sided and it puzzles me that Matthew does not notice. Matthew plonks himself down next to Makoro. Makoro ignores him and continues with his argument.

"There's no honesty here. People are not honest. It's a game people are playing ultimately," he says. "Think about the murder that happened here. I think to the white people it was a terrible shock. The alleged murderer would be identified as the trusted one among the blacks. So you ask yourself who can you trust? You come to the conclusion that all people have secrets, deep secrets, they are never truthful."

Makoro holds my gaze and I feel like my mind is being read aloud.

"It's even more so for a white woman," he says, his sardonic smile returning. "When she sees a black guy, she sees a penis, someone who has come to rape her. I think those are psychological divisions which South Africa still has to deal with. Maybe a side effect of this apartheid, which will stay with us very long."

That evening we gather with the Brothers in their television room to watch the 8 o'clock news on SABC 1, the main channel of the South African National Broadcaster. The news is preceded by a short address from the President Jacob Zuma calling for calm from the nation. In the main broadcast, the newsreader reads the facts: Eugene Terreblanche had been killed by a 15 year old and a 21 year old after an argument on the farm. They killed him in his bedroom with a panga and a knobkerrie – both traditional Zulu weapons. Both boys had been arrested for murder. There is no analysis, no discussion, but the innuendo is in the next segment which cuts to Julius Malema, then leader of the ANC Youth League at a Zanu-PF rally in Zimbabwe, wearing a shirt patterned with Robert Mugabe's face. Mugabe had made international headlines time and again for supporting the violent, forced removals of white farmers from their Zimbabwean farms.

I am about to turn in when Father Bernard pops his head around the television room door.

"Would you like to join me for a coffee?" he asks.

I follow him into his study, a cosy room full of books. He switches on the kettle, offers me an armchair and asks me about my marriage and my family. I feel like I've been summoned to the shrink's office. Slowly we move the conversation back from the state of my soul to the soul of the old Transkei.

"It's as if we have no government," he says. "I ask myself where does Mariazell feature in South Africa? Nowhere. Sure, people get a pension, but that's it. The Xhosas are very corrupt people. During apartheid they ruled themselves and the Eastern Cape had nothing. They say they were deprived of resources, but now they are in charge and the Eastern Cape still has nothing. Maybe the Eastern Cape could have developed, but they are very selfish, thinking about the profits, not about their lives."

I am shocked by his frankness, by the way he openly writes off Xhosa people as corrupt and selfish, and by my own reaction. If he was a white priest, my hackles would be up and I would be mentally clocking him as a racist. But he is a black Kenyan who works and lives in this community. He is a black man criticising other black men. And so what does that make him? Simply a critic?

"What about Mandela?" I say, "He was from the Eastern Cape. As were many of the other great leaders."

"Yes, Mandela did a lot. But you need a team. You need defenders, strikers. The goalkeeper alone cannot win the game. Now the economy is still in control of the whites, but there will come a time when South African blacks have to take over that job. And there is a psychological problem. To be a black person in South Africa means to have low self-esteem. They see an outsider as being better, as a competitor rather than an equal, rather than as someone who can help them. During apartheid there was a lot of help from other African countries, but now they do not want to help those people back. Now we see a lot of Xenophobia. They do not want anyone to be above them."

"Does it make it difficult for you, as a Kenyan, to be the priest here?" I ask.

"I'm not friends with the South African blacks. They say this is your mother, I say no, I do not have a mother, a brother or a sister. I am very conscious of this. They say if you steal from your brother, it is not stealing. I work with them, but I am not one of them. On the surface they are sweet and nice, but the majority, in the bottom of their hearts…" his voice drifts off and he shakes his head. "Out here it's survival of the fittest."

That night I sleep uneasily, wondering how long and steep is the road ahead of us, how long it will be before our wounds begin to heal. My mind drifts back to the veld. Standing there, under those big skies, soft grasses tickling at your ankles, you feel safe, but it only takes a tiny spark to start a fire that will burn for miles and miles, destroying everything in its path.

....

Chapter 19

The End of the Road

W E LEAVE THE MISSION on Easter Monday, swapping a monastery full of secrets for a country full of uncertainty. Matthew drops Linda at the Greyhound bus stop and me at Willowdale Lodge and takes his leave for his home in Pietermartizburg. I am alone again.

I handwash my clothes and transcribe my notes and then sit in an armchair on the wraparound *stoep*, overlooking a shaded lawn, a crumbling old tennis court, and distant cow fields, breathing in the birdsong, the gentle breeze and the calm. The peace of the land is one of the great ironies of South Africa. Through all the years of fears and political turmoil, the land has stood still, like an experienced, enormous breasted mother who listens deeply to all her children's cries, soothing our tears with the morning song of the hadida and the evening chorus of the cricket. She watches benignly over us as we play our foolish, dangerous games, fighting over our toys, failing to learn to share. I catch myself singing an old song that I have not heard in years, the South African version of an old Woody Guthrie tune.

"This land is your land, this land is our land, from the Brown Limpopo to the Transvaal Highlands, from the Tsikamma to the Kalahari, this land was made for you and me."

For years we shared the apartheid way, the Transvaal for me, the Transkei for you, shoring up huge chunks of the country so that the tribes of Africa

– ancient and recent – could "develop" separately, according to their cultures, traditions and so-called needs. It was a textbook theory that overlooked the most basic human fact: that like our bodies, our cultures, traditions and needs are living, breathing things. You cannot define them, label them and confine them. Our spirits naturally soar, especially over a land as beautiful as this.

I scroll idly through my mobile phone and find an SMS sent a few weeks earlier from Sibusiso Kwamini. *"The village is preparing for your visit and wants you to feel our culture... Welcome home!!!"* Sibusiso runs a cultural group in his small village of Rhwatsana close to Lady Frere in the northern part of the Transkei. I had read about his initiative, *Siyazingca Ngenkcubeko Yethu* (We are proud of our culture & heritage) in the Daily Dispatch newspaper. They are a rural village co-operative whose aim is to create income through promoting traditional Xhosa music, dance and craft and use surplus funds to provide homecare for the elderly and those living with HIV/AIDS. I smile at the text. It is a lovely message. When I first received it a few weeks back, it had felt like a chink of sunshine at the end of a dark winter. But as I re-read it now, I read it for what it is: a kindness but not a truth. The Transkei is not my home. Its ways are as unfamiliar to me as the hinterlands of Russia and my months here have done little to change that. It may have been different if I could speak the Xhosa language, if I had heeded Mandela's call in 1994 for us all to start learning to speak to each other in our native tongues, but I did not. I flew the coop and learnt French instead.

I stare across at the big copper beech tree and admit a truth to myself: the thought of venturing to another village to hear how the villagers feel let down by government, democracy, chiefs, and God fills me with gloom. I am sick of this broken place that no one seems to care about. I am lonely, miserable, and tired of this deep-seated anxiety that rears up whenever I am alone. It is so much easier to be abroad, thousands of miles from all of this, thousands of miles from myself. In my diary I jot down these words: "As I am here now, I'm starting to forget why I wanted to come. I'm starting to forget what it was I didn't know. The stories seem to repeat themselves. They are like the landscape, layered, hills upon hills, often shrouded in mist. There are no landmarks. I am lost and I don't know the way out."

That night I eat dinner in the lodge dining room with a young black geologist who is surveying the Transkei for a mining company. We talk about the land, its people, its poverty and the ethics of mining this wild, unspoilt place. We are two young, educated South Africans, talking in earnest about the future of their country and later as I put myself to bed, I wonder if I have been looking in the wrong place all along. I have been so hell bent on talking with those without a voice that I have forgotten to talk to those who have a voice, but are also never heard. South African newspapers are full of the chest-beating rhetoric of politicians, and the comment pages on news websites teem with angry racist slurs of Internet trolls, but there exists a growing class of smart, educated, black South Africans whose spirits have risen over the past and who are quietly building its future. The philosopher Bertrand Russell wrote about the curious quirk of writers, especially moralists, to tend to think well of sections of society to which they themselves do not belong. "Liberals", he writes, "tend to idealise the rural poor." Had I done that? Had I hoped that I would find some pre-colonial, pre-apartheid purity in the old Transkei that would overshadow all the old divisions and fears? That would make it all better? I think I had.

The next morning I wake before dawn for the journey to Rhwatsana. I pack the car, climb behind the wheel and turn the key. Nothing. The engine will not start. A fellow guest, also up early, has jump leads. We try to open the bonnet to connect them. It will not open. We try again. And again. We ring the local mechanic, but he is away on his Easter holidays. We do everything we can think of, but the bakkie is going nowhere. I climb down from behind the wheel and slump to the gravel floor and start to sob. Tears pour down my face and my body shivers and shakes and I feel every last drop of energy ebb out of me and disappear into the ground beneath my feet. I am crying with frustration and I am crying with relief. I am crying because the bakkie has broken down. I am crying because I have broken down.

For the past three months I had pushed on and on, suppressing my weariness and wariness, desperately digging in the dusty earth of this forgotten province looking for everything and nothing. I had wanted to know what rural African village life was really like. I had wanted to prove to myself, to everyone, that you just had to get close enough, and then all those divisions would magically vanish. I wanted to exorcise the past from within me, save me forever from its twisted fingers, and I had succeeded in doing the opposite. All the tales of bloody betrayals and corruption had fed into the racist stereotypes that lingered at the back of my brain. Yes, I had met individuals who I could trust and respect. When I thought of Nonhle and Jimmy and the Queen and Nurse Qaukeni and Mr and Mrs Mangala, I saw noble individuals who cared about this country. But the stories they told of corruption and violence rang even louder in my ears and the overarching feeling in me was disappointment, disillusionment, disgust – and fear. That fucking fear. Never to be exorcised. Never to be stricken. This country was a knot upon a knot upon a knot. It was a coiled serpent that lives in your stomach, tied in cunning knots over centuries of betrayals, a parasitic worm at the back of your mind. Everything about it repulsed me. Including and especially me. I wanted away from all of this. Away from this fucked up place that defies the mind, that defies reason. What a naïf to think that my little sojourn, my little dosey-do sponsored by George Soros would change anything. I despised myself for failing. And I scorned myself for daring to dream otherwise.

I pick up the phone and through sobs I call my parents. Could they come and pick me up because I cannot carry on. When they arrived a few hours later the strangest thing happened. The bakkie started with one turn of the key. I had always joked that my dad had sent his bakkie to take care of me and now it seemed it was true: it was protecting me from a journey without an end.

Chapter 20

....

Sicambeni

MY PARENTS PUT ME to bed in their home. I feel like a baby bird without plumage: vulnerable, defenceless, exposed. As the week passes I make little dalliances out of the nest. At first just as far as the television, then to the porch, and then to the beach where the sun works its magic and I feel my strength ebbing back. One lunchtime, after a week of doing nothing and thinking nothing, I start making noises about wanting to go back on the road.

My father cautions me kindly, "There's no rush. You're not well. Take your time."

He was right, but I need to tie the threads in my mind. On my travels I had heard about a radical developmental activist, a white South African guy called Luke Boshier, who had set up home in Sicambeni village in Pondoland, and was trying to effect change in his home country from the ground up. It intrigued me that he was not just driving down dusty dirt tracks, he was living down them. I called and asked if I could visit him.

The fact that I had no hesitation or anxiety about going to stay with a white male stranger did not pass me by.

I set off on a Sunday morning, for the last time to the Transkei. It is a peaceful day, very few people, animals or cars are about, and the bakkie and I enjoy the silence and the sun as we meander down these now familiar roads.

I stop in Flagstaff to buy a few groceries. The town is usually frenetic, but the only person today is a young black guy sitting in the sun on a bollard outside the Spar.

I park the car and get out, and he smiles at me.

"It's nice to see you," he says as I walk past.

"It's nice to see you too," I reply.

Just a line, a quiet greeting, but as the country tip-toes around each other in the wake of Terreblanche's death, it feels a gentle light.

I arrive at Sicambeni just after lunch, and am welcomed by Luke who is a brash, arrogant, easy-to-like, easy-to-loathe, beardy intellectual who jumped *veldskoen* (hiking boot) first out of the ivory tower of development politics into Pondoland soil. Together with his partner, Diane, and an eclectic bunch of volunteers from all corners of the globe, they transformed an empty piece of land into the so-called Centre for Appropriate Rural Technology (CART), something of a model *kraal*.

"This used to be a rubbish dump," Luke says as he shows me around. There is a permaculture garden where they grow a diversity of fruit and vegetables, a cluster of rondawels built with handmade clay bricks, and a homemade biodigester which anaerobically digests human and animal waste, preventing the local water supply from becoming contaminated, and which releases methane gas that they harvest for cooking. I am shown to my own hut, with a little bed, and a little window. It is like being welcomed to Eden.

Luke invites me for a coffee in the CART office. It is a tin-roofed square hut furnished with a patchwork couch and curtains, a raffia rug, iPhones and computers. As he speaks, Luke rocks back and forth on his chair, filling the small space with his big ideas. He explains how he was first inspired to come here after working with communities affected by HIV/AIDS in Khayelitsha.

"I got the sense that people just wanted to come home to the Eastern

Cape, but the infrastructure had failed them. I came here to see for myself and saw nothing but abundance – fertile soil, water, clay and Eucalyptus forests for building. The amount of land versus what is being utilised is ridiculous. We could feed the country," he says.

Luke's assessment echoes that of the agri-entrepreneur Graham Casalis who tried to plant the canola in the fields of the Jumba tribe, but while Casalis' solution is economic, Luke does not believe the answer lies in the creation of infrastructure or jobs, but rather in restoring the self-esteem and dignity that was eroded (first by colonialism, then by apartheid, and further crushed by a government trying to redress inequality by handing out food parcels and social grants), rather than the more difficult task of establishing a solid education system and a rural agricultural industry that would empower people to lift themselves out of poverty.

"The ideas of the ANC are lying shattered on the ground," he says. "They have lost their ideological purpose and created a culture of dependency. The land here gets farmed for one year, then they sell their produce, but they don't reinvest in the project, they go back to the government and ask for more money. What we need to change is the mindset of people who are waiting for the government to build them a house or put the water on."

CART is his attempt to do just this. It is a rural life-skills demonstration centre that attempts to show people how it is possible, *without* the help of government, using the resources they already have – the land and them-selves – to build a sustainable, rewarding life in the Transkei.

"Planting food gardens is an amazing way to get grounded, to get back into your understanding. It's consciously doing something to feed yourself and in the process you learn that unless you feed the soil, you won't suc-ceed," Luke says. "If we ask a guy what he wants, he says he wants money. If we ask them what he is going to do with the money, he says he's going to buy food. If we say you can grow food yourself, he says no, he doesn't want to do that. Why not? Because it means being African. That's the saddest, saddest thing. Our governance has turned to a democratic capitalist system and there is a complete detachment from the self through this process. Everyone is trying to be westernised or European. I'm not saying that we must go back to loincloths, but we need to look for solutions that belong here, in Africa. Who were these people before colonisation? Were they savages? Or did they have a beautiful, honest sense of self in their environment?"

I thought back to Mrs Mthwa and her dignity that was caught up inextricably in the land and in her ancestors. Of how Nonhle's grandfather had fought against the Betterment Plan, and refused to exchange a bag of soil for a bag of money. Throughout apartheid there had been parts of South Africa that had managed to keep its integrity intact, parts of the country that had never allowed itself to be part of the white man's solution to how black and white people could co-habit. The problems that exist in the rest of the Transkei accrue from the white man's project. Could another white man, even one as passionate as Luke, ever understand this world deeply enough to inspire and evoke real change?

"Do you honestly think you can make a difference by being here?" I ask.

Luke runs his hands through his floppy hair, leans forward in his chair and stares at me with piercing blue eyes.

"It is difficult. And one of the reasons why it's difficult is because people think that being white equals money. But I go on these missions and I explore them because it's the only way I can make a difference. I take this incredibly seriously. I have a beautiful home near Cape Town but it sits empty because I choose to be here because we have serious problems. I need you to understand I do not necessarily say what we are doing here is right. I'm not saying it is wrong either. I don't know. We don't have the answer yet. We are still on that journey. We are exploring and exhausted and grappling. Whether I am welcome here or not, I will actively participate in trying to shift the way things are being done here because it's not working, it's failing. We have to have the courage now to go in a different direction."

Luke pauses for a breather. I scribble down a few words in my notebook.

"You know, I don't expect you or anybody else to understand it," he says. "It's a journey. We've got to get to the absolute bottom of it and it's ugly. It's about confronting all sorts of stuff that we don't want to. Life is not about Zuma or Malema, but about Claire and Luke sitting on the top of a hill, talking about Africa's problems, and the belief that if we really care, we can have a part to play."

"Can we?" my inner voice wondered. *"Can we really?"*

I stayed for a couple of days, talking to villagers, walking village paths. In the early morning, a few days later, as I drove away from Sicambeni, I spot a hitchhiker, an elderly black man, standing outside a house, on the brow of a hill.

I slow down and wind down the window.

"Do you need a lift Tata?" I ask.

The old man holding a suitacase, nods. "To Mthatha."

"I am going Lusikisiki way, but I can give you a lift as far as the turn-off," I say.

He climbs in and puts his bag on his lap.

"Were you visiting family?" I ask as I pull off.

"A wedding," he says.

We both smile at the happy thought of a marriage and then turn to watch the road, simultaneously rolling our eyes and shaking our heads at the potholes.

At the main road I stop to let him out.

He shakes my hand, and he smiles kindly at me.

"Hamba Kahle," he says, as he climbs down. *Go well.*

"Hamba Kahle to you too," I reply.

Betweenword

I RETURNED TO SCOTLAND DETERMINED to move back to South Africa. I need to be back there, I tell my husband. I want to be part of the change that is happening.

Fate has other plans.

Within a week of returning to Scotland it arrives. In the post. Dog barking. Sun out. Nice day. It is not addressed to me. I tear it open. It is an appointment for an MRI scan. I pick up my phone. He does not answer. He has gone running on an island with a friend. Last week he told me about the blood test. And the biopsy. Just routine.

Not routine. In a moment, an exhaled breath, my life contracts. Thoughts of nation building, morality, democratic rights and wrongs evaporate. In their place slips malignancy, Gleason scores, PSA levels. Cancer. The punctuation mark that interrupts all other sentences. We cope by clinging to each other and redecorating. As if the cure is to be found in tins of Farrow & Ball paint, with their strangely labelled tins. *Savage Ground. Blackened. Arsenic. Borrowed Light.* The doctors say there is no need for treatment. Not yet. "Watchful waiting" they call it, and so we ride out that year, trying to avoid eye contact with the gremlin that now sleeps nightly in our bed.

I submit my story on the women chiefs to *Time* magazine, and with no more commitments, no publisher or literary agent pointing to a deadline clock, I am left alone with the stories of the Transkei. I begin to write around them, quietly prodding at the dark places in my heart, but my heart has new shadows and I spend most afternoons, under my desk, asleep at my own feet.

The distance between me and South Africa grows.

How can I write about this country if I am not there? How can I say I care and be so far away? The inner voice takes on a new tone.

"Who you are to write about South Africa? Shut up, white girl. Shut up, foreigner."

Cackling voice, the censor from within.

I need to get away from this desk. I need to do something.

In South Africa I had come across The Bookery, a NGO in Cape Town that collects good quality second-hand children's books to build libraries in disadvantaged South African schools. During apartheid, so-called Bantu education was designed to intellectually dispossess black people, and so non-white schools did not have libraries because they didn't "need" them. Since the end of apartheid, no new school libraries have been built which means 92 per cent of South African schools – 20,000 schools – still do not have libraries with the worst affected in the Eastern Cape (wherein lies the old Transkei) where only 166 out of 5,723 schools have libraries. Do libraries make a difference? Yes. In 2009 in the Eastern Cape, only 13% of students actually passed matric, South Africa's school leaving exams, compared to the 47% pass-rate in the Gauteng province. What makes this worse is that in 2009, Basic Education Minister Angie Motshekga commented that a stand-alone library for every school "would be unattainable, considering the historical neglect". Though it is possible to build stadia for the World Cup.

When I was a kid, books were my salvation. I would never have escaped the strictures of Benoni without them. When I first arrived in the UK, it thrilled and amazed me how the country was flooded with second-hand books, often costing less than a Coke, whereas in South Africa a new book costs a whole day's pay.

With a fiery, cancer-defying energy, I set up the Scottish wing of The Bookery. I write about the project for *The Times Educational Supplement*, the newspaper read by most teachers in the UK. The response is immediate. I receive calls from teachers at secondary schools in and around Glasgow. Boxes of books begin to arrive. I tear into the boxes. I sort them. I organize mass volunteering days where Chinese students from Glasgow university help to classify books for school children in South Africa. Energy begets energy. There is more publicity. Within a year we have a team of volunteers, we have formed partnership with Glasgow's central library and every secondary school in the city. We have a partner who collects the broken books so they can be recycled. We have a partner who brings us the unsold children's books from all the city's charity shops. In January 2011 we send our first shipment. We turn the back of an old barn in a city park into a bookshop so we can sell adult fiction and non-fiction to fund the shipping. We grow. We grow.

And while this is growing, something else is growing too.

Another gremlin.

This time a monster.

In September 2011 he finds a lump on his neck. By Hallowe'en we know what it is. A secondary tumour of a cancerous lump at the base of his tongue. This time there will be no watchful waiting. The strategy will be two-pronged: nuclear and chemical warfare. Radiation for the throat, platinum for the blood. Within three weeks of the offensive he has lost a third of his body weight. By January he is no longer able to swallow and a feeding tube is inserted through his nose into his stomach.

"It was designed by NASA," the nurse says proudly. "It's how astronauts are fed."

And so I become a space wife, an inter-galactic cancer-fighting drug lord pushing morphine and anti-sickness concoctions into the body formerly known as my husband. As the months go by, and winter becomes spring becomes summer, I can neither read nor write. Words are too painful, too sharp. I want to be insulated from how I feel. I do not need to live twice in one day what I am already living once, so instead I knit. I knit every day they blast his body with platinum and radiation. I knit every day they poison him from sickness into health. It is not until the end of 2012 that I am ready to return to writing, and it is not until the spring of 2013 (after he has been in remission for a year), that a first draft of this book is finished and ready for feedback. I select friends with literary stripes. Something strikes me about their feedback. Those who are not South African, and who do not feel that their personal lives have been shaped and shifted by apartheid, are drawn to the book.

"I like the way you're writing with such an honest voice about your personal perspective, it really opens up the feeling that everyone's experience and viewpoint is valid," says the Scottish artist.

"It makes me think about growing up in Perth in Australia, and about how ignorant we were about the Aboriginal population, how we too were lied to," says the Australian global press freedom campaigner.

But the South Africans react differently.

"I just don't see the need for this kind of book. I don't want to read this stuff. I've made my peace. I don't want to go here," says the UN documentary maker.

"I thought it was disturbingly intimate. I must admit that it made me uncomfortable," writes a black friend from our neighbouring state of Lesotho, who studied in South Africa.

"I felt that you were blaming me," says one of my best friends, an Afrikaner. *"You immediately got my back up."*

Raw, raw, everybody raw. These are our collective hurts and when one of us dares to push on the welts, we collectively cringe. We were taught not to go here. Apartheid taught us not to question and Mandela instructed us to forgive. No one has given us permission to pick our scabs. Do not touch them. If they bleed, they will scar.

It was not just South African friends who prickled. Towards the end of 2013 I submit the manuscript to the head of a South African publishing house who passes it on to an anonymous reader. Rejection is a normal part of the writer's life. Half the job requires a permeable skin through which to absorb the world and the other half requires an alligator costume. But the three-page rejection letter that followed was different, personal, laced with venom.

This is an extract: *"There is nothing exceptional in this account which rehearses no more than conventional 'liberal' positions but set as it is as a counter-theme in the essay it raises some uncomfortable questions. For example is it, and the essay itself, anything more than a self-congratulatory and exculpatory gesture? Her social life among her friends in London seems to have done as much as Rhodes [i.e. nothing] in bringing her to a more enlightened view of herself and the country. She wants 'to do something to help – to fix it' but she's not sure what. She finally joins the NGO Equal Education and puts herself to work collecting used books in Britain to send to South Africa – one of the traditional liberal activities of foreign sympathisers though often carried through with ambiguous results."*

To the accusation that my attempt to care, to become an active citizen and try and participate in the building of my home was just the traditional behaviour of a foreign liberal, for that I only had two, unpoetic words: Fuck you. During apartheid I had been banned from going to school with black children, from sharing my love of books and reading with my fellow South Africans. And now an anonymous voice was similarly banning me, judging me, criticising me for trying to get close, for trying to care. Their words reminded of apartheid itself – anonymous orders to stay back, to not get too close.

But the other criticism kept me awake at night. Did it have some credence? I played my journey over and over in my head. Every time someone had criticised the ANC and riled against corruption, I had shared their frustration. But was it also true that every time someone moaned about the corrupt actions of the current government, it had made me feel a little less blameful, a little bit more, to use their awkward language, "exculpated"? Maybe it was. Maybe like everyone who is mired in guilt, I had been looking for someone to blame.

By the end of that year I was wrung out. Tired of being a cancer nurse, a failed writer, a lost white, I disappear with a backpack to India. I am there when Nelson Mandela dies, an ordinary person once again cut off from an extraordinary piece of South African history. I travel from the semi-desert, Karoo-like state of Rajasthan through the amiable chaos of Mumbai to the tranquil backwaters of Kerala. India is the ideal antidote to my melancholy. The clanging of pujas at sunset, the blinding yellow opium fields, tractors driving the wrong way down motorways, meditative cows, grinning gangs of school girls and buzzing swarms of tuk-tuks. Life – alive, present, pulsating – drags your gaze from your navel and immerses you again in the heartbeat of the world. Without the facts, I drink from a well of sense impressions.

The teenage girl from a motorway slum kissing her dog on the lips.

The rich and poor and the poor and rich sitting and walking side-by-side, unafraid, unencumbered by each other, as the moon rises over Mumbai's marine parade.

The family of seven who live on the street around the corner from a five-star hotel, laughing and playing as they make lunch on the pavement.

The taxi driver who vigorously pumps my hand when I say he can keep the change – a mere seven pence.

A country where energy and generosity seem to bubble up from a never-ending underground stream.

A nation of doers and make-doers.

In India, the poverty and divisions are even more stark than in South Africa, and yet while the old Transkei had felt depressed and dejected, India pulsated with vibrancy and energy and I began to wonder why. Was it me? Had I only seen misery and despair because that is what I had been looking for? Had I been asking the wrong questions, leading people in the Transkei to tell me what I wanted to hear so I could feel *"exculpated"*?

I had to go back.

In January 2014 I began making plans. I got in touch with Luke Boshier to see how things were going at the Centre for Appropriate Rural Technology in Sicambeni. His email response was stark: *"After six years of seriously getting to grips with the deep-rooted issues, I came to the sad conclusion that the illusion of transformation is perpetuating the enslavement of people by parasitic politicians and money junkies. The problem goes way back hundreds of colonialist years and is fully engraved in everyday life. Personally I have retreated to an isolated corner of the Western Cape and am exploring sovereignty, selfish but liberating."*

I tried again with Sibusiso from *Siyazingca Ngenkcubeko Yethu*, the rural co-operative I had been on my way to meet when the bakkie broke down. At first he was enthusiastic though I got the sense that things weren't going well. By our next phone call I realised that he was trying to use my visit to attract local government and tourism officials to his village of Rhwatsana in order to relaunch Siyazingca. I felt that old feeling ebb back: the useful white.

I went anyway. In February 2014, I took a propeller plane from Cape Town, and with my husband, thinner, quieter, still alive, we drove up to Rhwatsana, via Queenstown, stopping en route to give a lift to three women on their way to a funeral. Our conversation, as ever, turned swiftly to politics.

"I will never vote for that white woman," Leticia Mrobo, 50, says, referring to Helen Zille, leader of the Democratic Alliance (DA). "She thinks she can rule this country, but there are some of us black people, we still have that in our minds, we still hate the whites."

We had hoped to spend the night in Rhwatsana, but as soon as we arrive, dropping off our hitchhikers outside a hut where people are already drinking, Sibusiso's aunt warns us that she thinks it unwise.

"A white person has never been attacked before but these people are unpredictable. They think you are Afrikaans."

The Afrikaners. Collectively remembered as the architects of apartheid. I feel like turning on my heels. Being a white South African is not a life, it's a life sentence.

Sibusiso, though, welcomes us with warmth, and takes us eagerly to see the local pre-school. It is a small white building, with dirty floors and upturned benches.

"But how can this be the pre-school? It is derelict," I ask.

And so unfolds another tale of disappointment and corruption. A small crowd gathers.

"They want to know what you can do to help us?" Sibusiso says.

The white in shining armour.

The next day Sibusiso and I take a walk to a waterfall. As we sit on its edge, listening to its thunder and eating sandwiches, Sibusiso talks about upcoming elections that will mark the twentieth anniversary of democracy.

"I said to my brother, for the love of this country and for the love of the ANC, I will not vote for the ANC. They have the best principles but they are the worst in practice. Just like in apartheid, we do not know what is happening to us. We are being oppressed by the ones we love."

I can barely stand to listen. I am not one of the ones he loves. Four years have passed, and nothing has changed.

Back in Scotland, I try to write it all down, try to find a new way of seeing, but it is not there. I try a different tack. When philosophers get an idea stuck in their heads, they write obsessively on a single point. As a philosophy student you are taught the art of decoding these long, meandering arguments, reducing pages and pages to a list of bullet points so you can assess whether the argument is sound or valid or neither. I had written pages and page about the old Transkei, but I was still lost, so I tried the old philosopher's trick.

This is what I deduced:

1. From the other side of the world I had grown afraid of South Africa, afraid of my home. I felt lost, lonely, homeless.
2. My fear was a result of the stories of violent crime that I heard from afar.
3. My fear was compounded by my apartheid conditioning and my lack of first-hand experience.
4. In order to quell that fear, I believed I needed to get close to that which I feared most of all.
5. What did I fear most of all? What apartheid taught me to fear: black South African strangers.
6. I chose to travel alone to a place that was synonymous with black South African strangers, strangeness. The Transkei.
7. I hoped that if I plugged my ignorance with first-hand experience, my apartheid conditioning would be overridden and my fears would vanish with it.
8. Relieved of my fears, I would no longer feel lost and homeless. My journey was to be my cure.
9. Supposition number 4 was correct. The closer I got and the more familiar the Transkei became, my fear did thin out. But in its place I found something else, something more intractable, that undermined supposition 7 and 8.
10. Underpinning the fear was a system of apartheid-instilled beliefs about what it means to be white and to be black. In post-apartheid South Africa, our identities are not our own, but are imposed on us by our collective past and held in place by our present.

11. In the Transkei I discovered that my white skin determined how I was treated by others. I was not seen as an individual, but an archetype. I was not treated as an equal. I was regarded as a useful outsider.
12. At the end of my 2010 trip, this realisation made me feel even more lost. My journey was not my cure. It was my undoing. I collapsed.
13. Back in Scotland, life was waiting for me with an even bigger lesson. Cancer showed me that healing is neither simple nor linear. Sometimes we have to get more sick before we can get better. And even when our bodies have healed, our minds and hearts may still limp behind. Healing takes time.
14. Four years later, I return to the Transkei, to try again. Once again, I am reduced to my skin colour. Once again I am confronted with the intractable vice of our collective past.

What now? The South Africa of my childhood had been a theatre of deception. We had all been assigned roles in a story greater than our own. The years had gone by, the Truman Show was officially over, and yet we were still on set, still stuck in these old parts. I was trying to escape mine, but it was not permitted. Or rather, I was looking towards my fellow citizens for an escape route, but it wasn't theirs to give.

Back in the northlands I begin to have a recurring dream. I first have it in a hotel room in Leipzig, eastern Germany. We are there to have his cancerous prostate cut out by a surgeon wielding a robot. Another journey continues. In the dream I am walking around downtown Johannesburg, looking for the train station. I am not in an anxious state, rather a state of wonder and curiosity. I cross roads and bridges. I gaze up at tall buildings, admiring their stature. I navigate, orientate, and eventually, always, I find the station and my train. As I take my seat, the train pulls off, destination Benoni, my childhood home, and as we begin to move and the view turns to blur, a sweet contentment washes over me.

Week after week I have this dream. And then one week the dream changes. Mid-journey I discover that it is not an ordinary passenger train but a tourist train, aimed at foreigners; here my fellow black South African passengers are not real citizens but actors. I am incensed. This is not the train I am supposed to be on. I am supposed to be with real South Africans. "I am a real South African. Let me off!" I shout. My anger floods my dream.

When I wake up, I finally get it. The answer is not in the Transkei. For years I had been motivated by own sense of homelessness, my own sense of loss. And like all walking wounded, I had been looking for someone to blame, and someone to save me.

That day I began to wonder what would I have seen, what picture would I have painted of the old Transkei, if I had been someone else, someone with a different past?

At last I understand that to move forward, I needed to confront what had shaped me. I need to go to where the seeds were planted. Where they grew.

Benoni. Johannesburg.

PART 2

Chapter 1

·············

Johannesburg: August 2014

CABERNET ROAD IS BARRICADED. A green, spiked metal fence topped with barbed wire cuts off the residential street from the main road. I put the car into reverse, and ride the clutch while I follow the fence with my eyes. It carries on past Shiraz and Bellingham streets, an imprisoned suburb.

I turn around and drive the perimeter, seeking a way in to Alphen Park, one of Benoni's most affluent suburbs. I find it at Vintage Road: two booms and a guard house. I remember this road. This is where Jenni came to live when her mum left her dad for a much richer man and we were disapproving but delighted with her new double-storey house and the quiet streets that were perfect for joy riding on Jacqui's bright red scooter. They would be even quieter now.

I stop at the boom and the female guard instructs me to press a button. I press, she looks me in the eye, I smile, she does not, she presses another button, the boom rises, I pass. Inside, everything is the same. The birds sing the same songs. The sky is still parched. The air on this late winter morning still sandpapers your nostrils, still smells of yellow grass starved by months without rain. Jenni's facebrick double-storey, still there. But she is not. Long gone. Away to Australia, with so many others. As far away as possible from the sadness, the anger and the fear of this green, spiked barricade.

I pull up outside number seven, and ring the intercom. The electric gate glides to the right, the front door opens, the security gate unlocks, and out comes Lorynn, one of my first friends, blonde, smiling, as smart, kind and welcoming as she ever was.

Like me, Lorynn could not get out of Benoni fast enough. She studied architecture at Wits and decamped to Jo'burg's northern suburbs. Cupid, though, had other plans, piercing her with an arrow from a boy from Boksburg, Benoni's neighbouring suburb, and once babies came along, they moved back east to be close to family.

"It's not too bad," she says, as we sit drinking instant coffee in a patch of sunlight on her grey modernist couch, while her African parrot eyes me with suspicion and Ellen the Malawian maid drinks her own tea at the dining table.

"In the northern suburbs, it's all about money, money, money," she says. "Here, at least, it's a simpler life. The kids can swim and play outside. Like how we grew up. I want that for my kids."

What? An illusion of safety? A cultural vacuum filled with sport and meat? The inner monologue is back.

"When did they put in the barricade?" I ask out loud.

Lorynn thinks.

"It has been there a long time. Maybe eight years. They put it after a spate of really terrible crimes. Someone was killed in a hijacking in their driveway."

Once upon a time to survive in Africa, white people believed they had to imprison black people. Now, to survive, we imprison ourselves. Ordinary streets become fortresses. The public becomes private. Lock up, shut away, push back, keep at bay. I do not judge. I cannot - my barrier is an ocean. A huge moat with ships and sharks and islands.

"Tell me about your plans. Why are you here?" Lorynn asks.

"I realised I have been avoiding Jo'burg," I confess.

I have done the calculations. In the past five years I have spent nearly a year in South Africa, and only five days in Johannesburg.

"All the crime stories, all the barricades, I've become afraid of my own home. Sometimes it feels like so that everyone else could be free, we had to sacrifice our freedom. So that everyone else could have a home, I had to lose mine," I say.

"I've never thought of it like that," Lorynn says. "Maybe you're right."

"I don't want to be right," I say. "That's why I am here. I need to push against the prison in my mind. I need to walk through old memories, talk to our old school teachers, walk through the places that this society says I shouldn't walk. I need to deconstruct what I was taught and rebuild this country in my head. I need to find my way home."

Chapter 2

....

Benoni High School

THE YELLOW BRICKS, THE grey chapel, the covered quadrangle that our Catholic headmaster affectionately nicknamed the Vatican. Twenty-one years later and it all looks the same. Alison Knoop is unlocking her office door as I arrive. The same jangly bunch of keys, the same blonde birds nest, the same black kohl eyes and upturned nose. Miss Piggy, we used to call her, back when she was Miss Kennedy and I was Miss Smith.

"Do you remember me?" I ask.

She stares. She thinks, offering me a seat in front of a desk cluttered with a quarter of a century's paper and books.

"Hmmm… there's been too many faces," she says, shaking her head.

Born in England, Alison Knoop has lived permanently in South Africa from the age of 11. She grew up in Nigel, a farming district about half an hour's drive from Benoni, studied teaching at the Johannesburg College of Education (JCE), and went on to become one of Benoni High's best loved biology teachers. Spiky, sarcastic, impervious to our adolescent menace, she was the one assigned to teach us sex education. I am here to ask her what else she was instructed to teach us. Was she told to hide things from us? I need to know if it was in her job description to keep us ignorant and make us afraid?

She listens to my questions and answers without pause. Miss Piggy, as frank as she ever was.

"We were the most conservative bunch out," she admits, her accent still with faint traces of England. "The Wits bunch protested against racism. At JCE, radicals were frowned upon. We were all good little products of our government."

"What did you think about apartheid?" I ask.

"It was nothing you thought of," she says. "Black people were just there. We learnt a little about the different education systems, but you didn't talk about it. Racism was theoretical for us. People don't get that."

"So how would you have treated black people back then?" I ask.

She laughs, slightly uncomfortable.

"I remember when I was in matric, my sister brought a black friend home and I remember talking to him like he was special needs kid. But racist was a word that wasn't used. We weren't racist. Racist implies that you hate another race. We didn't hate them. Our parents might have hated them, but we were apathetic. They just weren't part of our lives," she says.

She rocks back in her chair.

"This sounds terrible," she says.

I ask her about 1993, the year the first black children came to Benoni High.

"Simon Tshabalala," she says, shaking her head. "Do you remember him? A short, bright little boy. I think now of how brave he must have been. Even that year's school photograph couldn't handle the black and white faces in the same frame. They got the contrast all wrong and the black faces disappeared. We just weren't prepared. We didn't know what to expect. They were odd and strange and...black... We sort of expected them to start doing things, foreign things. We didn't know their culture. We didn't know what was in their lunchboxes. We had no point of reference. There was a girl called Goodness who became the star of Latin reading. To say that we expected them to be stupid is not right, but we expected them to be so out of place, we didn't think they would understand us, our language, our pronunciation..."

"What about fear?" I ask, reminding her of the bomb scares that plagued the school in the run up to 1994. "Were you afraid?"

She purses her lips and wrinkles her nose.

"We were warned by the police that there might be trouble and we assumed we were going to be overrun by black people with pangas. But what did we know? We were of the type that if we saw four black people walking together, they were coming to attack you. We were naïve. Totally unknowing. People may have become racist by events that happened after rather than before. Before we didn't have anything to be racist about."

It is an odd, but insightful comment, perhaps getting to the heart of why so many English-speaking white South Africans still regard themselves as blameless. In their minds, they did not actively hate blacks, they just actively participated in a society that was built to exclude them. Where was the harm in that?

I thank her for her time and she walks me over to the school library. I am curious to know what is on these shelves. What did they once try to teach me? I find my way to the history shelves where old, dull-covered tomes are tightly stacked. As I prise them out, their spines creak, like old men, waking up, groaning, their bodies untouched for years. Before I have a chance to write down the title of the first book, my ears prick up. A history lesson has begun in the classroom space at the front of the library. A thick, high-pitched South African voice, is reading, stilted, from lecture notes.

"Afrikaner Nationalism was invented because the Afrikaners believed that they were the chosen people…"

The voice stops. Papers shuffled.

The voice begins again.

"Afrikaner Nationalism was invented because the Afrikaners believed that they were the chosen people…"

I take a step sideways and peer around the shelves. A young white male teacher, with a voice of a woman, is standing unconfidently in front of fifteen slouched teenagers. At the back of the classroom, another male teacher is filling in some forms.

"Afrikaner Nationalism was invented because the Afrikaners believed that they were the chosen people…" the voice repeats for a third time.

I am surprised, a little bemused. Why, in a country obsessed with gold and money, is the history of Afrikaner Nationalism being taught as a twisted religious ideology? Where is the version of the story that begins with the English colonialists setting fire to Afrikaans farms and imprisoning women and children in concentration camps in the Anglo-Boer war? Where is the version that begins when destitute Afrikaners began to organise around a rallying cry of nationalism to pull themselves out of poverty? If we only blame religion, aren't we forever in danger of demonising the other and falsely believing that we are not capable of the same?

He rattles on. According to him, Afrikaner Nationalism was supported by the BoerieBond. I stifle a laugh. The Broederbond (The Brotherhood) are the Free Masons of South Africa. A secret club to which only Afrikaners can belong. Boerie, however, is a South African sausage. Not quite the same thing. I want to interrupt, correct, but the man in the tracksuit top speaks first.

"Are you listening kids? You better be listening to this. You need to know this. Look at me. Look at me," his voice is insistent, delivered like bullets to the head. "Afrikaans culture infiltrated every aspect of South African life. Are you listening? Into business, into rugby. They had secret handshakes and if you didn't know the handshake, you couldn't be part of that club."

There is anger in him. These are bullets of blame. Someone must take the hit.

"Do you know kids your age had to learn to march at school? Like Nazi youth," he says.

He carries on firing bullets. Telling them about the South African rugby team who refused to select a brilliant rugby player because he refused to join the Broederbond. What followed was a national outrage, uproar, protest.

"They had gone too far. That's when we knew it was nearly over," he says.

Torture, forced removals, detention without trial, we could overlook, but injustice to rugby, that was the last straw.

I doorstop him outside the library and ask if we can talk. He eyes me warily, caught off guard, but beckons me to follow him to his classroom.

"You were telling them about marching. I was one of those kids." I say. "Do you know why we were made to do it?"

He rocks back on his chair.

"The 1980s were open warfare in this country. It was no longer passive resistance," he says.

"But as kids, we knew nothing about this. They kept us in the dark," I say. "Why did they keep us ignorant?"

"What would the truth have done?" he replies. "You might have been one of the few that would have liked to have known, but most of them wouldn't."

He starts to say something and then stops himself.

"Please tell me," I say.

"I don't want this quoted," he says.

I nod, knowing that in a few months' time I will email him and ask if I can write it anyway. We will agree that I will not name him.

"In 1990 I was a teacher, but for one week that February I was called up on national service to be a plain clothed soldier in a bakkie, with a 9mm strapped to my leg, undercover in the township in the southern part of Johannesburg, looking for ANC operatives. And the next week I was back as a teacher. We had a dinosaur mentality. Adapt or die."

"How did you put that straight in your head?" I ask.

"You just accepted it. You made it right in your own mind," he says with a shrug.

"So was there a mandate on what you could and couldn't tell school kids?" I ask.

"There was nothing written on paper. That was just the way things were done, and if you broke rank, you were frowned upon. People who refused to fight were ostracised. I was an Engels (English) man in the army. The guys would get sauced up because it was so cheap to drink then and they would say their real feelings. They've got nowhere to go, they'd say. This is where they are going to stay. Rightly or wrongly. The white flight has been the saddest part of all of this," he says softly.

"Why do you say that?" I ask.

"They turned off the heat and they ran. I lost a lot of respect. I hate to use the word, but selfish is right," he says.

There it is. The undercurrent between white South Africans who stayed and those who left. Traitors. Absconders. Runaways.

"You seem really angry," I say.

"I was very angry with those who did nothing. But time is a healer. As we go, we mellow."

He falls silent.

"Protect the volk," he says, quoting one of the political slogans of the National Party, and rocking back in his chair. *Protect the people*. "Isn't that what adults do? Protect the children. Maybe that's why your teachers didn't tell you."

I shrug my shoulders.

"You know, I think you are unique of your generation," he says.

"Why is that?" I ask.

"Not too many people are asking questions."

Chapter 3

....

Benoni Library

MORNING IN BENONI. THE rush hour is over, the roads are quiet. A light wind hops in through the window, catching my hair, thinning the sunshine. I turn left out the school gates, down Dalrymple past the Afrikaans school and the technical college, left past the house with the maze-like garden where I once dreamt of living, right at the traffic lights where I once got rear-ended by a scooter, flying off my bicycle, face-down across the tarmac, the skin on my hips merging with the road. These are the roads of my childhood, imprinted on my brain. The bike shop, the ex-modelling agency, Jurita's bakery, the tin-roofed bungalows built during the mining boom. No matter how many years I stay away, I can never lose my way here. Being here is as familiar as being in my own body.

I turn into Tom Jones Street (named after a former local Labour Party leader, not the hairy Welsh pop star) and as I drive under the motorway bridge, I roll my eyes at the monstrosity floating on the Benoni Lake. A newcomer. Not part of the imprint. Once upon a lifetime, a sloping green field stretched from the library down to the lake. Today, it is a car park, serving a shopping mall designed in the shape of a white Mississippi steamboat complete with tall black funnels and a waterwheel destined never to turn. Themed architecture is common in post-apartheid South Africa. When you cannot face your own past you borrow someone else's. So we have Tuscan office blocks that emulate the grandeur of old Europe, Venetian casinos that encapsulate the romance of a bygone era, Kefalonian housing estates that diffuse Greek island Zen behind six foot electrified walls, and this: a fake steamboat imported from America's Deep South, its decks filled with shops, restaurants and movies. The Ku Klux Klan would be delighted.

I park the car in the Civic Centre car park and wander up into the town centre.

"It's got very black, you know," my mum told me over the phone.

"That's because it's in Africa," I replied.

"Don't get cheeky with me," she said, clicking her tongue.

I walk up Rothsey Street towards the Benoni Plaza, to see what is still there, what has gone. The fabric shop, still there, still playing country music. But now, outside on the pavement, a woman is braaing pork on an open fire. The banks are gone. Edgars, Jet, Foschini, the branded clothing stores of my youth. Gone. The shops are now hair salons, tombstone dealers, Chinese clothes merchants. In the pedestrianized zone where fountains once flowed, the water has gone. In its place, rubbish. I walk to Milky Lane, the Fifties-style ice-cream parlour where, when we could afford it, I spent Friday nights, eating pink and white cones before going to the movies. Its curved walls are still there, its once jolly pink and white checked floor is still there, but there are no doors, no windows, no furniture. On the walls are abortion posters: "Safe and Pain Free Dr Nandi, From R250", and graffiti: "Respect this P" in white paint, "Welcome all Thugs Nevermind" in silver. A child's sandal hangs from an old light fitting. I walk towards the cinema, now the Universal Church of the Kingdom of God. Wealth has retreated, turned its back on this town. Everything shiny is now inside the steamboat mall.

I walk back down through the town to the library, a squat, 1960s building, built of cement, glass and steel over three floors. Once upon a time it would have been considered cutting-edge design. Now it is another apartheid relic. Two black teenage girls sit gossiping at the entrance.

The girls look up as I walk past. I smile and nod. One smiles back, the other regards me coolly. Inside, no time has passed. The air is warm with the scent of old carpets, varnished wood and yellowing paper. The universal smell of libraries. I wander over to the teenage section which at age twelve I was certain contained all the world's secrets and everything I ever needed to know. I touch the books, now grubby and tired. I wonder if they might be the same editions that I once curled up with in bed, in the bath, on a blanket in the garden.

Today, though, I am wondering what else I could have known, if only I had looked, so I carry on up to the third floor reference section, to the South African history shelf. The books are of war and gold, old tomes that document the development of the Reef, the collective name for the gold mining towns that stretch out from Johannesburg in all four directions, to the north, south, east and west.

One book catches my eye: *Benoni, Son of My Sorrows*, published 1985, the story of how my hometown was founded, about the hope of gold in a time of desperation. I take a seat at one of the study tables and begin to read.

"Benoni received its name from the Bible and in its early days of the town the title Son of my Sorrows (its translation from Hebrew) was amply justified. The city of gold in Africa tempted miners and shopkeepers to escape from poverty and suppression in their homelands in the hope of finding wealth and freedom. But the bankruptcy of the early mines resulted in unemployment and the newcomers who had spent their all to journey here were rewarded only by hunger and social humiliation."

They were not alone. The town also lured Afrikaans farmers, broken and desperate, their farms destroyed from the droughts of 1903 to 1905 and the scorched earth policy of Lord Kitchener during the Anglo-Boer War.

"The town was renowned for lawlessness and violence" and the *"poor white problem became a source of daily conversation"*.

The solution, explains the book, was to introduce a whites-only labour policy in the railways, police and civil service as a way to create jobs for rural Afrikaners. The mines were already whites-only employers, importing miners from Cornwall and Wales, and with them, a very British classism.

"Between the upper strata and the miners and commercial people was a rigid social division which was maintained by economic snobbery and enforced by economic pressure. If any member of the lower strata on the mine asserted himself too much, he was dealt with by being dismissed."

And the lower class whites found their own way to assert themselves.

"If a Cornish miner saw a black man on the same pavement as him, he would order him into the street"

A firework goes off in my head. I keep reading.

At the founding of Benoni, when South Africa was still a British colony, districts were already segregated into black, coloured, Indian and white areas. The black, Indian and coloured areas were slums, the book says. Full of filth and disease.

I put down the book and look around. I am the only white face in the room. All around me, black faces are bent over books, writing, thinking, dozing. Why has it not registered in my head before that the segregation and denigration of black people began long before 1948, before apartheid? That before it was law, it was common law. That although the Afrikaners built the walls, the British laid the foundations. I close the book and shake my head. I am like one of those Russian dolls. My ignorance encased by more ignorance. How do I not know? Have I not been told, or have I not listened? Was it easier for me to hear that it was the Afrikaners' fault, their idea? Did it make it bearable, acceptable, a fact of life, if my ancestors were guiltless? I go online. I look up the founding date of the ANC: 1912. I look up the founding date of the National Party who introduced apartheid: 1914.

The key movement that fought black oppression pre-dates the founding of the political party that our modern, collective, global memory holds entirely accountable for racial discrimination.

How come it is so easy for us to forget what we do not want to remember?

I return the book to its shelf and walk downstairs to the other African history section. More than 100 books. I scan the spines. Mfecane Aftermath. General Louis Botha. Nigerian Civil War. What else is here? An orange spine catches my eye. I pull it out and open to the title page: Robben Island, *Out of Reach, Out of Mind*.

I turn to the introduction and begin to read.

"This is an unusual book because it documents for the first time the part Robben Island has played in the history of South Africa."

Robben Island, it says, was a refreshment station, a leper colony and a lunatic asylum. Full stop. Is that it? I turn to look at the publication date. 1971.

In the winter of 1964 Nelson Mandela was sent to Robben Island to begin eighteen of his twenty-seven years in jail. I glance again at the subtitle. Out of Reach. Out of Mind. I keep reading.

"They were out of sight of the public and thus out of their minds. They suffered in filth and squalor and were never allowed to return to the mainland, simply because they were unwanted..."

1971. In this year Govan Mbeki, Oliver Thambo, Mac Maharaj were imprisoned on Robben Island. *"This book will be of use to the student of society and of interest to the general reader because it stresses the difference between the crude methods of the past with the more enlightened practices accepted today as a matter of course."*

I keep paging. It must be in here somewhere. I finally find it in the Epilogue. 66 words. An afterthought.

"In June 1965 the Prison's Department took over the island from the Navy. No matter what prison it may be in South Africa, the prisoners are rehabilitated by teaching them a useful trade or occupation so that when they are released they are able to find work and become useful members of society. They have transgressed, but have paid the price demanded by a well-ordered society..."

I drop into one of the torn leather chairs that line the room, next to the shelf. I feel queasy, airless, trapped. I am a puppet who has seen her strings.

A toy built by the British and fine-tuned by the Afrikaners. I am the product of two political systems who pretend to be so different, but value the same thing above all else: order, not humanity.

I want to throw this book across the room. I want to shove it in someone's face. Instead, I get another idea. I ask to speak to the Chief Librarian.

I am directed down a corridor at the back of the library, to the office of Petra Rathebe. Petra looks up from her desk as I knock. She is a black woman in her early 40s, and it is clear from the look on her face that she does not often receive – or desire – visitors. I ask if I can sit down. She nods, reluctantly. I tell her about the Robben Island book and ask why it is still on the open shelves. Why with its glaring lies, has it not been put in a museum or in a special display of apartheid-era books? Should we not be striving to fix the inaccuracies of the past instead of allowing these lies to linger?

I am not trying to accuse. I am accusing. I am a white South African angry with the past and trying to find someone to blame in the present.

"We cannot take books off the shelves," she says. "They are part of our history."

I feel sour. Sullied. Stymied.

"If we remove those books, it is another kind of censorship," she says.

I calm down. She is right. If we only fill the history shelves with approved facts, we will be acting no better than the apartheid government. For history to have any chance at truth, all the stories have to breathe.

I switch tack. I need someone to talk to. I need someone to help me make sense of this. I tell her about my book.

"Who are you writing for?" she asks, suspicious.

"For no one. For myself. For whoever will read the book," I say. "I grew up here but when I think back to those days, I feel like I didn't notice what was going on. It was as if apartheid was invisible to me. I am trying to make sense of it."

She eyes me coldly, quizzically.

"You didn't notice apartheid and you grew up here?" she says, a scorn filtering through her voice.

"Yes, in Crystal Park, Rynfield..." my voice trails off, suddenly hearing her scorn and the stupidity of my own words.

"Well," she says, coolly, "you might not have seen it, but we saw it every day. We knew white people thought they were superior to us. When we saw them, we had to show them respect."

"Where did you grow up?" I ask.

"In Katlehong," she says.

I nod. I know the name. An East Rand township. I have never been there. I don't even know how to get there.

"What was it like for you during apartheid?" I ask. "I mean, what did you really understand of what going on?"

Her eyes narrow, and she shakes her head.

"No. I can answer questions about the books, but this is my place of work and I will not answer questions about things that are not of the library," she says.

I see my impertinence. I am like an unexploded grenade that has landed out of nowhere in her office. I am the white woman of her childhood, marching in, unannounced, demanding. I try again to explain.

"I am sorry. It's just that, I ask these questions of everyone I meet. I... I am just trying to understand. I really want to talk about these things, hear other people's stories. I feel like we need to be honest with each other, see the world through each other's eyes, so that we can move on."

"We *have* moved on," she says, firmly. "You *have* to forgive and forget. We *have* to, otherwise we cannot work with the whites."

I look through her window at the car park of the Steamboat Mall. Stupid, unwanted tears prick at the back of my eyes. I am ashamed and embarrassed. This was probably my most stupid ever attempt at an interview. I am a blundering sore, fixing myself onto the nearest body. I stand up and bow my head in an apology, backing towards the door. I turn on my heels and steer myself down the corridor, back through the library, out into the winter sunshine.

Back in the car I see my anger and I see Petra's. Hers is worn, mature, quietened. Its offender was obvious and forgiveness was a necessity, a pragmatic choice in order to live, to eat, to be. My anger is only just finding its voice.

Chapter 4

......

Northfield Methodist Church

I EAT LUNCH IN A sandwich shop across the road from the library, and listen in as the white woman owner orders her black staff around in *that* voice. The apartheid voice. The patronising tone that speaks to black men in the way you might speak to a child. Still here. .

I drive up through town, and wind down the window at the lights to hand R10 to a young man begging with this sign.
"Hello. Smile. My wife has been kidnapped by 3 American Ninjas. Plz help me with a donation 4 me to learn kung fu. LOL! HAHAHA! God Bless."
He gets more than the white man I saw earlier this morning, between the traffic, his shoulders sagging, his eyes closed, simultaneously begging and shutting off the world. He only got a weary shake of my head.

I pull up in the car park at Northfield Methodist church and stare at the mine dump as the clock ticks towards 2pm. As a teenager I spent nearly every Sunday evening at this church, envying the rich girls fancy new church outfits, trying to flaunt my own homespun creations, praying for the courage to talk to the boys I liked, or at least, for them to talk to me. After the youth service we would break into small conversation groups to talk about how to be moral, how to be good, how to do right by the Lord. Never once did we discuss race, inequality, South African social injustice. At Northfield on a Sunday evening, apartheid was invisible. An accepted order of which there was nothing to say. I have made an appointment with Reverend Trevor Hudson, head of the church. I want to ask him why.

I am ushered into his office. Four rattan armchairs with blue velour seat cushions are arranged around a low coffee table, close to the window. The curtains are drawn. There is a thick quiet to the air, a room at ease with grief, anger, the burdens of being alive. Trevor sits across from me. His face has weathered from the one I keep in my head, from twenty-three years ago, when I wore navy blue trousers, a white blouse and polka dot high heels as he placed the body and blood of Christ on my tongue, confirming me into the Methodist church.

I tell him about my journey so far. "I need to know," I say. "Was there an instruction from the church or from parents that race issues were not to be discussed?"

He crosses his legs and leans forward in his armchair, curving his spine towards me. His right hand plays with the worn skin on his face. He hesitates, looking for the right words.

He begins by taking me back in time, through his own story, beginning with a sheltered life in Port Elizabeth, a political awakening at an inter-racial Methodist youth camp, and a stint in jail in 1979 for taking part in an illegal anti-apartheid march. But it was not the experience of being in jail that scared him most.

"It was the reaction of the white congregation," he remembers. "All the black guys who got arrested were heroes, but for me it left me with a sense of homelessness in the white community."

I ask him to explain the church's actual stance.

"The Methodist church made a declaration in the 70s, saying that it was one and undivided. Have we been faithful to the vision of being a one and undivided church?" he sighs. "I think that's another story. I think that formerly the Methodist church took a clear stance, but whether it filtered down depended a lot on local ministers."

As a youth minister at Kempton Park Methodist Church in the 1980s, Trevor explains his solution was to take teenagers on an eight day immersion into the *real* South Africa, into townships and resettlement camps.

"We wouldn't go as tourists taking photographs, but really put ourselves in the position of listening to the stories of others and reflecting on those stories. That had tremendous reaction from parents, especially as kids came back," he says.

"So why didn't you bring this with you when you came to Northfield?" I ask.

"I was 41 and I didn't have responsibility for young people. I came here with a very clear job description," he says.

Not in the job description. I feel like kicking up the little coffee table.

Instead I say quietly, politely: "Part of me feels really angry. It was only when I went to Rhodes that I found out that people had been tortured and imprisoned. That our media had been censored. As a child, you had no idea. That there was this huge deception. We were brought up in a lie."

"Would you be able to say a little bit more about that anger?" he says, like a psychologist, coaxing a patient.

I stare at the coffee table. What does the anger feel like? Blank. Empty. Unfamiliar. An anger not permitted. A wavering, directionless anger.

"It's like part of your life was a dream. It makes you question what is real," I say.

Trevor smiles softly.

"Personally I feel quite encouraged by your anger. I usually hear it more from young Afrikaners. They feel a sense of betrayal by the NG Kerk who did give the religious rubber stamp on apartheid, and they particularly express that sense of being betrayed. But I have missed it in the English community," he says.

"Really?" I say.

"Really. I think we are in massive denial," he says. "When I think of my own generation, I never meet anyone now who said they supported apartheid, but I knew people who were abusive to my wife, myself, our

218

family. We don't want to confront that we were formed by a very deeply racist society. I think the component of prejudice is something that is very hard to face in one's transformation as a human being."

His words are oddly comforting. I had started out in the Transkei trying to be brave and quickly became lost, lonely, fearful, confused. Again and again I had blamed myself. Not good enough, not courageous enough, not smart enough, weak, pathetic, stupid. I had railed against myself and chucked all the world's insults at my feet, chastising myself for going around and around in circles. And now here was Trevor, saying that was normal. With his words, something in me softened and something else strengthened. For the first time I felt I was somehow, blindly, moving in the right direction.

Chapter 5
....

Cosmo City

IN THE FAR NORTH of Johannesburg, in the fields of an old farm, is a new city: Cosmo City, short for cosmopolitan. In 2004, the foundation stones were laid for what was to be Jo'burg's first purpose-built integrated suburb. There would be bigger properties for the middle classes (on streets named after American states: Alabama, Tennessee, Georgia), smaller builds for first-time home owners (on South Korea, Bangladesh and Cambodia Crescents) and clusters of squat, square RDP houses – free government housing for those who previously squatted in shacks (built on Angola, Zimbabwe and Congo streets). It was to be a post-apartheid model suburb, to accommodate all races.

What made it even more of a new South Africa tale, was the land it was built on – the old farm of Boer nationalist Robert Spiller van Tonder.

Van Tonder was descended from Boer war commandoes who felt betrayed by the outcome of the Anglo-Boer war – they did not want a unified South Africa, and felt the Boers were better off on their own. In 1977 van Tonder published his book *Boerestaat*, in which he laid out his philosophy for a new Boer republic, earning him the nickname Taalbul (one who fights for their language). Taalbul's dream remained an illusion and when he died in 1999 he was buried on his farm, now a short walk from the Cosmo City Kentucky Fried Chicken. On his grey marble tombstone, next to his thatched farm chapel, is the inscription: '*Vryheid Aan Alle Volke.*

Ook Aan die Boerevolke. Die Stryd Duur Voort.' 'Freedom for All People. Also for the Boers. The Struggle Continues.'

I doubt he is resting in peace.

At first the idea seemed to work. White families joined black families in buying new homes. Those higher up the economic chain moved to America, those at the poor end stayed in Africa, but when shops, schools and services, needed to glue together a community, were slow to be built and when the crime rate began to escalate – fuelled in part by a never-ending stream of builders who made it easy for criminals to mask their comings and goings – the whites retreated.

Today Cosmo City is home to 100,000 people and only 10 of them are white. Trevor Hudson suggested that I might want to meet one of them, the self-proclaimed "only blonde in Cosmo City", Adri Marie van Heerden.

I meet her at her small three-bedroom home on South Korea Crescent. She is dressed in turquoise trousers, a sparkly blue, white and purple top, her long blonde hair hanging loosely across her shoulders. I sit across from her on a brown couch, beneath a picture of the Johannesburg skyline, nursing a cup of coffee. She sits on the piano stool, and behind her, on top of the piano are three carved wooden words: Love Live Laugh.

Adri Marie grew up fifteen minutes away in the upmarket Afrikaans suburb of Ruimsig. Up until July 1999, her life was one hundred per cent Afrikaans. She had gone barefoot to Afrikaans schools, had only Afrikaans friends, had attended the strictly Afrikaans Dutch Reformed Church, and had chosen to study at the Rand Afrikaans University (RAU).

All that began to change when she attended a Christian missionary gathering in Mozambique in her first university holidays.

"I felt like I woke up to the fact that I lived on the African continent," she says.

Back at university after the camp, Adri Marie began making friends with Lerato, one of the few black girls in their halls of residence.

"I could see she was a bit resistant to me in the beginning, but I kept going to visit her, and I began to realise that her experience of being at RAU was very different to mine. It was this that sparked me to relearn our history."

Although it was 1999 and the democratic government was into its second term, Adri Marie did not feel she had a clear sense of the country's history.

"Our school history was how we fought the English and the Zulus, it was my culture against the rest. Only then did I start waking up," she says.

Adri Marie's political awakening was deeply entwined with a shift in her religious consciousness, and she began to draw parallels between the apartheid system and the injustices and hypocrisy that Jesus had observed in his lifetime.

"If you're Afrikaaans, it's like being Irish and Catholic. You go to the Dutch Reformed Church, you do your catechisms, you pray for the poor people, but the detrimental part of it, and it's still detrimental now, is that salvation is connected to some mystical thing that happens on the cross. You can have a spiritual life and some funny belief, and then you can have a real life, and they are not even connected. And that's what started breaking down for me. If you really learn about Jesus, you will see he was a revolutionary. He challenged systems that were excluding people."

But it was a visit to the apartheid museum in downtown Jo'burg that shifted her consciousness forever.

"I realised…" she says, shaking her head as if to try and expel something that she wished wasn't there. "…I realised, the starting point is that I am a racist. I can't say: 'No, no, I wasn't part of apartheid', I can't say that. I must say: 'I benefited from apartheid and I grew up in ignorance'. I woke up to the fact that if I wanted to live my life in the real South Africa, I couldn't stay ignorant anymore."

As Adri Marie opened to a new way of looking at the world, the world opened to her. Close friends from her schooldays had been working abroad for Oasis, a Christian organisation that works towards restoring dignity in people who have suffered from economic oppression. The friends had initially worked in India, but were now back in South Africa, had set up a project in Cosmo City, *and* had moved to the neighbourhood.

"Their philosophy is that there are so many barriers already, if you want to work in the community, you may as well try to become part of that community."

When a job came up they encouraged Adri Marie to apply, she did, and in 2008 also decided to move to Cosmo City.

"I knew moving to the neighbourhood would be a massive stretch for me. By then, I knew what the realities of South Africa actually looked like. How unintegrated everything is, how few people I knew had any cross-cultural real relationships. You have some shit to deal with if you make friends in the same economic class across the cultural barrier, but if you go cross-cultural and cross-economic, it's a whole different ball game. I knew I was going to be a small fish in a massive dam."

It was not just Adri Marie's worldview that was about to get shaken up. Her conservative Afrikaans family also found their worldview put to the test.

"They weren't okay at first," she admits. "It was really tough for them. No matter what your house looks like, you are now a white Afrikaans girl, by yourself, going and staying in this neighbourhood. My mother was worried and didn't know what to do. But now she loves telling people."

"What changed her?" I ask.

"She got exposed to this life. It's so much about exposure. People are just ignorant. Even myself, it wasn't like I wasn't nervous. I was. It's the mental thing of it. My work was totally in the community all day, but to live here, literally felt like a different world."

I am curious to know what it is like being here, day in and day out.

"How do people treat you?" I ask.

"When I bought this house, my neighbours said: 'Oh, are you buying a house for your maid?'" she remembers, laughing. "Still if people knock to sell something and I open the door… the shock on people's faces, that will never get old. People treat you in extremes. Either you get preferential treatment, or you get shunned and treated not in a good way. So I would arrive somewhere and they would make a seat for me right in the front. Or people would automatically treat me as an enemy, or somebody they could get something from. I started realising people aren't ever honest with me."

Her words remind me of my Transkei journey. People's perceptions of me were never rooted in my reality, or any fundamental truth about me, but rather a perceived reality that exists outside of us all – an inflamed, suppurating perception, based only on skin colour.

"What do you think whiteness symbolises in this country?" I ask.
"You know, in a poor community, there is a deep belief that it is better to be white," she says. "There are little kids around here who we ask: 'What do you want to be when you grow up?' and they will answer: 'white', because it has a picture that you are going to be okay. Being white means you have a safety net. It means you have inner resources and family members to bail you out. It means you know how to access a job and work the system because you have grown up in that system."
We sit quietly for a moment, staring at our white hands.
"In the beginning I would say I moved to Cosmo City because I didn't know what it was like on this side. It was an experiment. But now I would say to people, I live here for my own salvation, it saves me to stay in the real South Africa, it gives me perspective every day. Culture, be it western culture, media culture, it tries to make us blind to what the real world looks like. South Africans are all trying to put up walls, keeping themselves safe, but it's that safety that is killing us. Proximity changes everything. Why can't the world see that our wellbeing is connected?"

Talking with Adri Marie gives me that feeling you get when you first notice winter is over. It has been a lonely road, examining this strange South African life from the other side of the world. It feels good to find a fellow searcher.

I suggest we take a walk around Cosmo City, but Adri Marie has another idea: she wants me to meet Nobuhle, a 24-year-old black woman who works with her at Oasis and who has also thought a lot about these issues.

As we leave her house, Adri Marie points out her new lawn.

"A friend planted this lawn as a surprise but I haven't done anything to maintain it. The other day my neighbour came around and asked if he could mow it for me. I think I'm an embarrassment to the community," she says with a giggle.

The Oasis centre is in America, next to the grave of Taalbul van Tonder. His old farm chapel has been converted into multimedia centre for local youths. Adri Marie introduces me to Nobuhle, a beautiful young woman, with an open and instantly likeable presence. It is nearing lunchtime and Nobuhle agrees to walk with me across the veld to the supermarket, so I can buy something to eat. As we walk, across the scrubby land, cut through with footpaths, littered glass and tin cans, she is open with her story.

Raised in an entirely black community in Hillbrow in downtown Jo'burg, by a mother who died from HIV and a father who was mentally unwell, as a child Nobuhle says she was entirely unaware of her race. It was not until she was in high school that something began to niggle.

"There was this thing you became aware of – that white people are more privileged and that they can help you in any situation. There was this psychologist who would come to school and I remember going to her because it felt like she felt more sorry for me than a black individual would be. If I told a black person my story, they would tell me I had to be strong. But if I told her, she would feel sorry for me, and it kind of made me feel good, and like she was going to help me out with something," she says.

Nobuhle's perspective began shift in 2010 when she took part in the Oasis' Bridge the Gap, a programme which aims to build self-esteem among school leavers, equipping them with the technical and life skills they need to find employment. The programme strives to deliver the message that everyone is equal, but it was a message that Nobuhle found hard to swallow.

"I remember feeling like I had to respect Adri Marie more than any of the other black programme leaders," she says. "Afterwards when I started facilitating, I would hear myself saying: 'We are all human beings', but at the same time, an inner voices would say: "Except Adri Marie. She is a god". It was like that. You are black, you are a human being. You are white, you are a god."

I buy a pie at the supermarket and we start walking back through the car park. A little black boy waves to me from the backseat of his parents' car.

"See," Nobuhle says. "He's waving at you, not me."

"Isn't he just being friendly?" I ask.

"He thinks you're a god," Nobuhle laughs.

Nobuhle's perception finally began to shift when she befriended Lorna, a young girl from Scotland who had come to South Africa to volunteer at Oasis.

"I associated her with being rich, but then when we became friends and I learnt her story and I realised she is living a life just like I am. She is struggling in terms of self-esteem issues. She experiences heartbreak, she is wondering: 'Where should I go in life, What type of guy do I want? Do I want to get married and have kids?' She gets broke like I do, she earns the same amount like I do. I realised I have excluded a lot of white people because I think they are not in the same situation as me. That they are the people that give, instead of the people that also get."

Her friendship with Lorna helped Nobuhle take Adri Marie off the pedestal.

"And with my friendship with Adri Marie, came a bit of freedom," she says sagely. "It feels normal. It *is* normal. It feels like you are just talking to someone who is a woman like you."

By now we are sitting back in the garden at Oasis.

"I think we have a very long way to go, and we can't take these kinds of situations lightly," Nobuhle says. "The fact that we respect white people more than we respect each other is a painful thing. We have not come to that point where we say: 'I am equal to another white person whether or not we are rich or poor'. We do not say: 'I am creative, I have skills, I am gifted like that person'. We have not learned to value ourselves as black individuals. We do not think we are equal."

I think of this long after our conversation ends. Perhaps what disturbs me most is her belief that a lack of self-esteem is a black-only problem, rather than a normal part of the human condition. Every white person I have got to know, in Europe and South Africa has at some point confessed their doubts. Am I good enough? Am I really a doctor, or am I just pretending? I am just a kid from Benoni, can I really write? Can I really have a voice? Doubt is a fundamental aspect of being human and for black South Africans to think that only *they* doubt themselves, is one of the biggest *un*confidence tricks of all time. White South Africans robbed the black population of its self-esteem. We kept it for ourselves, turning ourselves into fake gods, who supposedly fear nothing, and ironically fear everything.

Chapter 6

History lessons

THERE WAS SOMEONE ELSE I needed to speak to. Twenty-one years ago Graham Howarth was my high school history teacher, the first person in all my years of school who had asked my opinion, who suggested that education was more than just regurgitation of facts. I had emailed him, asking if we could talk about what it was like to teach history during those last days of apartheid.

We agree to meet in a coffee shop at the Bedford Centre, an upmarket shopping mall close to Johannesburg. It is the kind of place where wealthy white housewives gather on weekends to flaunt their jewellery and leave lipstick stains on cappuccino cups.

The years have not aged him. Still the same crinkly eyes, still the same moustache. The only thing that sets him apart from the brown-dressed man who lives in my memory is his clothes: a pink shirt and light blue jeans.

"Do you want to ask me things?" he says, uncertain, as we order coffees and I switch on my Dictaphone.

"If you prefer, you can just start talking," I say.

"When I got your email I thought I would be fascinated to know how you perceived me at the time," he begins "I'd come out of Wits, history for me was a philosophical thing, but those school text books by Joubert and Brits, that wasn't history, that was national party propaganda."

"I'm trying to find out if there was some kind of official mandate, a rule book that told you what you could and couldn't tell us?" I ask.

He shakes his head.

"There wasn't a mandate. But there was a hierarchy. The department of education kept a very close check and balance on what was happening in the schools. That's why they had this big inspectorate. Look, there were some good things, the education was disciplined, it was structured, but it had this overture of 'we are actually an extension of the state'. I remember throwing a textbook out of the window one day, very, very controversially" he says laughing to himself.

It rings a bell in my memory. An urban myth once traded in the playground, now proved true.

"We were going through Joubert and Brits," he remembers, "and there was a heading that said: The Social Impact of the Discovery of Minerals on Whites, and it listed them, and it was beautiful, it was like manna from heaven. We did this, and we did that… which was right, that is what happened, and then it had a heading: Blacks, and it said: 'It also affected Blacks. There was social dislocation.' Full stop, end of story, and Claire, that got up my nose. So I said to a young guy or girl sitting next to the window, "please open the window", and I took the book and I threw it out. Everybody was shocked."

"Did you get into trouble?" I ask.

"No, the head never found out," he says.

"Were there other teachers who you could talk to about how you felt?" I ask.

"I've got to say no, these were not things we spoke about. A lot of my colleagues didn't question because they were just part of the system and we are very comfortable being part of systems, because that's our comfort zone. Do you remember cadets?" he asks.

I nod. Every Friday, like good little soldiers, we were taught to march on the school playground. Left, left, left, right, left.

"I remember as clear as day, I made an appointment to see Mr Lotter (the headmaster) and I said to him: 'Sir, I stand on the cusp of my career, you expect me to come twice a week in a military uniform. I've never refused things in my life, but I refuse to do this. I'm a teacher, and my job is to get people to be thinkers. What I'm doing is nothing more than a mouthpiece for the National Party, and now you've got me marching kids up and down. I mean, what is that saying to children? First it's saying there's a threat. Secondly that we've got to stand together. This is a school. I cannot be in a profession that expects me to be what every fibre in my being says I shouldn't be.' So he said: 'Okay, let's compromise. You don't march children, you don't wear a uniform, but when we have cadets, you go and sit on the grandstand.' And I said: 'I can live with that' but it made me even more aware of my responsibility to students. To say guys, this book we are studying from is not history, it's one person's version of history."

"Do you know why they started making the girls march?" I ask.

He shakes his head. "I can't answer that. I can imagine it was an intensification of that doctrine, of creating that disciplined approach. It was akin to what happened in Nazi Germany, in a sense. Everybody was Sig Heiling, and those who didn't were too scared to question. I don't know if we were too scared, I just don't think we were ever questioning individuals. Nothing in the school system was designed to get anyone to think, teachers nor students. It was an autocratic system. Everyone deferred to the head, so there was a very paternalistic or maternalistic approach to education."

"And today?" I ask.

Since Benoni High Mr Howarth has served as deputy headmaster of an Ivy League private school and more recently has taken up the reins of a tough, inner-city convent that counts orphans and vulnerable children among its students.

He shakes his head. "There is such an elitism in this country, especially in education. When people found out I was going to an inner-city school, someone said to me: you're going from mink to manure. I still don't think most white people have bought into the new South Africa. I think they like it and they like Mandela and Tutu, because they speak reconciliation which white people love, but it's a reconciliation with a caveat: I'm very happy to reconcile as long as it doesn't take me out of my comfort zone or affect me in a negative way. My previous PA is a black lady, and she says, you cannot believe, even today, how people look at me in a certain way, speak to me in a certain way because I am black, and it's assumed I can't know certain things, or I can't have certain feelings."

My mind flickers to my flight from Glasgow to Jo'burg. The first leg was a British Airways plane from Glasgow to Heathrow. As I disembarked I glanced into cockpit, as I always do, to pass on my thanks and sitting at the controls was a black pilot. My first reaction was surprise at seeing him, my second reaction, surprise at myself. Ugly little racist, flying around the world, my bags packed with my filthy brainwashing.

I turn the conversation back to the past one more time.

"I remember one day we got sent home early from school," I say. "I wanted to know why and I asked you, and you wouldn't give me an answer. You told me just to go home. If you were so worried about educating us, why wouldn't you tell me?"

"But Claire, I think that's normal," Mr Howarth says. "Most children today don't know the realities. They live in a bubble and I would say it's everywhere in the world because the school is about that, the school protects, it shelters."

"But we were so lied to," I say. "Who can I be angry with?

Mr Howarth thinks it over.

"I think you can be angry with the system and with people who never challenged the system, because what we have as people are minds, that's what separates us from animals. We weren't allowed to think, we weren't allowed to put our minds to things, and if we did, it was stopped at source."

We pay for our coffees and walk from the coffee shop into the bustling corridor of the shopping mall.

"I am just trying to find a way to make sense of this country," I say with a resigned sigh.

"The way I do it, I just try to live by my hopes, not by my fears," he says, shaking my hand.

I walk out into the rooftop car park. The morning has brightened, the sun has broken through. In the distance, I can see the skyline of Jo'burg, book-ended between Yeoville koppie and a mine dump. I am heading to Melville, the leafy suburb popular with the city's bohemians and intelligentsia, on the opposite side of the city. There are three ways to get there. On the motorway, over Sylvia Pass, or through the inner city. Safest, safer, potentially not safe. I put the car into gear and head towards the inner city. From Kensington to Troyeville, Jeppestown and onto Commissioner, the three-lane one-way road that cuts through the tall buildings of downtown Jo'burg. Each block is punctuated with traffic lights and as I approach, every light turns red. My little white face in my little grey car is sandwiched between taxis, and buses, skyscrapers and pavements filled with black faces. My white face feels like a beacon. My tongue goes numb. A lone black man walk slowly in front of my car. I have no reason to fear him, he is just passing by, but I have no way to trust. And so it is: the white South African life. Caught between the spinelessness of shopping malls and the spinechills of the street.

The lights turn green and I turn right into Rissik. The street opens up, the claustrophobic buildings recede, in front of me, a beautiful white colonial building, a pretty old dame, to my right a building painted with the South African flag, and alongside it, a burnt out colonial building, how apt. I put down my foot and speed through the orange light. I drive over the railway tracks and up to Constitution Hill, away from the inner city.

Away from the *gevaar* that lives in my mind.

Chapter 7

Afrikan Freedoms

FOR THE NEXT FEW days I am to stay with an old friend. Polo is a black, 30-something university lecturer, with whom I once shared a digs in Johannesburg. Polo grew up in Lesotho, the daughter of a doctor and went to private school with children from South Africa's political and intellectual elites which she admits made her conscious of the anti-apartheid struggle movement. She has a PhD in comparative Francophone-Anglophone literature from the Sorbonne Nouvelle, and before returning to Jo'burg lived in London, Hong Kong and Paris. As I pull up outside her Melville home, the house hidden from the road by a seven-foot wall topped with barbed wire, I notice something is missing: a doorbell.

"Don't you have a buzzer?" I ask, calling her phone.

"Oh no," she laughs. "Nobody does. Jo'burg living. If you don't have a buzzer, no one can work out if you are in. It's supposed to be much safer."

I drop off my bags, and we head straight back out in her giant Mercedez Benz, once the choice car of apartheid ministers and now popular with those who don't care about appearances but do care about crime – nobody steals these outmoded, fuel-guzzling monsters. It's Women's Day, and Polo has found us an afternoon gig at the Afrikan Freedom Station, a tiny music venue in an old shop-front close to Sophiatown, the legendary hub of black music and culture that was destroyed during apartheid. Inside, it is like being back at university. The furniture is a mish-mash of wooden benches and old couches, patrons are welcome to smoke – whatever they like – out back, and the bar serves a mixture of strong coffee and gentle teas. We order two coffees and settle down on wooden benches to watch Nkoto Malebye, a soulful, voluptuous Jo'burg singer dressed in a red, peacock-feather print ballgown and matching turban, warm up. Malebye orders us to talk amongst ourselves as she tries out her songs, and so our conversation turns to my book and my reason for being back in Jo'burg.

As I try to explain my need to push myself into places that frighten me, to reclaim my home, I feel Polo's distaste and unease grow. Another mutual friend – the daughter of a white father and black mother – had already expressed her anger, through a Facebook message, at my suggestion that places exist where white people are not permitted. For decades black people were forcibly prevented from being in parts of this land. No one has ever stopped a white person from going anywhere. Polo adds that our friend despises events like Nike's "Take Back the Night", a 10K road race, when for one night each year white people return en masse to downtown Jo'burg.

"What's wrong with that?" I ask.

"The problem is that it gives people permission to taste that life, but then retreat to their white spaces and for things not really to change. For the status quo to remain the same."

"But surely for people to begin to transform, they need to start some-where. At least it gets people into the inner city."

"She would say that if you want to go into the city, no one is stopping you. You don't need permission from Nike. You can just go. The idea of 'Take Back The Night' is offensive. Take it back from whom? All the people who live in it? The people who live in Hillbrow and Yeoville and Berea? The city is still there. People live there all the time."

I hear her. I can see why it could be construed as offensive, but there is another truth that her argument is ignoring.

"You could see it as taking back the night from fear," I say.

Polo does not look convinced.

"You know, with all respect, I don't think you understand how brain-washed we were. Do you know we marched at school? Like little Nazis."

Polo shakes her head.

"Nobody wants to think they were affected by this shit," I say. "And so we pretend we weren't. We push it all away. We act like it is all fine. But is it? What's in your head is not always the same as what's in your heart. We all want to be nice liberals, but are we? That's what I am probing at."

Malebye's set begins and we retreat into the music. Her voice is all-soul, all-heart. She lifts us up and carries us over the city and its stories and gently drifts us back down into this small room with its scuffed red floor, overlooking an old supermarket car park. As she sings, I remember a recent phone conversation with one of my best friends, who grew up in Welkom, in the Orange Free State, the bastion of Afrikanerdom.

The month before, she and her sister had visited Constitutional Hill for the first time. This is the site of an old jail where, during apartheid, political prisoners had been held for months, years, without trial. Today the bricks from the old cells have been used to build the Constitutional Court, South Africa's highest court, which rises up, beautiful and inspiring, next to the old prison.

"I was so disturbed," she told me. "South Africa treated its blacks like animals. I couldn't believe this was going on all the time while we were living our normal lives. It was just like what the Nazis did to the Jews. They dehumanized them. It's painful and it's shameful. I'm Afrikaans and to confront that... that's what my people did."

I listened gently, knowing only too keenly how uncomfortable and dis-tressing it is to face this for the first time. And what moved me most about her account was what she chose to take away from her visit.

"It is so peaceful there," she said. "It's almost like a complete transfor-mation has happened. I felt like we saw how humanity can triumph over atrocities, how people really can move on. Since we've been, we've told everyone about it. None of them can believe what used to go on. It's had a ripple effect from us being there. My sister and I are going to go to Robben Island next."

As each of us transform, we all transform.

Malebye takes a break and my conversation with Polo turns back to the book.

Polo's analytical literary mind is fired up and she wants to flag up more problems she foresees.

"You will be criticised for your appropriation of voices, taking on stories that are not yours to tell," she says referring to my travels through the Transkei, documenting the voiceless of the rural poor.

"What because I have a white skin, I am not allowed to tell the stories of my fellow South Africans? Even if their stories are a frame for my own? What else do you think people will say?"

"You'll get criticised for the commodification of the apartheid story, from profiting from it," she says.

All white people ever did was profit from apartheid, and so for me to profit from reflecting on it is tarred with the same brush.

"Who knows if the book would make any money? But even if it did, would it make a difference if I gave the money away, or gave some of it to projects to help build more school libraries in South Africa?" I ask.

"It's about more than that. It's about the fact that because you are white, you have access to London publishers and therefore that this voice, of yours, can be heard above others," she says.

At this I emit a cold laugh.

"Do you know how hard it is to get the attention of a London publisher? Just because I am white does not mean I have automatic access. You send your work in, it ends up on a slush pile and you end up on medication because you are so damn anxious."

"Yes, but even the fact that you can write, that you can use language, that you know how to write in a way that a western reader reads means your story gets heard above others," Polo says.

"So what are you saying? That I shouldn't write because others can't write? That I should silence my voice because other voices are silent?"

"I'm just saying you need to be aware of your privilege in being able to do this," she says.

Malebye returns to the stage and our conversation goes back on hold.

We finish it back in the Mercedez Benz. Or rather, I finish it. I begin to rant.

"You know Polo, you say I am privileged, but I think you need to realise that is another apartheid lie. Apartheid treated all black people as the same, and it does the same to whites. I am not rich, I am not well connected. I am from a working class family. My dad worked in a factory and at the end of the working week, there was just enough money to buy food and put a roof over our heads. We never went out to dinner, we never had money for treats. You are much more privileged than me. You went to a private school with the Mbeki kids. The only reason I could afford to go to university was because I got a bursary and worked in a pizzeria most evenings and every holiday. And besides, that isn't the point. Do we really think that only poor people are allowed to introspect? That if a wealthy person tries to question their life and make sense of themselves, it's invalid because they are privileged? If anything, the wealthy are the ones often blamed for injustice in society so we should celebrate when rich people are spending money on introspecting rather than on private yachts. I'm trying to give a shit, I'm trying to question myself and this society, and all the bullshit, and you are saying I'm going to be judged for even trying. That doesn't seem fair."

"I am just saying you need to be prepared that you are going to get hurt by doing this. You need to know that," Polo says.

There is a hierarchy of suffering, a hierarchy of victimhood in our post-apartheid story, and my seeping wound is at the back of the queue.

Do I know that? Yes. But we do not read or write memoirs simply to tell our own stories. As we page through how another human came face to face with their truth and with all their complex, messy emotions, it creates a space for us to reflect on our own. Our collective story is pulsing under this nation, demanding to be heard, and until it is, it will not go away. We need to talk about that which we do not want to talk about.

Back at Polo's house, I shut myself in the spare room. I stare into the abyss of my journal, feeling lost, friendless, despondent.

"I am sinking," I write. *"The energy leaves my arms. I should be aware of my privilege but what of yours? I don't have the privilege of being blameless. The moral privilege. History is not on my side. Silenced by a society that does not want me to reflect, that questions my right to make a story out of my relationship to this society. If you don't have the right to question yourself, then what, then what?"*

The next day is Sunday. Polo's friend Vangi Gantsho organises a monthly poetry sharing in the gardens of the Union Buildings, South Africa's administrative seat of government. We pack our sunglasses and picnic blankets and board the Gautrain, the high-speed, high-security train that was built for the World Cup and that connects the airport to Jo'burg, Rosebank, Sandton and Pretoria. Being on the Gautrain is like being in Singapore. Security patrols. No feet on the seats. No chewing gum. No sipping water. There is another older, cheaper train, the Metrorail, that serves the same route between Jo'burg and Pretoria; and also connects other urban centres. but the Metrorail is considered slow, unreliable, and most crucially unsafe. Throughout the nineties the Metrorail continued to be used by white South Africans. In the 2000s however, as violent crime gathered pace and trains were sometimes set on fire (as a protest against the lack of delivery of key services including electricity, water and basic sanitation to poor communities), white South Africans retreated from the service. Today most white South Africans would regard the Metrorail as too dangerous to travel on. The Metrorail website does little to encourage otherwise, cautioning passengers to avoid dark corners and to not talk to strangers, rather than promising additional security. Today if you are rich you take the Gautrain. Why, you wonder, did the authorities build a whole new train, put it behind barbed wire and price it for the rich, instead of investing in this old public service, and improving security and access for all? Because despite our lip service to equality, and our world-class constitution, South Africa doesn't really believe its own story.

In the gardens of the Union Buildings, we gather beneath a conifer tree, not far from a new statue of Nelson Mandela and an old statue of Barry Hertzog, the Boer general who was Prime Minister of South Africa prior to World War II. We are a small group of ten: eight black, two white. The other white is a South African academic who works most of the year in Angola. She treats me as so many so-called enlightened whites (her) treat other white South Africans (me): with contempt. She ignores me when I speak, pretends not to hear my questions, talks over me. She is so desperate not to be associated with me, for her identity not to be polluted by mine, that she repels me with every word, every gesture, every glance.

I know this behaviour well because I do it too. In Glasgow, there is a group of white South Africans who regularly organise braais through a Facebook page. Instead of being curious about them, I am wary, I keep away. We see ourselves as innocent and each other as guilty.

Vangi begins. Others follow. The poems are honest scribblings, musings on days spent, love letters to Africa, the ordinary framed against the extraordinary of this bewitched, beloved country. As their confidence grows, so does mine, and I stand up and share the poem that I wrote when my words returned, after the cancer.

I made a new best friend this November
As we counted down to Day One.
I could not shut my eyes on yesterday, today or tomorrow
Until I had knitted a square

Knit one. Purl one. Slip Slip Knit Pearl 20

Then came that first day and my fierce determination to knit us out of this crisis

Was usurped by an even fiercer determination to cook us out.

I packed the pantry with superfoods, alkaline, organicWheatgrass and slippery elm, seaweed and tofu

While the nurses just smiled and said: "It doesn't matter what he eats,

He can eat cream puffs, just as long as he eats".

But he didn't eat.

That first week he vomited.

The second week everything tasted like vomit.

Then a cement-like gunk began to pump from the back of his throat

Coating every mouthful with a bitter gloop.

I whizzed juices.

I whizzed soups.

I gave him a straw and cheered and cajoled as he stared at half-empty bowls

Until the sounds of my footsteps leaving the kitchen filled him with dread.

And as the days slipped away, so did he, until he stood lighter than me in his socks, and the nurses shook their heads and said: "He needs to eat. He can eat cream puffs."

But he couldn't.And so they put a tube down his nose and like Neil Armstrong and Buzz Aldrin before him, he was fed like a spaceman.

And I started knitting again.

I bought a cable needle and made like an Arran fisherman.

I bought camel wool. Angora. Swedish yarns. No acrylic.

I knit one. Purl one. Knit two together and slipped a stitch.

I worked the wrong side and the right.

I cast off Continental style.

7 days. 6 weeks. 42 squares.

I knitted a square for every day they pressed pause on our lives

And catapulted us into a parallel cancerous trajectory
To which we are blinkered until it happens to us.
And now the knitting is done.
And the squares must be stitched together
And when the final stitch is made
We will have a beautiful blanket
And he will be healthy and warm.

As I finish I sense the mood has shifted. The eyes looking back at me are different than they were earlier.

As I sit down, one poet reaches out and touches my arm.

"I'm sorry," she says.

The others smile softly at me from across the blanket. I see it in their eyes. In this moment, I am not a white person, I am just a person.

In our suffering, we become the same.

Chapter 8

....

To Cape Town and back

I AM EN ROUTE TO Cape Town to visit a friend. At a coffee shop at Jo'burg airport, I grab the last table and nurse a morning coffee. A middle-aged white woman behind me in the queue surveys me with an unmasked resentment. A businessman man notices and offers to share his table with her. She declines and pulls up two chairs to create her own patch.

"Why can't she just share?" I think, hoping she'll be nowhere near me on the flight. She is in the seat next to me.

As we take off, I switch on my laptop and start writing, trying to pin down impressions from the day before.

"Are you writing a book?" she asks.

I nod.

"What's it about?"

My answer changes every time, depending on who's asking. I decide to give her the long answer. A litmus test. What will a white South African woman make of this kind of book? "Would you read it?" I ask her.

"It's very difficult for me to pick up one of those books and read," she says.

"Why?" I ask.

"Tangled emotions of guilt and regret and deep, deep sorrow," she says.

I wait quietly, waiting for her to say more.

"We're in a bit of haze, perhaps we've had to develop that to survive. I'm sorry that we are so dulled, that there is a dullness of interest, it's just as though…" she thinks for a while, "I think we had to fall asleep. For survival. To live with guilt and regret is too painful."

She makes another play, trying to be optimistic.

"If the author has written from a genuine place, and you allow yourself to break through that barrier, and it can be very cathartic, very healing," she says.

"But…"

"We knew that we lived in deplorable circumstances and yet they were so loving and loyal to us. If you follow that thought through, it's deplorable and yet we did not follow that thought through, and we told ourselves that was how it is. That we were helpless. Most South Africans felt helpless."

*

My friend picks me up from Cape Town airport. It was this friend who recently visited the Constitutional Court and confronted for the first time the horror of our history. She keeps a blog documenting inspiring spaces and design in South Africa. Ever since her visit she has been trying to write about Constitution Hill, but as we sit in her garden, sipping coffee with Table Mountain as our backdrop, she tells me how she has writer's block.

"I don't know what's wrong. I can't find the right words. Every time I try and describe it, it sounds flat, empty, trite. I can't capture in words how that place made me feel," she says.

"I think I know what's wrong," I say. You cannot describe how something affects you unless you are wholly honest about yourself.

"For it to make sense, you have to write about your ignorance. You have to tell people you are an Afrikaner from Welkom who grew up afraid of the 'bloody kaffirs'. You have to tell people that it has taken you twenty years to learn about the fact that detention without trial and torture were used to keep our so-called safe apartheid world intact."

"I can't do that," she says. "It's too embarrassing. I don't want to admit that."

"I know," I say. "Me neither."

*

Back in Jo'burg the airwaves are alive with the news that the city has been voted the most unfriendly city in the world, unfriendlier than Moscow and Paris.

"I'll tell you what it is," my friend's husband says, whom I am staying with tonight. "It's these bloody *zots* (blacks) with their unsmiling faces."

My friend protests. I protest. She remarks how the black ladies behind the till at the local supermarket are always kind and friendly to their tearaway children. She defends. I defend. Her husband sulks. A typical conversation in a white South African household. A line of casual racism, hackles rise, hackles fall, a quick switch of topic in the name of familial peace.

The next morning, on the phone, she is talking to a plumber. She comes off the phone, her face red, her blood boiling.

"We are building a toilet in a small space. The onsite builder – a black guy – says he thinks there is enough room. The plumber just said down the phone: 'What does a kaffir know about toilets?'"

"What did you say?" I say.

"Nothing. It happens all the time. I have to do business with these people. I never know what to say," she says.

We make coffee. We sit on the couch.

"I hate being put into the same box as racist whites," she says. "I can tell you most of the people I know have never been to the apartheid museum. I want people to go there and be affected by it, but half the people we went to school with are exactly the same as they were then. My husband has a friend. He doesn't have a proper job, has illegitimate children, and then he says: 'Those blacks, breed like flies'. How is he different? I have to hold my tongue," she says.

"Why do you have to hold your tongue?" I ask.

"It would be the end of a friendship," she says.

"Is it a friendship worth having?" I ask.

She shrugs. "He's my husband's friend."

*

Sunday morning. The black smoke of a veld fire billows alongside the motorway. It is a typical end-of-winter Jo'burg scene. We destroy so that our world can grow again.

I head to Maboneng, an enclave of design, creativity and multi-culturalism in old Jeppestown. Industrial warehouses refashioned into cafés, fashion stores, a food and design market, the new Museum of African Design (MOAD). A mural of Jan van Riebeek looks down from up high: the original colonialist observing the new generation of cultural colonialists, reclaiming the city, building a brave new world.

At MOAD it is the last day of the 21 icons exhibition. Black and white portraits of this country's legends, accompanied by interviews, sharing their wisdom. One insight inspires me above all the others. Gcina Mhlope, South African storyteller, poet, writer:

"I tell stories in order to wake up stories in other people."

Chapter 9

···········

Milisuthando

MONDAY MORNING. JOHANNESBURG. MY bed for the week is a couch in the home of an old university friend and her two dachshunds, Scratch and Sniff. Not their real names, but the names they deserve.

Scratch is curled under my left leg. Sniff with her Billy Idol eyes is glaring at my toast.

I check my emails. Nothing. Today I am supposed to be meeting Milisuthando Bongela, or MissMilliB, a 29-year-old hip, smart black girl-about-Jo'burg-town who writes a blog about fashion, feminism and race. She has not confirmed a time or place and I feel irritation welling up in my chest.

African time, whispers the inner monologue. Still there.

I first came across Milisuthando in the midst of an irate Facebook debate on a mutual friend's Facebook feed. Milisuthando was venting her spleen about the content of a blog written by Discopants, a white Capetonian blogger. Like many South Africans, Discopants had been living abroad for a number of years, in her case Sweden. Missing the sun and the good life, she had finally moved her family back and was now living comfortably once again under Table Mountain – and writing about it.

The tone of the blog is awkward – partly frank, describing the life of unreconstructed white South Africans going about their privileges with a slight nod-nod-wink-wink-isn't-this-mental tone, and partly unapologetic, i.e. what's the point of moving out of your comfort zone as that won't change anything. Africa will be as Africa is, so you may as well just enjoy the sunshine for as long as it lasts. Until that is, she went out of her comfort zone.

Discopants' maid invited her to her birthday party in her township home. Discopants was afraid to go. She asked everyone she knew for their advice, and in the end she went with her kids and her mum, and lo and behold, she had an amazing time. Her maid introduced her to all her neighbours. All her maid's friends – all women – were there, and they spent the afternoon singing, "about their life, their pain, their struggles," recounts the blog. Discopants was deeply moved by the welcome. Milisuthando Bongela was furious. Why was she spitting mad about a white woman going out of her comfort zone, and writing about it. Surely that is what we want to happen?

I contacted Milisuthando away from Facebook. I asked her if she would read the first few chapters of my book. Would my writing fill her with similar bile?

She agreed to read them, thanking me for reaching out, but then never got back to me. I tried again before I left on this trip. *"I want to write about that rage you felt towards that blogger, and about the stuck mindsets that infuriate you. Irritation that you may even feel towards me for even trying to write about this topic, or for the fact that this topic still exists 20 years down the line,"* I wrote.

I suggested that she could show me Jo'burg through her eyes – her version of the city that she thinks a white woman from the suburbs would never see. I wanted to learn her perspective so I could shift mine, and with her permission, write about it. She agreed, but had not responded to my recent emails. I track down her phone number and she picks up. She sounds wary, apprehensive, but agrees to meet at lunchtime at a coffee shop in Braamfontein. She does not want to walk with me around Jo'burg though. Today we can just talk.

We meet in Post, a trendy café in Braamfontein popular with Wits students and the cool kids of Jo'burg. I recognised her as soon as I entered the café. Her hair is unwoven, her gaze questioning and wary, her short frame clothed in a stylish, shapeless dress, the kind of dress that frames your mind, not your body.

Milisuthando Bongela was born in Mthatha in 1985, but grew up in Butterworth, also in the Transkei. Her father was an author, her mother a teacher, and she grew up on a middle-class street in an entirely black community of doctors, nurses, teachers, town planners. Her primary school was ten kilometres out of town, a beautiful campus with rolling hills and a river running past. There were only three white kids in the class, and one Indian boy. Everyone else was black. Did she understand apartheid?

"We knew something was up, our parents had a curfew, and whenever we tried to go to South Africa we had to get passports and if one of us did not have a passport, we had to be put in the boot, but we were children, we didn't know the full extent of it," she recalls.

Milisuthando's life changed forever in 1993. With the end of apartheid, the Bongelas moved from Butterworth to East London, the only black family in the neighbourhood of Amalinda.

"That was my first encounter with my race. That was when I knew I was black," she says.

On the first day after everything had been unpacked, the family went to church and came home to find the house had been egged.

"We had never even conceptualised such an act, we just thought it was funny as children, but of course, it was a bigger deal than that," she says.

Her mother and father went door to door around the neighbourhood, demanding to know who had done it.

"My mother and father are not militant, but they understand their own self worth as people. They were not seeking an apology, they were there to say, we're here, you are going to have to deal with it. From then on it's been a life of being othered, and dealing with being othered. Every part of my body, every morsel of me constantly has to get into a space and be reminded that I am black."

Milisuthando's words hook me in my chest. My instinct is to comfort her, to touch her arm, but her anger does not exclude me. I am part of it, so I keep my hands to myself, and listen instead.

At primary school Milisuthando, together with the other black students, were put in a remedial class because they could not speak English as well as the white girls.

"That created a dichotomy in the society of the school. You had this constant feeling of you are not good enough because you don't know the language, you don't know the culture. You have to learn how to do everything. Lunch: having cheese and fruit and a nice little juice rather than polony and brown bread and oros. What starts happening is you start to go back home and discredit the value of your own culture, your own language, the way you look."

By the time Milisuthando reached high school, they had moved again.

"We moved because there were too many black people in AmaLinda, all the people from the Transkei started moving there and my family thought it was becoming ghettoised and less good quality. As educated as they were, they were victims of that apartheid thinking," she says.

Life at high school was harder than ever.

"Our hair was wrong. Our language was wrong. We couldn't swim. There was no black teacher, except for the Xhosa teacher so that institutionalised the idea that a black teacher could not be a science or maths teacher. And we were indoctrinated into the white history of the country. Jan Van Riebeek. Founders Day. It was not until standard nine that modern South African history of apartheid was taught. We don't even have a history. We don't because we were stupid and didn't write anything down. It was all oral. So imagine what that does to dignity and identity? You grow up in a culture where the value system is completely foreign and there's too few of you to fight it, you don't even know how to fight it. You just think that's how life is."

"When did you become angry?" I ask.

She looks down and nods.

"2012. Angry with a purpose. Angry with a cause. Angry at knowing why I am angry," she says.

"What happened? What was the spark?" I ask.

"I read *Frontiers* (Noel Mostert's tome about how South Africa was created). It paints a picture of how we got to be here, and I felt very betrayed by family, my people. Why didn't they fight it?" she says.

I nod. I know what it is like for your anger to wake up.

"And then this year, I woke up to how little we've done to address our very, very severe wound, as a nation. Not just black people, white people too because in order to dehumanize others, you have to dehumanise yourself. You have to strip out all the things that make you human, in order to strip them out of someone else."

Her words are like a white light, firing through my heart. She speaks a truth that I feel. That I felt when I fell to my knees, sobbing, at the end of my time in the Transkei.

We are a nation with so little compassion – for each other, and for ourselves. Yes, tourists remember us as friendly, welcoming, warm. We have a superficial charm that is undeniable, but beneath our sunshine veneer, our hearts are stony. When we try complex reflection and introspection, we get stuck. Defensive anger is our go-to emotion. We cannot feel the pain of others, because we have not yet been able to fully feel our own.

As her anger grew, Milisuthando tried to talk about it with her white friends.

"'Let's talk about the white elephant in the room, I'd say, the race thing, and they say: 'We weren't there, we didn't do anything'. And I was like: 'I wasn't there either, but it doesn't mean we can close our eyes and pretend that nothing happened.' And then I realised that their parents had the same attitude. They told themselves: 'We are not discriminating against anyone, we give money to our domestic worker, we are not doing anything bad.'

That's how people absolve themselves. They say they didn't do anything."

Deny. Deny. Deny. Again, I nod at the truth she speaks.

"It wasn't me. The other boy did it," I say with a wry smile.

"I'm fucking mad right now to be quite honest," Milisuthando says. "This is not a black problem, this is a national problem and nobody is doing anything to sort it out. And when I talk to my white friends about it, they say: 'Well, what can I do?' I can't tell you what to do! You've got to talk to your people. Figure it out! The way I'm trying to figure it out. My black friends, we read, we talk, we purge, we try to heal ourselves, we're not the only ones who are sick. When you get together with your friends, you must also figure out how to move on. Talk about these deep-seated problems that has created this problem for the rest of us. And if you are not willing to do that, fuck you!"

Milli's anger and two empty cups of coffee stare back at us.

"We really want to close our eyes and say it's all going to work out," she says, her voice softer. "But it hasn't worked out. It's not working out. It's actually getting worse. And I feel like the goodwill – the ability to forgive, to not do anything violent – of black people has been taken for granted. It's not appreciated. We gave you Mandela for gods' sake."

Dear Tata Mandela. His heart was bigger than all of ours. His capacity for compassion so immense, we passed the buck to him, outsourced our healing to an icon. He transformed so we didn't have to. Our very own Jesus Christ, who was persecuted and died for our sins.

It is my turn to speak. I tell Milli how difficult it is for me, too, to have these conversations with white people. How you feel the barrier go up, the judgement come down, when you try to speak about anything to do with apartheid. You are the bore at the party, the person they wish they hadn't invited.

"You mustn't stop," Milli says. It's going to be very hard, it's going to be very lonely. More people have to do what you are doing, which is uncomfortable, you will become a pariah, you will become unpopular, even to yourself at times, you will probably be excommunicated from your community and not invited to things, but that's okay."

"Is it?" I say, laughing. "It sounds horrible."

"But I ask myself, at what point are white South Africans ever going to be uncomfortable in this country?" she says. "I think people are running away from the discomfort of our history"

I nod. "And you have to be uncomfortable in order to transform," I say, thinking of my trips in the Transkei. Putting myself again and again out of my safe zone.

"And it's not just doing the things that physically make you stand out, it's about going inside, into your head and heart. The whole fear thing for me, that's very odd to me," she says. "If there really was a real reason to feel fear, then there would be no white people here. Black people would have killed your children they look after every day and the security guards that guard your houses would have murdered you in the night."

"Don't you ever feel fear?" I ask.

"I'm just aware, I'm not afraid," she says at first, but then changes tack. Through our frank conversation we have a created a space where only honesty will do.

Milisuthando admits her truth: "I have to train myself not to be afraid of the black man, because I was. But I cannot be afraid of my own brother or my own father. I cannot."

She tells me a story about sitting alone on a Transkei beach, 5am, on New Year's Day. She is writing in her diary, reflecting. Down the beach are six young black guys, still drunk from the night before. Two of them come towards her and her first thought is: "Fuck, they are drunk, I am here by myself. I don't want to be raped." The young guys just wanted to talk, but she asks them to leave her alone, saying she is writing, and they back off, but still stay close. A few minutes later, two white men arrived on the beach, and that is when she feels her whole body relax.

"I had to say: 'no, no, no, no', that cannot be your relaxant. You cannot condition yourself to be more relaxed now that white men are around. That is playing into that whole system that has been created," she says.

"I thought it was just a white thing to be afraid of black men," I say.

"Oh no, of course not," she says. "We are all victims of the same system. Every single one of us. The narrative where the black man is the robber who is going to come in the night and rape you and your kid, it's the same narrative. Yes, it's true, the criminals that are out there, that are angry, that are stealing, yes they are black guys but the system was designed so that only black men would have the need and the anger to go and smash someone's window and threaten their lives. That's how you have to look at it."

"It's hard to be analytical when you are terrified," I say.

"Of course, but you can't let that fear run off on its own without reason. You know, a black man has never invaded white countries and said we're going to kill you, he's never done that. He's never said I'm going to rape your women en masse. There's a collective amnesia. A naturalised white superiority and black inferiority."

We have been talking non-stop for hours but we are not ready to stop. We order more coffees.

We talk about the first time Milli went to Europe and saw a white woman cleaning.

"I was like, what the fuck? I had never seen a white girl holding a rag, wiping anything, ever."

We talk about Mandela. "Our poor old father of the nation sold us out as people. We love him, but it is a very complicated love. The ANC led us into the wrong hands. It wasn't an Africa for Africans, it was oh shit, we need to protect the foreign investors."

We talk about how white Europeans look down on white South Africans.

"The nerve of them," says Milli. "The Brits are the absolute worst because they have somehow managed to magically absolve themselves of something that they have done to the entire world. It's incredible how they blamed apartheid on the Afrikaners. What? They are the ones who created apartheid in the whole world in the first place. They've told themselves all these myths about colonialism, and they don't teach their children the true history of exactly how much they thought it out, how at the same time as they did plants and animals they created a whole science around what the negro is. They animalised this person."

We talk about how Milli will never vote for a white person.

"Never. In my whole life. No matter how liberal they are. I don't trust white people."

And we talk about the firebrand Julius Malema, and Frantz Fanon, about the hip black scene in Jo'burg, about European blacks and American blacks who are moving to Jo'burg, who have come here looking for a home because they hate being black in America and in England and Paris.

"When they come here and they meet me and my friends, conscious blacks, they feel like this is a cauldron of something wonderful for black people, the only place in the world where being black is a good thing."

And I tell her how jealous I am of the scene they have going on. Art, poetry, late nights at Kitcheners and Great Dane. The scene that I cannot be part of, that excludes me because I am not young, hip and black.

She agrees. "You *want* to be black in Jo'burg."

"So I have a question," I say. "I think about coming back to Jo'burg, but like you say, it's a great time to be black here, but is it a great time to be white?"

"No it's not," she says.

"I feel like I need to be a human," I say. "I don't want to be always defined by my skin colour first. I want to be me. I want to grow in this life, and I don't want to be held back by this legacy. I am prepared to confront it, and prepared to talk about it, but I don't want it to define my whole existence. So it feels in some ways I can't live here now."

"Hmmm…" Milli says, listening closely.

"But I don't want to let go of South Africa, because I do define it as my heart space, but, and I'm not asking you as a counsellor, but do you think in some way it's better that I'm not here? That a white South African isn't here?"

"No, I don't like that at all," Milli says, her reaction immediate. "I've been thinking about this question as well. That's why I said to you earlier, when are white people ever going to be uncomfortable in South Africa? Absolutely, it's not nice to have to confront the guilt that comes with having white skin. I can understand how anxiety can emanate from that feeling, but if you are truly an African, if you are truly a South African, when are you going to roll up your sleeves and say fuck, we fucked up, let's fix it? Yes, it's hard to be white. But it was hard for all those years to be black and we still lived. And here we are. I feel that in order for white people to save themselves and bring back the humanity that they kind of parked on the side for a long time, they have to go through the shit. Because then you grow and you meet other parts of yourself, and you meet other parts of the human self that have been switched off by whiteness. So if I had to be making that choice, I'd think fuck it, I belong here."

Loud music has been playing in the café, all through conversation. As she finishes I notice the song. "Should I Stay Or Should I Go" by The Clash.

"Listen to the song," I say.

"You see!" Milli laughs.

"If I go there will be trouble. And if I stay there will be double," I sing.

"You know it gives me faith that you are doing something like this," she says. "Once you become conscious, you become constantly conscious. And the problems of apartheid are all just reoccurring, as if it's natural. We have to create the remedy."

The café is closing. The floor is being mopped around. Chairs upended onto tables. The waiter comes over and suggests it's time to leave.

Out on the street, I ask Milli one more question.

"What would you need to see to know that transformation was really happening in white society?"

She cocks her head and thinks.

"It shouldn't be on the outside. There's been so much energy spent on pretending that this transformation is happening, but it hasn't happened, so I don't know what it looks like, I don't know how it would present itself. And besides, it's not for me to say or prescribe. It's a white people thing. If it's truly happening, it will show itself."

I give her a hug.

"Good luck," she says. "You guys have a lot of work to do, hey. At least we've already started our work."

It is rush hour as I get into the car. Within minutes I am in a snarl of minibus taxis, jammed at odd angles, hooting. Instead of getting irritated I find myself smiling. Here I am, caught in the chaos of trying to get somewhere but going nowhere. Exactly where I want to be.

Chapter 10

....

Hillbrow

W HAT THE FUCK?" A middle-aged black man shouts from the pavement, shaking his head in disbelief.

"Go to the gym!" laughs a young black guy, a few metres on.

It is Sunday evening, a few hours after sunset, and I am on a bike, alongside thirty other cyclists – mostly women – riding through the streets of Hillbrow, one of Jo'burg's inner-city neighbourhoods, infamous for high crime rates and widely regarded as a no-go area for middle-class South Africans.

It was not always this way. Up to and during the 1980s, Hillbrow was one of Jo'burg's hippest neigbourhoods. It was here, in its art deco apartment blocks and vibrant clubs and bars, that the young came to escape the claustrophobia of apartheid suburbia, where Jo'burg's gay scene thrived, and where white and black bohemians mingled and sometimes lived side by side, flouting the Group Areas Act. To label the area radically liberal though would be to ignore the fact that Hillbrow was also home to a large, elderly and conservative Jewish population. As the collapse of apartheid gathered speed in the late 80s, the authorities rebranded Hillbrow a "grey area" (deemed an area with a significant illegal black, Indian and coloured population) and rumours of rising crime rates in other "grey" or "open" areas caused house prices to plummet. As talk grew of Hillbrow, or even the whole of Johannesburg being reclassified as a "free" area, where all races could live side by side, the apartment-owners of Hillbrow found themselves trapped – prohibited by law from selling their apartments to black buyers, but unable to find buyers among racist white buyers. Their reaction: panic, lock up and flee to the suburbs. By the early nineties, many apartment blocks lay empty, and without revenue from rates and taxes, the city was unable to maintain infrastructure and the neighbourhood fell into decline. In the early nineties, when South Africa began to relax its border controls with other African nations, these abandoned inner-city homes fell into the hands of some of Africa's most enterprising businessmen – illegal landlords, drug dealers and pimps. White fear and flight had bolstered the prophecy: the once hippest neighbourhood in Africa had become a dangerous, urban slum that soon earned the sobriquet Killbrow.

"Keep going, keep going," shouts a voice from the back, so we keep peddling, as the lights turn red over a four-lane intersection. A row of waiting minibus taxis, normally hot off the mark, wait, immobile, letting us pass. I throw back my head and laugh, a deep belly laugh. In London, New York, Paris, Glasgow, Rome, the city comes alive at night, the middle classes take to the streets to cavort and shake off the working day, but in Jo'burg we retreat, bolt our doors, hide. Tonight as we fly down Claim Street, past the pink neon star marking the Summit Club, one of South Africa's oldest 'adult entertainment' clubs – it feels as if we have escaped from prison. Someone howls at the full moon. The rest of us howl back and ring our bike bells.

Meet the Monthly Cycles, a gang of women bike riders who take to the inner-city streets once a month to challenge two South African perceptions: one, that women aren't "street" enough to ride bikes, and two, that being in Jo'burg after dark is a death sentence.

"I am trying to unpack my own internal perceptions of fear based on living in Johannesburg," comments Meghan, one of the regulars. "I feel that the more I explore, the more I understand what should be feared and what should not. And so far, without a doubt, I can say that there is more to not be fearful of than there is to fear."

We started our ride in Braamfontein, or Braam as the locals call the inner-city neighbourhood just across the road from Wits. Braam together with Newtown and Maboneng have led the inner-city's cultural renaissance – although not without controversy. In the decade after apartheid, as violent crime began to soar, the middle classes retreated to the suburbs, turning former residential streets into bars, clubs and cafés, while the inner-city became home to the urban poor. Today, those with capital are turning their attention back to the inner-city, buying up old buildings and transforming them into artists studios, loft apartments, rooftop bars and craft markets, stoking up debate about the ethics of gentrification. Is South Africa, once again, forcibly removing the poorest, the most powerless, this time in favour of a multi-racial elite?

The pavements of Hillbrow heave with black men, very few women are about.

A little boy dashes out of a shop and runs next to the bikes, cheering us on.

"Where is the finish line?" he shouts.

"If only I knew," I shout back.

The bustling streets of Hillbrow disappear and we head into the silent streets of the CBD, the storefronts shuttered, no sound but the wind, and turn down Jeppe, through the vast empty car park of the Market Theatre, under the motorway bridge and towards Fordsburg, the old Indian inner-city neighbourhood where, of an evening, the streets bustle with traders and food stalls. As we ride down a half-lit street, two newspaper billboards catch my eye:

"African Women Defining a Continent".

"No Free Ride for ANC Man".

Indeed.

I return to Hillbrow early the following morning for an appointment at Ponte, Jo'burg's iconic circular skyscraper with the red Vodacom crown, built in 1976 to be the tallest, and most sought-after, residential address in Africa. During the late 80s and 90s, Ponte suffered the fate of the rest of Hillbrow: the drug dealers and pimps moved in, the respectable citizens fled, the lifts stopped working, and its hollow centre became a dumping ground for rubbish, including dead bodies. In 1998, the Kempston Group (the building's owners) were approached by South African Correctional Services with the idea of turning it into a prison. That never transpired and by 2001, Ponte was declared Africa's first vertical urban slum, a reputation that lives on. The truth, though, is very different.

In 2011, Nick Bauer, a journalist with the *Mail & Guardian*, South Africa's weekly liberal newspaper, was sent to Ponte with the brief to find four things: a Nigerian drug lord, a prostitute, the pimp who owns the prostitute, and an old white man who has refused to move since the Eighties. He found none of them, and instead left with a signed lease for an apartment on the 51st floor. So what had changed?

In the mid-2000s, Kempston hired the Red Ants, a fully armed security and eviction services company with a military background, to evict illegal squatters. The evictions got the attention of foreign investors who wanted to reinvigorate Ponte. They set to work excavating the three stories of detritus that had accumulated in the central core, fixing the lifts, renovating the upper floors and launched a massive marketing campaign to sell the idea of a new Ponte to the bright young things of Jo'burg. The response was positive and people put down deposits on apartments, but when the global financial crisis hit, the foreign investors got cold feet, packed their bags and left, leaving Kempston to pick up the pieces. Instead of selling the flats, Kempston took the decision to redecorate the apartments – think Italiante tiles and melamine kitchens, more suburban townhouse than design in the sky – and rent them out to people they deemed respectable. Today the building is at full capacity and run with more discipline than a Catholic girls boarding school. The caretakers are armed, residents access the building with fingerprint ID, visitors are forbidden after 9pm unless residents have written permission from the caretakers, and all Nigerians – branded the druglords of Jo'burg – are banned from the building. It is like a mini-apartheid state where personal freedoms come second and order comes first.

I am here to meet Mike Luptak – aka Loops – a white South African who has made his home on the building's 52nd floor and established the business Dlale Nje in commercial units on the ground floor. Dlale Nje began life as a recreation centre for the 500 kids who live in Ponte, providing them with arcade games and a space for creative expression, but it has since grown a second *raison d'etre*.

"If you go to a braai or a dinner party, there will always be someone who has something disparaging to say about Hillbrow, Yeoville and Berea," Loops says. "I don't have a problem with their opinion, but with how that opinion was based: it's all second-hand experience that comes through the washing machine, and it completely pisses me off. People live in a bubble in Jo'burg. I want to be the guy that sticks the pin in that bubble."

Loops' idea was to start a perception-busting business, leading guided walks through Hillbrow and Yeoville, and challenging corporate executives to immersion weekends in the urban jungle. In a typical South African office environment, a white face will often still hold rank over a black face. Put a mixed race team on an urban street though, and the power dynamic quickly shifts.

"My personal thing is to get as many South Africans onto this thing as I can as they are the ones who have all the discouraging things to say about this area, but that's proving to be the biggest challenge. So far 80% of people who come on these tours are foreigners."

I feel pathetic paying a fellow South African to walk me around my own city, especially after the conversation I had with Polo about Nike's Take Back the Night. I ask Loops how he feels about these kinds of events. "I've got a very firm stance on this," he says. "The transition of South Africa as a nation doesn't start from what government is doing, it starts from within. People sit in their homes, watching the rugby on a Saturday, and expect the service delivery to be improved, but nobody does anything. But the fact that you've come into the inner city on a Nike 10k, or a walk with me, is a massive thing because you weren't here before because you had this inherent paranoia within yourself that you were going to get raped or murdered. Let's not get academic about what this really means. Yes apartheid happened, but what ability do we have to move on from that, and where does it start? It starts here," he says, pointing to his heart. "And that's why you are here, you are confronting those fears you had when you were younger."

"But do I really need you?" I ask. "Shouldn't I just be a big girl and just go by myself?"

Loops shrugs. "You could. But there are real reasons why people fear these streets. Not everyone is a criminal but you need to learn to know what danger looks like, and you need to walk these streets in order to learn that."

"How did you start?"

Loops laughs.

"When I am in a situation where I'm uncomfortable, that's my happy place."

We set off accompanied by Franck Leya, a 19-year-old Congolese guy who arrived in South Africa as a political refugee from the DRC as a child. In 2014, Yeoville is more like Little Congo than South Africa, and Loops has hired Franck to lead night walks through Yeoville. As we walk, Loops chats about how critical it is that South Africans start to understand how the structure of our society makes crime the easiest option for immigrants.

"They have no access to a bank account, no identification, so no job possibilities. It gives them a feeling of carte blanche. They can do what they like because they can't be identified, and if they get caught, they won't be put in a South African prison, they'll just be deported. And then they come back in and do it all over again. Zimbabweans have a very bad reputation around here because of that."

We turn into Abel Road and walk past the Italianate façade of the La Rosa Hotel, an infamous post-apartheid inner-city brothel, which has been refurbished by the Johannesburg Housing Company and now, according to its website, offers affordable rental accommodation and a gym. I have noticed this building so many times, always through a car window, and the sense of being right here, on this pavement, fills me with a childish, fizzy joy. It feels like the first time I ever stood outside Grand Central Station in New York City and had to pinch myself because in that moment, life felt more real than real. Of course, the sad and crazy thing is that this is not New York, this is my hometown. What should be ordinary is extraordinary, what should be normal is abnormal.

We stride on – "you've got to walk with purpose," Loops advises – past street fruit and veg sellers, up the bustle of Pretoria Street, Hillbrow's main thoroughfare, past Indian-owned shops selling blankets, mobile phones and computer repairs. Nothing happens. Nothing to report. We walk, people shop, in the paved square at the bottom of Constitutional Hill a few guys sit under a tree. I stop to take a picture of a carved tree trunk, a wooden totem pole to Africa, with the words "South Africa" inscribed at the bottom, supporting the names of the other African nations higher up.

"Right, keep going," Loops says, keeping an eye around us.

We cut past the Constitutional Court, through the peaceful silence of the old prison and down into Braamfontein, to the gentrified pocket around De Korte and Jorissen streets, where we order flat whites at Velo Café and reflect on my first inner-city stroll.

"How was it?" Loops asks.

"Fine. Normal. Ordinary," I say. "Makes me think I could probably walk on my own."

"There's a German woman who lives in Ponte and walks that route every day. But she knows what she's doing," Loops says.

"What is it I need to know?"

"The most reliable info on the streets comes from the female traders. If you get lost, ask them. If you walk the same route every day, buy from them, make friends with them, they will look out for you," Loops says.

"What else?"

"If you get asked the time, don't answer. They just want to see what kind of watch or phone you have. Most people get mugged because they don't see the signs."

"But also, don't hide your phone, especially if you have a rubbish phone like yours," says Franck, laughing at my old Nokia. "No one will want it. I used to hide my phone and got mugged all the time. Now I play music on my phone, so there's noise around me, and the last time I got mugged I asked the guy for my SIM card back, because I was waiting for my exam results."

"Did he give it to you?" I ask.

Franck nods. "You have to be relaxed on the street. A smile is a passport to wherever you're going."

"Another trick, if someone looks threateningly at you, wave," Loops says. "Pretend you've seen someone you know further down the street. That totally throws them off."

We spend the rest of our coffee break talking about Loops' younger life. Like me, he had arrived in South Africa age 5, an economic immigrant, him from the collapsing communist state of Czechoslovakia. Loops had grown up in the insular suburbia of the West Rand and was fascinated by the inner city. As a teenager he used to sneak out of his family home and take taxis into Jo'burg to ride a skateboard and explore the city by night.

"It was a forbidden zone," he says explaining the allure.

Coffee finished, we head back outside. Loops nips to the bank and Franck and I stand on a corner, chatting.

"Do you feel confident to walk anywhere in this city?" I ask. Frank has a very dark skin which makes it obvious he is not from South Africa. "When

264

the xenophobia kicked off, my dad forbade me from going to Soweto for a while, but I'd go back there now."

"And what about the whites? How do they treat you?"

"Most white people have only ever been nice to me. You do get the racist ones, who shout 'get out of the way you black fool' from their car windows, if you are late crossing the road or something, but calling me black, that's not an insult. I know I'm black. I see it in the mirror every day."

We laugh. Franck at the inanity of the insult, me at how refreshing it is to hear someone so unencumbered by his skin colour.

We flag down a minibus taxi and head towards Yeoville, getting out at the market. Inside, it as if we have been teleported to Kinshasa. Congolese tailors are hunched over sewing machines creating statement garments from vibrant African fabrics; food stalls are selling roots and fruits for which I don't know the names, never mind the recipes, and around the back, a wrinkly black South African man with kind eyes is selling tattered books for a few rand. That childish fizz inside me sparks up again, and I feel my roots unfurl and seek around for a little bit of earth. I have hitchhiked around Zimbabwe, travelled on local buses through Mozambique, but here, in my so-called part of Africa, I have never felt the bustle and vibrancy of the continent. Cocooned by shopping malls, safeguarded by trendy neighborhoods, here I exist in limbo, between a fading memory of an old South Africa and a blurred picture, still emerging, of what this country *should* look like, *should* be like. Instead of exploring what is, I have been obsessed with what was and what one day, might be. But in this moment, I don't care where our country is going. The present is good enough as it is. Especially the fashion, I think to myself, as I reach for a few skirts to try on.

Later that afternoon, after lunch of steak and chips on the upstairs terrace of the House of Tandoor, a Rasta-owned Yeoville institution, we walk up to the Yeoville Koppie, a scrubby hillside that overlooks the whole city. During the gold mining boom, this highest point in the city was where the colonialists came to picnic and escape the dust. Today it is where African Zionists come to pray, an open-air church as close to the heavens as you can get in this city.

A pastor in white robes stands in front of a group of people, women seated to his right, men to his left, their heads covered with white cloths.

"They are facing east, to pray," Loops explains.

We walk to the edge of the koppie and look across over the whole city: Ellis Park, Ponte, Park station, Carlton Centre. The word PROSPER is flashing on top of a distant skyscraper. That is why people come here. That is why people have always come here. I glance down the hill and see a group of men standing in a circle among the Aloe trees, voices lowered, an intense discussion. "Drug deal," I think, but within minutes they begin clapping, a gentle rhythm, and I realize they are praying. My prejudice hits me in the face. Ashamed, I look down at the ground beneath my feet. It is littered with broken glass. My critical voices hisses again. "Why this mess? If it's so holy, why don't they keep this place clean?"

"They break the glass to release their prayers to the heavens," Loops says, reading my mind.

In a sentence, my twisted thought flies away. Littering to glittering, grime to divine. How much more beauty will I find if I only stop judging and start looking?

We leave the koppie and walk back to Hillbrow, past once-grand houses and a wall spraypainted with the words: "How Goes the World Now, Sir?"

"I'm in love with art like that. Art that makes you ask questions," Loops muses. "I think the most interesting question we can ask right now is 'why do black people have the ability to move on, more than whites?'"

We make our way to our final stop for the day: Sunny's Tavern at the bottom of Abel Road, a popular haunt with senior ANC members. We order two beers and take a seat on old wooden benches on the fenced-in front terrace. It is quiet, just a few huddles of men, enjoying a post-work drink.

"So how was today?" Loops asks.

"Good. It's opened my eyes. Ordinary people living ordinary lives in an ordinary place. I feel like something has been peeled away," I say.

I'm intrigued by Loops though. He could live anywhere, and yet he chooses to be here.

"What kind of person do you have to be to live here?" I ask.

Loops sips thoughtfully on his beer.

"You have to be the kind of person that questions things. I think the fact that I don't have the answers to a lot of questions you are asking is why I live here."

We sit in silence and drink our beers. As Loops heads back to the bar for another, four black men, sitting on a bench to my left, wave me over.

"Where are you from?" asks one.

"South Africa," I reply.

"Noooo," he says, shaking his head.

"What do you mean no?" I ask.

"You don't look like it."

"Why? What does a South African look like? We all look different," I say.

He pats the seat next to him. I sit down.

"You know, I love and I like what you're doing," he says.

"What am I doing?" I ask, laughing.

"You have an aim of why you are here and I love it. Life, you see is about understanding and respect. No matter if you are white or black."

I ask his name and he introduces himself as Emmanuel Nyati, a 44-year-old construction worker, originally from Zimbabwe, who has been in South Africa most of his life.

He looks down at his watch. It is 4.30. "You can come on the streets until five o'clock…"

"Six o'clock," interrupts his friend.

"No five, five is better. After dark, the *tsotsis* (gangsters) come, but during the day, everyone can walk here. Here in Hillbrow, we can all be together."

Chapter 11

············

The Train

I T IS MIDNIGHT AND I am sitting on a stool on the 52nd floor of Ponte City, staring out over the city. Tomorrow morning, before sunrise, Loops and Franck are going to help me go even further out of my comfort zone, and so tonight, I am sleeping on Loops' couch. Except I can't sleep. The air is too dry up here and I don't want to close my eyes. I try to think, reflect on the day, but I don't want to be lost in thought either. All I want to do is look, stare, out at the lights of the city, the warm bulbs of apartments, the blue neon of the Telkom tower, the brief beams of head-lights as they momentarily illuminate a deserted street, the constellation glow of the suburbs like a distant Milky way.

It is oddly comforting. Normally, when night falls on this city, I am at street level, barricaded behind bars and fences and fears. As the skies darken, my body contracts, my breath shortens and I analyse every creak and bump, waiting for and wishing away my personal nightmare. I taunt myself with what has happened to others. Breaking glass, forced entry, a knife against my chest. I am not immune. But up here, towering above the city, among the lights, I feel part of something bigger, shifting, growing.

4.30am. The alarm goes off. Bleary eyed, Loops and I take the lift down the 52 floors to the entrance of Ponte. It is still dark and the air is terse, a sharp cold catching at the back of your throat. Outside on the pavement, a man is warming himself at a small open fire. Beside him, a car is waiting for us, its headlights on. Across the road I spot Franck's silhouette. Well timed. We bundle in and pull off, through the quiet streets. On the radio the DJ is playing "*Don't Worry, Be Happy*": a tribute, he announces later, to the actor Robin Williams, who has committed suicide. We shake our heads sadly and look silently out the window at the sleeping city, gathering speed on the motorway towards our destination: Benoni train station.

The first time I ever visited downtown Jo'bug, I was five years old. My mum, her friend, her daughters and I walked across the iron pedestrian bridge over the tracks and stood on the platform, waiting, excited.

"We are going to Jo'burg. We are going to Jo'burg," I whispered to myself, over and over. But when the train rolled in, it did not stop and so my mum, bewildered, incensed, ran shouting after it, cursing in her Yorkshire accent. And it stopped. Screeching to a halt with only the last carriage on the platform.

"*Wat maak julle?* What are you doing?" the train conductor shouted, sticking his head out of the window of the train.

"We want to go t'Jo'burg," my mum said.

The conductor shook his head in disbelief, but opened the last door and waved us aboard. Being white in the eighties was your ticket to ride.

Loops buys our tickets from the kiosk. R7.50 one-way. A similar journey from the East Rand to Johannesburg on the Gautrain costs R28. We cross the iron pedestrian bridge, glancing up at the near full moon, now beginning to wane, and make our way down to Platform 3. There are no lights on the platform, the only glow is from smart phone screens, reflecting on the faces of commuters. I close my eyes and scan the surroundings with my other senses. The smell of grease and grime from the tracks, the chatter of birds waking up in the trees, the fizz of anticipation in my belly.

The 5.26 is ten minutes late. Its Cyclops headlight momentarily blinds us before the yellow train wails to a halt. Doors open, we climb aboard. Loops turns to the left, his head hidden by a hoodie, to doze in a darkened corner. I turn to the right and sit on a soft grey leatherette two-seater, next to a sleeping man. Franck sits across from me, putting in his earphones and turning his attention to his phone. No one would think we are together. No one would know that my usual fears are assuaged by the presence of my travelling companions. To everyone else's eyes I am a lone white woman. The only one on the train.

Inside the train is clean. No graffiti on the marble patterned walls, no rubbish on the floor. The windows, like those of old trains in Glasgow and London, are cloudy, the outside world obscured by decades of grime. Our first stop is Dunswart, the industrial area between Boksburg and Benoni. Out of a dimly lit corner of the train, a white man emerges, wearing blue overalls. My face registers surprise, as does his. I smile, he smiles. Clocked by my tribe. The doors open and his body is exchanged for eighty others, every one black. There are giggling female students hustling for seats, quiet men in overalls, sleepy eyed office workers, and a mum in a leopard print headscarf, her little daughter in her school uniform, a blue blanket patterned with little cars wrapped around her shoulders. They stand next to me, a few people glance at me, one man in overalls offers a gentle smile.

Tak-tak tak-tah, clunk, urrh

Gada-gada gada-gada gada-gada

Dun-de-dun-dun

Dun-de-dun-dun

We pull away. The students chat. People close their eyes. The mother licks her fingers and gums down her daughter's hair. Her daughter grimaces and pulls away. I smile to myself. I also used to hate it when my mum did that.

Lum-be-lum lum-be-lum

Dadada dadada dadada

Dadada dadada dadada

The man in overalls stares into space. His expression is neither happy nor sad, pensive nor relaxed. I recognize that face, it is the face my dad had before he left for a shift. A man thinking about his family, his day, his bills to pay.

Shaka-shaka-shaka-shaka shaka-shaka-shaka-shaka

Sqqeeeeeeeeeechhhhhhhhhh

The guy alongside me wakes up to check where we are. He sees me, raises his eyebrows, shakes his head in a display of bemused disbelief, checks his watch and goes back to sleep.

Toto-lak-shaya ato-cetabaya

Hawa-hawa-hawa hawa-hawa-hawa

Sqqeeeeeeeeeechhhhhhhhhh

The train lurches and the man in overalls bumps into my leg.

"Sorry," he says. "I'm sorry."

"It's fine," I whisper. "It's fine."

As my words enter the space, so do I. I look again around the carriage. I look again at the mum protectively holding her daughter, at the dad in overalls, at the keen young students, laughing about their lives. I breathe in and put my hand to my heart, and as I do I *feel* this thought: They are just like me. I am just like them.

They are just like me. I am just like them.

It is something my self-professed liberal lips have uttered hundreds of times before. Something I have shouted at the television when I see reports of people committing brutal acts of racism on the evening news. A truism. And yet, sitting here now, tied by the rumble of the train, moving together on one track, I realise that for the first time in my life, I am not saying it because it is what I am supposed to say. I am feeling it. It is as if my mind has dropped from my head into my belly. As if a dirty old veil has fallen from my eyes and for the first time as I look around the carriage, I see you. Not a black person, but a person. Not black people, but people. The ordinariness of my face is reflected back at me in yours and I feel that thing which underpins our belief in equality: our common humanity.

The Buddhists talk about realizations. The Christians talk about epiphanies. Moments in our life when we understand something so deeply, so profoundly, it is as if something in our whole being shifts. We cannot force these moments. They come to us after years of search, usually when we least expect them.

I take a deep breath in. The air in the carriage is thick, warm. I need more air. I stand up and open the window. Outside the sun is rising, the dawn is turning purple.

Franck tugs on my arm and shakes his head. I look around. The mother does not want the window open. I acquiesce, and push it back up and sit down, trying to hold onto this feeling, trying to push away the question I do not want to ask: what does this say about me?

Throughout this journey, from the Tranksei to Jo'burg, I had been searching for something, but I was never certain what. At times I had thought it was a deeper understanding of politics and social culture, at times absolution, at other moments driven on by the conviction that all I needed was proximity. If I could just get close enough, familiar enough, something would shift, it had to. But the closer I had got in the Transkei, the further away I had felt and the more locked-in to that sense of being an outsider, an interloper, a tolerated white woman. My decision to return to Jo'burg had grown out of my failure in the Transkei, and it had come to me in a dream – the recurring dream of being on this train, on this Metrorail.

And so here I sit, another commuter on the early-morning service from Benoni to Park. We are wedged together in a state of early-morning bleariness, quiet except for the giggles of teenagers. We are moving in the same direction, on the same track and in this moment, there is no fear. That very South African barrier has disintegrated, dissipated. We are all in the same train, going the same way, wanting the same thing. And without it, I see you.

And I wonder, can you see me?

Chapter 12

....

Jozi spoors

BACK IN MABONENG. AT one of the art galleries at Arts on Main, a young black guy comes up to me. He looks hip, cool, interesting. We start chatting. I ask him which paintings he likes. He steers the conversation to his life. He finished school last year but cannot go to university yet. Why not? Not enough money. Could I contribute money to his studies? He is smart, you can see it in his eyes. He will go far. But not this way.

"No," I say, shaking my head. "That's not right. You can't assume that because I am white, I'm rich. If we want to be equals, you also have to treat me like an equal."

He nods. He gets it. He offers me his hand, and we shake. He walks away.

*

Franck and I are sitting on the balcony at the Guildhall Pub, one of Jo'burg's oldest pubs, overlooking Library Square Gardens. We spent the morning at JAG, the Johannesburg Art Gallery, then walked through town, playing our new favourite game: 'Count the white man'. By lunchtime we are up to 4. The people inside the Guildhall do not count.

Franck's parents came to South Africa as refugees fleeing from the war in Congo.

"I knew nothing about it," Franck says. "The first time I learnt about child soldiers was at school here. I felt so stupid. Everybody else knew what was going on in my country before I did."

I raise my beer glass and clink his.

"I know how that feels," I say.

*

Inside the Guidhall, the white owner starts a conversation with me.

"Where are you from?" he asks.

"From here. From Jo'burg. Well, Benoni," I say.

"Naah," he says. "You don't look like you're from here."

"What does someone from here look like?" I ask.

"Hmmmm, you just don't look like you're from here," he says, his eyes briefly glancing outside to where Franck sits.

"Where are you from?" I ask.

"I was born in Mozambique, but when that went to shit, we came here. Now this place is going to shit too," he says.

I tell him I am not so sure. That I have met a lot of young, educated, fired-up black people who really want to see change in this country. Who are also angry with corruption and lack of service delivery. Who see a different way to the ANC. They inspire me.

"But they are so angry. That Julius Malema…" he says.

"I know. But wouldn't you be angry if your parents and grandparents had been treated as theirs were?"

"No man. It's over. What have they got to be angry about? They have everything they want. This country is theirs now. Everything is for them."

Two young black guys come up the stairs.

"What do you want?" he barks at them.

"We're looking for jobs," says one.

"Wait a minute," he snaps. His tone makes my skin crawl. It is the old apartheid voice. Short, sharp, snide. He turns back to me.

"These blacks today, they've got an attitude problem," he tells me, with authority.

The young guys are standing less than a metre away. They can hear everything.

He keeps ranting. I stop listening. I have heard all this shit before. I look past the owner at the young guys, catching their eyes. They meet my gaze. I am not part of this, my eyes plead.

"My beer is getting warm," I mutter. "Asshole."

*

The Goodman Gallery. Jo'burg Art Week. Tonight it is showcasing The Brother Moves On, a contemporary performance art collective. A praise singer wearing a thick collar woven from dried grass, threads his way through a gathering of the great and good of Jo'burg. A multi-racial crowd. His hair is braided into a Mohican, patterned with shells, he is dressed in a red skirt and black tuxedo jacket, his face is smeared with white paint.

On a makeshift stage a young coloured man in an Arab Jalabiya, wearing a fez made of bank notes; another man is painted yellow, wearing only underwear.

With tins of gold spray paint, they graffiti the stage: *Something will occur again. Blank faces. Nelson. Fok Off.*

A band plays white noise.

The praise singer disrobes. Totally. His penis is tiny. One myth destroyed.

"*Isithabane!*" he shouts. Faggot.

"*Isithabane!*" the hip black kids chant back.

The hip whites stand there uncomfortable. What does it mean? What are they chanting?

"There was a man," words flash on a screen. "They made him a monster. PANIC!"

The fat praise singer begins to dance. A clumsy ballet. His 'teacher' joins him on stage. She denigrates him. "You cannot dance. You are fat. You are black. Go away!"

The yellow man and the jalabia man douse the stage with kerosene. They set it ablaze.

"We are suffering, rainbow child," the praise singer crows. "We are suffering from an apartheid *babelas* (hangover). We did not realise that freedom could be so daunting.

Because when you are free, you can do what you like. And I tell you, rainbow child, we don't know what we are doing. Because we are suffering from an apartheid babelas.

The beautiful ones are not yet born. We are just the beginning, rainbow child."

A white actor friend with me says: "I fucking hate this shit."

I disagree. I like it. I like the anger. We have to get it out.

*

Thursday night. Kitcheners, Braamfontein. Jozi's second oldest pub, and now the pub *de jour* for black hipsters and their white wannabe entourage. Cue me. I spent the day taking the intellectual pulse of the country at TEDx, the Jo'burg installation of the global conference movement that champions innovation in technology, entertainment and design. Tonight I am looking for a different kind of beat. As a writer, I come in two varieties: the oft seen Leave-Me-Alone-I'm-In-My-Navel and the lesser spotted Turbo-Girl. Tonight my latter switch is on.

At the bar I meet Thulani, red shirt, pink tie, who works for one of the investment houses.

I tell him briefly about my book. He is not interested. But he does not walk away. He keeps talking. We keep talking. Oh I see. He is interested in me.

Thulani is with his pals, a crew of gays and lesbians. The drunker we get, the more we fawn over each other. The gays and lesbians and me, that is.

"Your skin is so beautiful," says one. "Touch it, touch her skin."

They all touch my leg. Thulani included.

"I am married," I warn, raising my eyebrow.

"No!" "How can you be married?" "How old are you?" come the responses.

"37"

"No." "No way" "You don't look it."

"It's the light," I say. "Everyone looks good in a nightclub."

We keep fawning. We keep talking. They say something bitchy about white people. I am too drunk to remember what, but I remember saying: "I am white you know. I really am."

"No you're not," they say. "You're not like them."

"But I am still white."

Chapter 13

....

Thuthuga

MY LAST NIGHT IN Jo'burg. I want to be alone, but not. Tonight, at the Afrikan Freedom Station a pianist and saxophonist are playing homage to their idols: John Coltrane, Charlie Parker...

Inside it is cold. The back door is open so everyone can smoke. I order a coffee and snuggle into a couch, clutching my handbag like a blanket.

Next to me a young bespectacled guy is making a film. He introduces himself as Thabo Sixishe, from Lesotho. His grandfather used to be the kingdom's Minister of Communications. We chat about art, films, books, my book. The conversation turns to my epiphany on the Metrorail. Another litmus test. How will he react?

"I love it. No one ever speaks like this. No one is honest," he says.

He talks about how black people treat whites differently.

"Think about how white people are treated when they get into minibus taxis. They are treated like they will break. Like children. That's another kind of racism."

Is it? Perhaps it is. Like the relationship between an abusive father and child. Both want to love each other. Both want to protect each other. And yet, again and again, we undermine each other, trapped by old habits, unable to transform.

The pianist and saxophonist segue into their own compositions.

They play a song called *Gae*.

"What does it mean?" I ask Thabo.

"It means *home*. In SeSotho," he says.

I smile.

They play a song called *Thuthuga*.

"And that?" I ask again.

"That's a difficult one. It means to heal, to cleanse, to put back together, to make whole."

And then they play an untitled song, a composition for their friend who had died. As the mourning of the saxophone fills the space, hovering over the red, scuffed floor and seeping into my red, scuffed heart, my eyes fill with tears.

Back at university when I watched *Dry White Season* and *Cry the Beloved Country*, I had cried tears of shame. At the end of my first Transkei trip I had cried in frustration and at the end of the second, I had sobbed with anger. Tonight, these tears are different. They begin as tears for my brother, whom I lost to this city. I think of him long dead, on the verge of a motorway, a broken neck, a broken family. I stare out the window at the neighbourhood where I used to live, at the city beyond, its streets quiet in the darkness. Once upon my lifetime, a political system declared that the sadness of this saxophonist and my sadness were not the same, could never be the same. His poetry, his truth, his inspiration, were deemed of no relevance to me.

In this moment, I feel more than the loss of a brother. By virtue, or rather vice, of a political system I have lost more brothers, sisters, mothers and fathers than I can ever count. My life has been narrowed, confined, contracted, and it still is. The tears that were for one brother become tears for all. They burn hot rivers on my cheeks. They do not stop. I sit with my back straight, my heart open to the music, and I cry without shame for all of us. For the humanity we lost and that we are still struggling to find.

Epilogue

FEBRUARY 2015. JOHANNESBURG. I put on a pair of blue jeans and a white T-shirt, and pack a small calico bag with a pen, some tissues and a notebook in which I draw a map of downtown Johannesburg. In my left pocket I stash R300, in my right my mobile phone. I leave my friend's Westdene home on foot. It is a perfect summer's day. The sky is a child's drawing of bright blue with puffs of white cloud. The street is still, no wind in the *doringbooms* (thorn trees). The guard at the local church nods as I walk past. I smile and wave back.

I stop in at the local seamstress. I broke the zip on my carry-on bag by overloading it with books and I am hoping she can fix it. She buzzes me in through the security gate.

"Give me a week," 35-year-old Nozuko Ndinisa says. "I'll need to go into town to get the zip."

"Do you feel fine walking around town by yourself?" I ask her.

"I do. There are many who don't, including black people. But I have no clutter around me here," she says, pointing to her head.

We both laugh and I tell her that I know what she means. I have been trying to get rid of my clutter, telling her briefly about my journey.

Nozuko nods, saying she grew up in the Transkei, and that as a child, she too had been ignorant of apartheid.

"Now we are so touchy," she says. "I don't know why we are trying so hard not to see colour. I can't say I don't see it. I say let's see it and be done with it. I know how to behave with whites and with blacks."

"What do you mean?" I ask.

"For example, white people, they always want to know why. They like to know exactly what is going on and they always ask questions. You need to give them proper answers. Or like, in a white zone, don't stand in the middle of the road, it irritates them. Decide where you're going or stand on the side of the road if you don't know. And white people don't like noise. They are more intolerant than us."

We both laugh. There is truth in these stereotypes. But do these characteristics define us? Do they matter more than the fact that all of us breathe and hope and suffer and dream?

On the corner outside her shop, I raise a finger at a hooting taxi. Minutes later I am on my way downtown, away from the stillness of the suburbs.

My first stop is Braamfontein, just before the Nelson Mandela Bridge. Braam was one of the first parts of the inner city to rejuvenate, helped by a lively student population and by the Neighbourhood Goods Market, the Jo'burg version of the hipster food and craft market that began in Woodstock in Cape Town. It is the safe part of town, the right side of the tracks. I order a late breakfast at a table in the sun, and as I eat I notice a familiar face at the next table. At first I can't place it, but then it hits me. Five years ago, on the very day I set out on this journey, I had met Annene du Preez at Thea's Wild Coast Kitchen. Annene du Preez is a self-proclaimed wild child and the daughter of Max du Preez, one of South Africa's most prominent political commentators. On that day, Annene, Thea and I had spent an afternoon drinking beers at a local shebeen and driving to the beach in Thea's 4x4. I tell Annene my plan to spend the next few days walking alone around downtown Johannesburg.

Annene nods. She gets it.

"*Entevrees*," she says.

I look at her quizzically.

"It's an Afrikaans word. It's a kind of claustrophobia that you feel from being pushed out. Here we only allow ourselves to be this big," she says, clasping her hands close to her body. "You know some people say our auras are three kilometres wide, but even though we have so much space in Africa, we think we can't expand. I'd go with you if I wasn't so busy."

"Next time," I say.

We hug goodbye and I walk to the edge of the Nelson Mandela Bridge and stand for a moment looking up at a skyscraper on the opposite side of the city emblazoned with the words: "Happy 20 years to our Rainbow Nation."

First one foot, then the other. I fall into step behind young black female students who are walking the bridge, each on their own. The bridge arcs over the railway tracks of Park Station. On the tracks below, the carriages of the Shosoloza Meyl, the long-distance train that once carried me from the heart of this city to the heartlands of the Karoo and beyond to the Mother City, lie silent, waiting their next departure.

As I walk, I am noticed, and I smile at everyone who offers me their gaze, looking them in the eye. I will not hide any more. I cannot live like that. I will not fear indiscriminately. I cannot thrive like that. I will trust and I will walk. We might not be able to change our past, but we can choose what we do today, and that will change our future.

Across the road from the Bree Street taxi rank, I smile at adverts in a chemist's window promoting "Vagina tightening" and "Kwik Up male performance boosters". On President Street where Asian traders sell a cornucopia of goods in low-ceilinged old buildings that once housed laundromats and warehouses, I buy a kaftan from Faruk Kagzi, a 34-year-old from India.

"How is business?" I ask.

He shakes his camouflaged peak cap.

"Business is not like before, it's been affected by the criminals. Back in 1998, the Indians, the whites, more of the blacks, all came to town. Because of the crime, you don't think you can live here forever. Here, the weather is good, the food is good, it's a historical country, there's interesting wildlife.

If it wasn't for the crime, this would be the best country in the world."

I continue up President Street, pausing in a shop that sells kitsch religious iconography and hologram pictures that morph from Nelson Mandela to Jacob Zuma as you move your head. I buy a cheap block-mount of Mary Magadalene printed with the words "Blessed Art Thou Among Women" and listen as shop owner Sharda Kassim, a 64-year-old Indian woman, born and bred in South Africa, speaks in defence of Jo'burg streets.

"We've travelled all over the world and it's exactly the same. Yes, before the safety was there. I used to walk from Jeppe to Eloff Street at night, window shopping in the OK Bazaars. But this is still home. Family is here. Ties are here."

I keep walking. Moving. Being. There is a slowness to this part of the city. People do not walk fast. Hustle without bustle. I tune into a tentative, quiet energy. I do not feel fear, instead as the sun shines on my back, I tune into a watery peace, a faint sadness. The old city has lost her people. She has grown quiet because her people have retreated.

Around the city, many of the old art deco skyscrapers are abandoned. Some are streaked with pink paint that has been poured down through empty windows.

Opposite the imposing grey façade of the Gauteng Premier's office is Clegg House, a white art deco edifice streaked with pink. I stop to ask the two security guards standing outside the building's car park whether they know what it means.

They do not.

"Maybe it was for a movie," says one, introducing himself as John Maswanganyi, 45.

He is more interested to know what I am doing there.

"What do you mean?" I ask.

"Most white women are in the malls of Sandton, not on the streets of Jo'burg," says John.

"And why do you think that is?" I ask.

"You white people do not like crime," John says, laughing.

I laugh too. "Don't black people also not like crime?"

"But you, you are more afraid," John says, clicking his teeth.

"Why do you think that is?" I ask.

He shakes his head. "I don't have an answer to that."

His colleague Raymond Thutlwa, 37, interjects. "It's fair enough. We are not like cars. If you get in an accident you can get a new car. But we only have one life."

"But if we live our lives hiding, caged in, what kind of life is that?" I ask.

"It's true, it's not a life. Even animals don't live like that," John says.

My mind tracks back to the day before, as I sat drinking coffee overlooking the car park of a shopping mall. What struck me was the faces and bodies of the white women, pushing their trolleys – haggard, their shoulders hunched, their hearts concave, pulled back from the world. We are not here, whispered their bodies. Do not notice us. We will make ourselves smaller. We will not intrude. Spare us. Let us be.

I stand for a while talking with John and Raymond.

"This is great," John says. "In the past we could never have spoken like this. You and I talking together about what we think."

I agree. There is so much to say, so much that has gone unsaid and unheard, so many conversations we have not had, away from political rhetoric and newspaper headlines. Our democracy promises the freedom to participate, but still we only taste it in fragments.

I walk up Fox Street, past the provincial legislature. The pavement is a haphazard chequerboard of flagstones, all different colours, some broken. A random collection of textures and tints, cracked and pushed together under a piercing blue sky.

At the corner of Rissik and Pritchard, a Jehovah's Witness sits behind a desk. He is an ageing white Frenchman who arrived in Johannesburg from Paris in 1967. I ask if he feels at ease on the street.

"There is a bad element, but you are mostly fine," Patrick Rube says.

"As a Jehovah's Witness, going door to door, you must meet a lot of people," I say.

He nods.

"How would you describe the state of the South African heart?"

He thinks for a while.

"After all those years of apartheid, people focus on their own things. It's difficult for them to open up to people of other races and cultures," he says.

"What do you think it will take for us to open up?" I ask.

"Talking," he says simply. "Time. A willing heart."

I keep walking. I walk down Commissioner and find young fashion emporiums, as cool as anything in New York. I walk the length of Albertina Sisulu Street, shopping for African wax prints. For every smile I offer, I receive one in return. These are the smiles of my fellow South Africans, and with every step on these streets, I feel I am moving forward.

As the late afternoon arrives, I walk back through Braamfontein. The coffee shops are closing up for the day, the office workers and hipsters are making their way towards taxis and train stations.

As I cross the road to hail a taxi to Westdene, I get caught on the white line between two lines of traffic. I am not the only one.

Standing next to me is a kindly middle-aged bespectacled black man. We look at each other and he offers me his arm, like a father to a bride, and I link my arm with his, and we stand together, smiling, waiting.

When the road is clear, we laugh and scuttle across and as we reach the pavement he offers me his hand, introducing himself as Levy, an IT worker from a nearby office block.

"And you?" he asks. "What do you do?"

"I'm a writer," I say.

He nods. "I knew you were a writer. I could tell."

"How?" I ask.

"I can see that you are following your purpose. You are trying to find your truth."

I hold onto his hand. Tighter.

"You see me," I whisper.

He smiles.

"Thank you," I say.

We chat for few minutes until the taxi comes, and as it pulls away I notice three black words spray painted on an old white wall. "Anything is possible."

Maybe.